BLUEPRINTS:
A PROBLEM NOTEBOOK

FUNDAMENTALS
OF
FINANCIAL
MANAGEMENT

EIGHTH EDITION

EUGENE F. BRIGHAM
and
JOEL F. HOUSTON

University of Florida

The Dryden Press
Harcourt Brace College Publishers

Fort Worth Philadelphia San Diego New York Orlando Austin San Antonio
Toronto Montreal London Sydney Tokyo

Address for Editorial Correspondence
The Dryden Press, 301 Commerce Street, Suite 3700, Fort Worth, TX 76102

Address for Orders
The Dryden Press, 6277 Sea Harbor Drive, Orlando, FL 32887
1-800-782-4479

ISBN: 0-03-024433-1

Printed in the United States of America

7 8 9 0 1 2 3 4 5 6   0 2 3   9 8 7 6 5 4 3 2

The Dryden Press
Harcourt Brace College Publishers

PREFACE

Blueprints has become an integral part of the material we provide to students. At the University of Florida, we teach a large class, with upwards of 700 students each semester. This large class size forces us to lecture, even though we prefer discussion-oriented classes. To get the students more involved, we have developed a set of integrated cases which cover the key points in each chapter and which we use as the basis for our lectures. For our classes, we use the computer slide show to present the material that is summarized in each integrated case. Early on, students began asking us to make copies of the slides available to them. We did so, and that improved the class considerably. With paper copies of the slides, students could focus on what was being said in the lecture without having to copy things down for later review. *Blueprints* includes a copy of each integrated case, copies of the slides, and space to write down additional notes.

We consider the current version quite complete. However, the <u>optimal</u> product varies from instructor to instructor, depending on how the class is conducted. Therefore, instructors are encouraged to modify *Blueprints* to suit their own styles and interests. For example, if one covers chapters in a different order, or does not cover certain chapters, or covers only part of some chapters, or has additional materials not covered in the text, or anything else, the *Blueprints* chapters can be rearranged, added to or subtracted from, or modified in any other way. Deletions and rearrangements are easy, but additions and/or modifications would, of course, require some typing and/or cutting and pasting.

Students always want copies of old exams. Also, we have review sessions, conducted by TAs, and those sessions are devoted to working exam-type problems. So, we have included a number of exam-type problems at the end of each *Blueprints* chapter. Students work them on their own or else go to review sessions where the TAs work them. The solutions for these exam-type problems are provided at the end of the last *Blueprints* chapter.

Currently, at Florida we provide an off-campus copy shop with the *Blueprints* chapter material. Of course, we provide materials only for those chapters which we plan to cover in the course.

Instructors can use *Blueprints* in conjunction with the computer slide show, which is based on the integrated cases. Also, we frequently use the blackboard, both to explain the calculations which lie behind some of the numbers and to provide different examples. Our students end up with lots of marginal notes which clarify various points.

One thing has become crystal clear over the years--the best lecture notes, and materials related thereto, are instructor-specific. It is difficult to use someone else's notes verbatim. However, there is no point in reinventing the wheel, and if the *Blueprints* wheel fits a particular instructor's wagon, he or she might do well to use it, spending time adapting it to his or her own style and coverage rather than taking the time to develop lectures notes de novo. Therefore, you are encouraged to look over the *Blueprints* package, decide if and how you might use it, and then go to it. If you are like us, you will change things from semester to semester--there is no such thing as static optimality!

If you do use the package, and find some modifications that work well for you, we would very much appreciate hearing from you--your modifications might well help us and others.

Eugene F. Brigham
Joel F. Houston

P.O. Box 117168
College of Business
University of Florida
Gainesville, Florida 32611-7168

April 1997

SUGGESTIONS FOR STUDENTS USING BLUEPRINTS

1. Read the textbook chapter first, going through the entire chapter rapidly. Don't expect to understand everything on this first reading, but do try to get a good idea of what the chapter covers, the key terms, and the like. <u>It is useful to read the chapter before the first lecture on it.</u>

2. You could also read the *Blueprints* chapter material before class, but that is not necessary.

3. *Blueprints* was designed as the basis for a lecture--the most important material in each chapter is covered, and the material most likely to give you trouble is emphasized. As your instructor goes through *Blueprints*, you should (1) see what we regard as the most important material and (2) get a better feel for how to think about issues and work relevant problems.

4. You could read *Blueprints*, in connection with the text, and get a reasonably good idea of what is going on in the course. However, the real value of *Blueprints* is as a vehicle to help the class lecture make more sense and to help you get a good set of notes. In class, your instructor will discuss various points raised in *Blueprints* and elaborate on different issues. Also, he or she will explain how formulas are used, where data in tables come from, and the like. <u>You will end up with lots of marginal notes on your copy if you use *Blueprints* as it is supposed to be used.</u> Indeed, these marginal notes will constitute your class notes.

BLUEPRINTS
Table of Contents

BLUEPRINTS: CHAPTER 1
AN OVERVIEW OF FINANCIAL MANAGEMENT

1-1   Jennifer Johnson went home for a quick visit early in the term, and, over the course of the weekend, her brother, who received his finance degree three years ago, asked her to tell him about the courses she is taking. After she told him that financial management was one of the courses, he asked her the following questions:

a.   What kinds of career opportunities are open to finance majors?

b.   What are the most important financial management issues of the 1990s?

c.   What are the primary responsibilities of a corporate financial staff?

d. (1) What are the alternative forms of business organization?

    (2) What are their advantages and disadvantages?

e.   What is the primary goal of the corporation?

    (1) Do firms have any responsibilities to society at large?

    (2) Is stock price maximization good or bad for society?

    (3) Should firms behave ethically?

f.   What is an agency relationship?

    (1) What agency relationships exist within a corporation?

    (2) What mechanisms exist to influence managers to act in shareholders' best interests?

    (3) Should shareholders (through managers) take actions that are detrimental to bondholders?

g.   What factors affect stock prices?

h.   What factors affect the level and riskiness of cash flows?

9/13

---

1 - 1

CHAPTER 1
An Overview of Financial Management

- Career opportunities
- Issues of the 1990s
- Forms of business organization
- Goals of the corporation
- Agency relationships

---

1 - 2

Career Opportunities in Finance

$< 1 yr$ $> 1 yr$

- Money and capital markets
- Investments — *maximize value*
- Financial management

key job opportunity
- financial analyst

---

1 - 3

Financial Management
Issues of the 1990s

- Use of computers and electronic transfers of information
- The globalization of business

Responsibilities of the Financial Staff

1 - 4

- Forecasting and planning
- Investment and financing decisions
- Coordination and control
- Transactions in the financial markets

Alternative Forms of Business Organization

1 - 5

- Sole proprietorship
- Partnership
- Corporation

Sole Proprietorship

1 - 6

- Advantages:
  - Ease of formation
  - Subject to few regulations
  - No corporate income taxes
- Disadvantages:
  - Limited life
  - Unlimited liability
  - Difficult to raise capital

Partnership

■ A partnership has roughly the same advantages and disadvantages as a sole proprietorship.

Corporation

■ Advantages:
  ● Unlimited life
  ● Easy transfer of ownership
  ● Limited liability
  ● Ease of raising capital
■ Disadvantages:
  ● Double taxation
  ● Cost of set-up and report filing

Goals of the Corporation

■ The primary goal is shareholder wealth maximization, which translates to maximizing stock price.
  ● Do firms have any responsibilities to society at large?
  ● Is stock price maximization good or bad for society?
  ● Should firms behave ethically?

Agency Relationships

- **An agency relationship exists whenever a principal hires an agent to act on their behalf.**
- **Within a corporation, agency relationships exist between:**
  - **Shareholders and managers**
  - **Shareholders and creditors**

(bondholders)

lend money to receive future interest payments

separation of management & owners' interests

bonds - most popular source of corporate financing in US

Shareholders versus Managers

- **Managers are naturally inclined to act in their own best interests.**
- **But the following factors affect managerial behavior:** *tied to performance*
  - **Managerial compensation plans**
  - **Direct intervention by shareholders**
  - **The threat of firing** – *debt/equity ratio*
  - **The threat of takeover**

stock options

bond coupon rate depends on economic interest rate

preferred stock - dividends
vs.   no voting rights
common stock - voting rights

In the event of liquidation 1) bondholders 2) preferred stock and 3) stockholders

debtor imposition financing can prevent liquidation

Shareholders versus Creditors

- **Shareholders (through managers) could take actions to maximize stock price that are detrimental to creditors.**
- **In the long run, such actions will raise the cost of debt and ultimately lower stock price.**

Higher debt creates higher stock value through higher tax deduction (because interest expense can be written off) by raising net income

Factors that Affect Stock Price

- **Projected cash flows to shareholders**
- **Timing of the cash flow stream**
- **Riskiness of the cash flows**
- Confidence in management

↓ further along in time requires more discounting

Factors that Affect the Level and Riskiness of Cash Flows

- **Decisions made by financial managers:**
  - **Investment decisions**
  - **Financing decisions (the relative use of debt financing)**
  - **Dividend policy decisions**
- **The external environment**

---

stock value = PV of future cash flow

cash flow
interest rate = present value

net cash flow = net income
       − noncash revenue
       + noncash charges

or = net income + depreciation

What is the interest rate to discount cash flow? Higher rate of return is higher to compensate for higher risk → higher interest rate

P. 23 Figure 1-2

EXAM-TYPE PROBLEMS

1-1.   Which of the following statements is most correct?

a.   Proxy fights and hostile takeovers are the two main methods of transferring ownership interest in a corporation.

b.   The corporation is a legal entity created by the state and is a direct extension of the legal status of its owners and managers, that is, the owners and managers are the corporation.

c.   Unlimited liability and limited life are two key advantages of the corporate form over other forms of business organization.

d.   Due in large part to limited liability and ease of ownership transfer, corporations have less trouble raising money in financial markets than other organizational forms.

e.   The stockholders of the corporation are insulated by limited legal liability, and the legal status of the corporation protects the firm's managers from civil and criminal charges arising from business operations.

1-2.   Which of the following statements is most correct?

a.   The proper goal of the financial manager should be to maximize the firm's expected cash flow, because this will add the most wealth to each of the individual shareholders (owners) of the firm.

b.   One way to state the decision framework most useful for carrying out the firm's objective is as follows: "The financial manager should seek that combination of assets, liabilities, and capital which will generate the largest expected projected after-tax income over the relevant time horizon."

c.   The riskiness inherent in a firm's earnings per share (EPS) depends on the characteristics of the projects the firm selects, which means it depends upon the firm's assets, but EPS does not depend on the manner in which those assets are financed.

d.   Since large, publicly-owned firms are controlled by their management teams, and typically, ownership is widely dispersed, managers have great freedom in managing the firm. Managers may operate in the stockholders' best interest, but they may also operate in their own personal best interests. As long as managers stay within the law, there simply aren't any effective controls over managerial decisions in such situations.

e.   Agency problems exist between stockholders and managers, and between stockholders (through managers) and creditors.

2-19 Donna Jamison, a 1993 graduate of the University of Florida with four years of banking experience, was recently brought in as assistant to the chairman of the board of D'Leon Inc., a small food producer which operates in north Florida and whose specialty is high-quality pecan and other nut products sold in the snack-foods market. D'Leon's president, Al Watkins, decided in 1996 to undertake a major expansion and to "go national" in competition with Frito-Lay, Eagle, and other major snack-food companies. Watkins felt that D'Leon's products were of a higher quality than the competition's, that this quality differential would enable it to charge a premium price, and that the end result would be greatly increased sales, profits, and stock price.

The company doubled its plant capacity, opened new sales offices outside its home territory, and launched an expensive advertising campaign. D'Leon's results were not satisfactory, to put it mildly. Its board of directors, which consisted of its president and vice-president plus its major stockholders (who were all local business people) was most upset when directors learned how the expansion was going. Suppliers were being paid late and were unhappy, and the bank was complaining about the deteriorating situation and threatening to cut off credit. As a result, President Watkins was informed that changes would have to be made, and quickly, or he would be fired. Also, at the board's insistence Donna Jamison was brought in and given the job of assistant to Fred Campo, a retired banker who was D'Leon's chairman and largest stockholder. Campo agreed to give up a few of his golfing days and to help nurse the company back to health, with Jamison's help.

Jamison began by gathering the financial statements and other data given in Tables IC2-1, IC2-2, IC2-3, and IC2-4. Assume that you are Jamison's assistant, and you must help her answer the following questions for Campo. (Note: We will continue with this case in Chapter 3, and you will feel more comfortable with the analysis there, but answering these questions will help prepare you for Chapter 3. Provide clear explanations, not just yes or no answers!)

Table IC2-1. Balance Sheets

	1997	1996
Assets:		
Cash	$ 7,282	$ 57,600
Accounts receivable	632,160	351,200
Inventories	1,287,360	715,200
Total current assets	$1,926,802	$1,124,000
Gross fixed assets	1,202,950	491,000
Less accumulated depreciation	263,160	146,200
Net fixed assets	$ 939,790	$ 344,800
Total assets	$2,866,592	$1,468,800
Liabilities and equity:		
Accounts payable	$ 524,160	$ 145,600
Notes payable	720,000	200,000
Accruals	489,600	136,000
Total current liabilities	$1,733,760	$ 481,600
Long-term debt	1,000,000	323,432
Common stock (100,000 shares)	460,000	460,000
Retained earnings	(327,168)	203,768
Total equity	$ 132,832	$ 663,768
Total liabilities and equity	$2,866,592	$1,468,800

Table IC2-2. Income Statements

	1997	1996
Sales	$5,834,400	$3,432,000
Cost of goods sold	5,728,000	2,864,000
Other expenses	680,000	340,000
Depreciation	116,960	18,900
Total operating costs	$6,524,960	$3,222,900
EBIT	($ 690,560)	$ 209,100
Interest expense	176,000	62,500
EBT	($ 866,560)	$ 146,600
Taxes (40%)	(346,624)	58,640
Net income	($ 519,936)	$ 87,960
EPS	($5.199)	$0.880
DPS	$0.110	$0.220
Book value per share	$1.328	$6.638
Stock price	$2.250	$8.500
Shares outstanding	100,000	100,000
Tax rate	40.00%	40.00%
Lease payments	40,000	40,000
Sinking fund payments	0	0

Table IC2-3. Statement of Retained Earnings, 1997

Balance of retained earnings, 12/31/96	$ 203,768
Add: Net income, 1997	(519,936)
Less: Dividends paid	(11,000)
Balance of retained earnings, 12/31/97	($327,168)

Table IC2-4. Statement of Cash Flows, 1997

Operating activities:
    Net income   (\$ 519,936)

Additions (sources of cash):
    Depreciation   116,960
    Increase in accounts payable   378,560
    Increase in accruals   353,600

Subtractions (uses of cash):
    Increase in accounts receivable   (280,960)
    Increase in inventories   (572,160)
Net cash provided by oper. activities   (\$ 523,936)

Long-term investing activities:
    Cash used to acquire fixed assets   (\$ 711,950)

Financing activities:
    Increase in notes payable   \$ 520,000
    Increase in long-term debt   676,568
    Payment of cash dividends   (11,000)
Net cash provided by financing activities \$1,185,568

Sum: Net decrease in cash   (\$ 50,318)
Plus: Cash at beginning of year   57,600

Cash at end of year   \$ 7,282

a.   What effect did the company's expansion have on its net cash flow and operating cash flow?

b.   Jamison also has asked you to estimate D'Leon's EVA. She estimates that the after-tax total cost of capital was $125,000 in 1996 and $275,000 in 1997.

c.   Looking at D'Leon's stock price today, would you conclude that the expansion increased or decreased MVA?

d.   D'Leon purchases materials on 30-day terms, meaning that it is supposed to pay for purchases within 30 days of receipt. Judging from its 1997 balance sheet, do you think D'Leon pays suppliers on time? Explain. If not, what problems might this lead to?

e.   D'Leon spends money for labor, materials, and fixed assets (depreciation) to make products, and still more money to sell those products. Then, it makes sales which result in receivables, which eventually result in cash inflows. Does it appear that D'Leon's sales price exceeds its costs per unit sold? How does this affect the cash balance?

f.   Suppose D'Leon's sales manager told the sales staff to start offering 60-day credit terms rather than the 30-day terms now being offered. D'Leon's competitors react by offering similar terms, so sales remain constant. What effect would this have on the cash account? How would the cash account be affected if sales doubled as a result of the credit policy change?

g.   Can you imagine a situation in which the sales price exceeds the cost of producing and selling a unit of output, yet a dramatic increase in sales volume causes the cash balance to decline?

h.   In general, could a company like D'Leon increase sales without a corresponding increase in inventory and other assets? Would the asset increase occur before the increase in sales, and, if so, how would that affect the cash account and the statement of cash flows?

I.   Did D'Leon finance its expansion program with internally generated funds (additions to retained earnings plus depreciation) or with external capital? How does the choice of financing affect the company's financial strength?

j.   Refer to Tables IC2-2 and IC2-4. Suppose D'Leon broke even in 1997 in the sense that sales revenues equaled total operating costs plus interest charges. Would the asset expansion have caused the company to experience a cash shortage which required it to raise external capital?

k.   If D'Leon started depreciating fixed assets over 7 years rather than 10 years, would that affect (1) the physical stock of assets, (2) the balance sheet account for fixed assets, (3) the company's reported net income, and (4) its cash position? Assume the same depreciation method is used for stockholder reporting and for tax calculations, and the accounting change has no effect on assets' physical lives.

l.   Explain how (1) inventory valuation methods, (2) the accounting policy regarding expensing versus capitalizing research and development, and (3) the policy with regard to funding future retirement plan costs (retirement pay and retirees' health benefits) could affect the financial statements.

m.   D'Leon's stock sells for $2.25 per share even though the company had large losses. Does the positive stock price indicate that some investors are irrational?

n.   D'Leon followed the standard practice of paying dividends on a quarterly basis. It paid a dividend during the first two quarters of 1997, then eliminated the dividend when management realized that a loss would be incurred for the year. The dividend was cut before the losses were announced, and at that point the stock price fell from $8.50 to $3.50. Why would an $0.11, or even a $0.22, dividend reduction lead to a $5.00 stock price reduction?

o.   Explain how earnings per share, dividends per share, and book value per share are calculated, and what they mean. Why does the market price per share *not* equal the book value per share?

p.   How much new money did D'Leon borrow from its bank during 1997? How much additional credit did its suppliers extend? Its employees and the taxing authorities?

q.   If you were D'Leon's banker, or the credit manager of one of its suppliers, would you be worried about your job? If you were a current D'Leon employee, a retiree, or a stockholder, should you be concerned?

r.   The 1997 income statement shows negative taxes, that is, a tax credit. How much taxes would the company have had to pay in the past to actually get this credit? If taxes paid within the last 3 years had been less than $346,624, what would have happened? Would this have affected the statement of cash flows and the ending cash balance?

s.   Working with Jamison has required you to put in a lot of overtime, so you have had very little time to spend on your private finances. It's now April 1, and you have only two weeks left to file your income tax return. You have managed to get all the information together that you will need to complete your return. D'Leon paid you a salary of $45,000, and you received $3,000 in dividends from common stock that you own. You are single, so your personal exemption is $2,550, and your itemized deductions are $4,550.

(1) On the basis of the information above and the April 1997 individual tax rate schedule, what is your tax liability?

(2) What are your marginal and average tax rates?

t.   Assume that a corporation has $100,000 of taxable income from operations plus $5,000 of interest income and $10,000 of dividend income. What is the company's tax liability?

u.   Assume that after paying your personal income tax as calculated in Part s, you have $5,000 to invest. You have narrowed your investment choices down to California bonds with a yield of 7 percent or equally risky Exxon bonds with a yield of 10 percent. Which one should you choose and why? At what marginal tax rate would you be indifferent to the choice between California and Exxon bonds?

creditor, investor, manager

2 - 1

CHAPTER 2
Financial Statements, Cash Flow, and Taxes

- Balance sheet
- Income statement
- Statement of cash flows
- Accounting income vs. cash flow
- MVA and EVA
- Personal taxes
- Corporate taxes

Creditors

1) why are they borrowing?

2) What is the capital structure

3) Outstanding debt

4) Past debt service rendered

5) Liquidity

2 - 2

Balance Sheet: Assets

	1997	1996
Cash	7,282	57,600
AR	632,160	351,200
Inventories	1,287,360	715,200
Total CA	1,926,802	1,124,000
Gross FA	1,202,950	491,000
Less: Deprec.	263,160	146,200
Net FA	939,790	344,800
Total Assets	2,866,592	1,468,800

Current assets { Cash, AR, Inventories }

Investors

1) Past performance

2) Future expectation

3) growth & stability of earnings

4) risk in the capital structure

5) how is the company performing compared to industry?

2 - 3

Liabilities and Equity

	1997	1996
Accts payable	524,160	145,600
Notes payable	720,000	200,000
Accruals	489,600	136,000
Total CL	1,733,760	481,600
Long-term debt	1,000,000	323,432
Common stock	460,000	460,000
Retained earnings	(327,168)	203,768
Total equity	132,832	663,768
Total L&E	2,866,592	1,468,800

Managers

1) How well it performed? why?

2) strengths/weaknesses

3) What change needs to be made

Income Statement

	1997	1996
Sales	5,834,400	3,432,000
COGS	5,728,000	2,864,000
Other expenses	680,000	340,000
Deprec.	116,960	18,900
Tot. op. costs	6,524,960	3,222,900
EBIT	(690,560)	209,100
Interest exp.	176,000	62,500
EBT	(866,560)	146,600
Taxes (40%)	(346,624)	58,640
Net income	(519,936)	87,960

operating costs

EBIT= earnings before interest & taxes

Other Data

	1997	1996
No. of shares (outstanding)	100,000	100,000
EPS	($5.199)	$0.88
DPS (dividend payment)	$0.110	$0.22
Stock price	$2.25	$8.50
Lease pmts	$40,000	$40,000

Statement of Retained Earnings (1997)

Balance of retained earnings, 12/31/96	$203,768
Add: Net income, 1997	(519,936)
Less: Dividends paid	(11,000)
Balance of retained earnings, 12/31/97	($327,168)

Statement of Cash Flows (1997)

OPERATING ACTIVITIES
Net income	(519,936)
Add (sources of cash):	
Depreciation	116,960
Increase in A/P	378,560
Increase in accruals	353,600
Subtract (uses of cash):	
Increase in A/R	(280,960)
Increase in inventories	(572,160)
Net cash provided by ops.	**(523,936)**

L-T INVESTING ACTIVITIES	
Investment in fixed assets	(711,950)
FINANCING ACTIVITIES	
Increase in notes payable	520,000
Increase in long-term debt	676,568
Payment of cash dividends	(11,000)
Net cash from financing	1,185,568
NET CHANGE IN CASH	**(50,318)**
Plus: Cash at beginning of year	57,600
Cash at end of year	7,282

Short term ←

What can you conclude about D'Leon's financial condition from its statement of CFs?

- Net cash from operations = -$523,936, mainly because of negative NI.

- The firm borrowed $1,185,568 to meet its cash requirements.

- Even after borrowing, the cash account fell by $50,318.

Handwritten notes:

Operating activities
+ Net income
+ Depreciation
+ Any decrease in current assets (except cash)
+ Increase in accounts payable
- Any increase in current assets (except cash)
- Decrease in accounts payable

Investment activities
+ Ending fixed assets
- Beginning fixed assets
+ Depreciation

Financing activities
- Decrease in notes payable
+ Increase in notes payable
- Decrease in long-term debt
+ Increase in long-term debt
+ Increase in common stock
- Dividends paid

Borrowing increases company value by:
- increased cash flow
- increased net income (via tax deduction)

What effect did the company's expansion have on its net cash flow and operating cash flow?

NCF_{97} = NI + DEP = ($519,936) + $116,960
= ($402,976).

NCF_{96} = $87,960 + $18,900 = $106,860.

OCF_{97} = EBIT(1 - T) + DEP
= (-$690,560)(0.6) + $116,960
= ($297,376).

OCF_{96} = ($209,100)(0.6) + $18,900
= $144,360.

Economic Value Added

Jamison also has asked you to estimate D'Leon's EVA. The after-tax total cost of capital = $125,000 in 1996 and $275,000 in 1997.

EVA_{97} = EBIT(1 - T) - After-tax cost of capital
= (-$690,560)(0.6) - $275,000
= ($689,336).

EVA_{96} = EBIT(1 - T) - After-tax cost of capital
= ($209,100)(0.6) - $125,000
= $460.

EVA = after tax operating profit
— after tax cost of capital

Would you conclude that the expansion increased or decreased MVA?

Market value added

$$MVA = \frac{Market\ value}{of\ equity} - \frac{Equity\ capital}{supplied}$$

During the last year stock price has decreased 73%, so market value of equity has declined. Consequently, MVA has declined.

Does D'Leon pay its suppliers on time?

- Probably not.
- A/P increased 260% over the past year, while sales increased by only 70%.
- If this continues, suppliers may cut off D'Leon's trade credit.

Does it appear that D'Leon's sales price exceeds its cost per unit sold?

- No, the decline in the company's cash position suggests that D'Leon is spending more cash than it is taking in.

What effect would each of these actions have on D'Leon's cash account?

1. The company offers 60-day credit terms. The improved terms are matched by its competitors, so sales remain constant.
   - A/R would ↑
   - Cash would ↓

2. **Sales double as a result of the change in credit terms.**

- Short run: Inventory and fixed assets ↑ to meet increased sales. A/R ↑, Cash ↓. Company may have to seek additional financing.
- Long-run: Collections increase and the company's cash position would improve.

How did D'Leon finance its expansion?

- D'Leon financed its expansion with external capital.
- D'Leon issued long-term debt which reduced its financial strength.

Would D'Leon have required external capital if they had broken even in 1997?

- **YES**, the company would still have to finance its increase in assets.

What happens if D'Leon depreciates its fixed assets over 7 years (as opposed to the current 10 years)?

- No effect on physical assets.
- Fixed assets on balance sheet would decline.
- Net income would decline.
- Tax payments would decline.
- Cash position would improve.

Other policies which can affect financial statements

- Inventory valuation methods.
- Capitalization of R&D expenses.
- Policies for funding the company's retirement plan.

Does the company's positive stock price ($2.25), in the face of large losses, suggest that investors are irrational?

- NO, it means that investors expect things to get better in the future.

Why did the stock fall after the dividend was cut?

- Management was "signaling" that the firm's operations were in trouble.
- The dividend cut lowered expectations for future profits which caused the stock price to decline.

What were some other sources of financing for D'Leon in 1997?

- Bank loans: Notes payable increased by $520,000.
- Credit from suppliers: A/P increased by $378,560.
- Employees: Accruals increased by $353,600.

D'Leon received a tax credit of $346,624 in 1997.

- This suggests the company paid at least $346,624 in taxes during the past 3 years.
- If D'Leon's payments over the past 3 years were less than $346,624 the firm would have had to carry forward the amount of its loss that was not carried back.
- If the firm did not receive a full refund its cash position would be even worse.

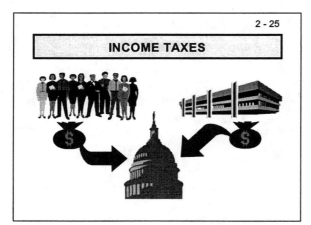

2 - 25

INCOME TAXES

---

2 - 26

April 1997 Single Individual Tax Rates

(after deductions)

Taxable Income	Tax on Base	Rate*
0 - 24,000	0	15%
24,000 - 58,150	3,600.00	28%
58,150 - 121,300	13,162.00	31%
121,300 - 263,750	32,738.50	36%
Over 263,750	84,020.50	39.6%

*Plus this percentage on the amount over the bracket base.

taxable income may not equal gross income

---

2 - 27

Assume your salary is $45,000, and you received $3,000 in dividends. You are single, so your personal exemption is $2,550 and your itemized deductions are $4,550.

On the basis of the information above and the April 1997 tax rate schedule, what is your tax liability?

Calculation of Taxable Income

Salary	$45,000
Dividends	3,000
Personal exemptions	(2,550)
Deductions	(4,550)
Taxable Income	**$40,900**

40,900 - 24,000

- **Tax Liability:**
  TL = $3,600 + 0.28($16,900)
  = $8,332.
- **Marginal Tax Rate = 28%.**
- **Average Tax Rate:**
  Tax rate = $\frac{\$8,332}{\$40,900}$ = 20.37%.

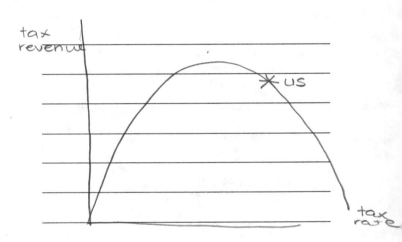

tax revenue

✶ US

tax rate

US - progressive taxation
higher income, higher taxes

January 1997 Corporate Tax Rates

Taxable Income	Tax on Base	Rate*
0 - 50,000	0	15%
50,000 - 75,000	7,500	25%
75,000 - 100,000	13,750	34%
100,000 - 335,000	22,250	39%
...	...	...
Over 18.3M	6.4M	35%

Plus this percentage on the amount over the bracket base.

Assume a corporation has $100,000 of taxable income from operations, $5,000 of interest income, and $10,000 of dividend income.

What's its tax liability?

Operating income	**$100,000**
Interest income	**5,000**
Taxable dividend income	**3,000***
Taxable income	**$108,000**

Tax = $22,250 + 0.39 ($8,000)
**   = $25,370.**

*Dividends - Exclusion
** = $10,000 - 0.7($10,000) = $3,000.**

Taxable vs. Tax Exempt Bonds

State and local government bonds (munis) are generally exempt from federal taxes.

- **Exxon bonds at 10% vs. California muni bonds at 7%.**
- **T = Tax rate = 28%.**
- **After-tax interest income:**
  Exxon = 0.10($5,000) - 0.10($5,000)(0.28)
  = 0.10($5,000)(0.72) = $360.
  CAL = 0.07($5,000) - 0 = $350.

At what tax rate would you be indifferent to muni vs. corp?

Solve for T in this equation:

Muni yield = Corp Yield(1-T)

7.00% = 10.0%(1-T)

T = 30.0%.

Implications

- **If T > 30%, buy tax exempt munis.**
- **If T < 30%, buy corporate bonds.**
- **Only high income people should buy munis.**

EXAM-TYPE PROBLEMS

2-1. Which of the following statements is most correct?

a. In order to avoid double taxation and to escape the frequently higher tax rate applied to capital gains, stockholders generally prefer to have corporations pay dividends rather than to retain their earnings and reinvest the money in the business. Thus, earnings should be retained only if the firm needs capital very badly and would have difficulty raising it from external sources.

b. Under our current tax laws, when investors pay taxes on their dividend income, they are being subjected to a form of double taxation.

c. The fact that a percentage of the interest received by one corporation, which is paid by another corporation, is excluded from taxable income has encouraged firms to use more debt financing relative to equity financing.

d. If the tax laws stated that $0.50 out of every $1.00 of interest paid by a corporation was allowed as a tax-deductible expense, this would probably encourage companies to use more debt financing than they presently do, other things held constant.

e. Statements b and d are both correct.

2-2. Solarcell Corporation has $20,000 which it plans to invest in marketable securities. It is choosing between AT&T bonds which yield 11%, State of Florida muni bonds which yield 8%, and AT&T preferred stock with a dividend yield of 9%. Solarcell's corporate tax rate is 40%, and 70% of the preferred stock dividends it receives are tax exempt. Assuming that the investments are equally risky and that Solarcell chooses strictly on the basis of after-tax returns, which security should be selected? Answer by giving the after-tax rate of return on the highest yielding security. (8%)

2-3. Purcell Corporation has operating income (EBIT) of $1,250,000. The company's depreciation expense is $300,000. Purcell is 100 percent equity financed, and it faces a 40 percent tax rate.

a. What is the company's net income? ($750,000)

b. What is its net cash flow? ($1,050,000)

c. What is its operating cash flow? ($1,050,000)

3-17   Part I of this case, presented in Chapter 2, discussed the situation that D'Leon Inc., a regional snack foods producer, was in after an expansion program. D'Leon had increased plant capacity and undertaken a major marketing campaign in an attempt to "go national." Thus far, sales have not been up to the forecasted level, costs have been higher than were projected, and a large loss occurred in 1997 rather than the expected profit. As a result, its managers, directors, and investors are concerned about the firm's survival.

Donna Jamison was brought in as assistant to Fred Campo, D'Leon's chairman, who had the task of getting the company back into a sound financial position. D'Leon's 1996 and 1997 balance sheets and income statements, together with projections for 1998, are given in Tables IC3-1 and IC3-2. In addition, Table IC3-3 gives the company's 1996 and 1997 financial ratios, together with industry average data. The 1998 projected financial statement data represent Jamison's and Campo's best guess for 1998 results, assuming that some new financing is arranged to get the company "over the hump."

Jamison examined monthly data for 1997 (not given in the case), and she detected an improving pattern during the year. Monthly sales were rising, costs were falling, and large losses in the early months had turned to a small profit by December. Thus, the annual data look somewhat worse than final monthly data. Also, it appears to be taking longer for the advertising program to get the message across, for the new sales offices to generate sales, and for the new manufacturing facilities to operate efficiently. In other words, the lags between spending money and deriving benefits were longer than D'Leon's managers had anticipated. For these reasons, Jamison and Campo see hope for the company--provided it can survive in the short run.

Jamison must prepare an analysis of where the company is now, what it must do to regain its financial health, and what actions should be taken. Your assignment is to help her answer the following questions. Provide clear explanations, not yes or no answers.

Table IC3-1. Balance Sheets

	1998E	1997	1996
Assets:			
Cash	$ 85,632	$ 7,282	$ 57,600
Accounts receivable	878,000	632,160	351,200
Inventories	1,716,480	1,287,360	715,200
Total current assets	$2,680,112	$1,926,802	$1,124,000
Gross fixed assets	1,197,160	1,202,950	491,000
Less accumulated depreciation	380,120	263,160	146,200
Net fixed assets	$ 817,040	$ 939,790	$ 344,800
Total assets	$3,497,152	$2,866,592	$1,468,800
Liabilities and Equity:			
Accounts payable	$ 436,800	$ 524,160	$ 145,600
Notes payable	600,000	720,000	200,000
Accruals	408,000	489,600	136,000
Total current liabilities	$1,444,800	$1,733,760	$ 481,600
Long-term debt	500,000	1,000,000	323,432
Common stock	1,680,936	460,000	460,000
Retained earnings	(128,584)	(327,168)	203,768
Total equity	$1,552,352	$ 132,832	$ 663,768
Total liabilities and equity	$3,497,152	$2,866,592	$1,468,800

Note: "E" indicates estimated. The 1998 data are forecasts.

Table IC3-2. Income Statements

	1998E	1997	1996
Sales	$7,035,600	$5,834,400	$3,432,000
Cost of goods sold	5,728,000	5,728,000	2,864,000
Other expenses	680,000	680,000	340,000
Depreciation	116,960	116,960	18,900
Total operating costs	$6,524,960	$6,524,960	$3,222,900
EBIT	$ 510,640	($ 690,560)	$ 209,100
Interest expense	88,000	176,000	62,500
EBT	$ 422,640	($ 866,560)	$ 146,600
Taxes (40%)	169,056	(346,624)	58,640
Net income	$ 253,584	($ 519,936)	$ 87,960
EPS	$1.014	($5.199)	$0.880
DPS	$0.220	$0.110	$0.220
Book value per share	$6.209	$1.328	$6.638
Stock price	$12.17	$2.250	$8.500
Shares outstanding	250,000	100,000	100,000
Tax rate	40.00%	40.00%	40.00%
Lease payments	40,000	40,000	40,000
Sinking fund payments	0	0	0

Note: "E" indicates estimated. The 1998 data are forecasts.

Table IC3-3. Ratio Analysis

	1998E	1997	1996	Industry Average
Current		1.1X	2.3X	2.7X
Quick		0.4X	0.8X	1.0X
Inventory turnover		4.5X	4.8X	6.1X
Days sales outstanding (DSO)		39.0	36.8	32.0
Fixed assets turnover		6.2X	10.0X	7.0X
Total assets turnover		2.0X	2.3X	2.6X
Debt ratio		95.4%	54.8%	50.0%
TIE		-3.9X	3.3X	6.2X
Fixed charge coverage		-3.0X	2.4X	5.1X
Profit margin		-8.9%	2.6%	3.5%
Basic earning power		-24.1%	14.2%	19.1%
ROA		-18.1%	6.0%	9.1%
ROE		-391.4%	13.3%	18.2%
Price/earnings		-0.4X	9.7X	14.2X
Market/book		1.7X	1.3X	2.4X
Book value per share		$1.33	$6.64	n.a.

Note: "E" indicates estimated. The 1998 data are forecasts.

a.   Why are ratios useful? What are the five major categories of ratios?

b.   Calculate D'Leon's 1998 current and quick ratios based on the projected balance sheet and income statement data. What can you say about the company's liquidity position in 1996, 1997, and as projected for 1998? We often think of ratios as being useful (1) to managers to help run the business, (2) to bankers for credit analysis, and (3) to stockholders for stock valuation. Would these different types of analysts have an equal interest in the liquidity ratios?

c.   Calculate the 1998 inventory turnover, days sales outstanding (DSO), fixed assets turnover, and total assets turnover. How does D'Leon's utilization of assets stack up against other firms in its industry?

d.   Calculate the 1998 debt, times-interest-earned, and fixed charge coverage ratios. How does D'Leon compare with the industry with respect to financial leverage? What can you conclude from these ratios?

e. Calculate the 1998 profit margin, basic earning power (BEP), return on assets (ROA), and return on equity (ROE). What can you say about these ratios?

f. Calculate the 1998 price/earnings ratio and market/book ratio. Do these ratios indicate that investors are expected to have a high or low opinion of the company?

g. Use the extended Du Pont equation to provide a summary and overview of D'Leon's financial condition as projected for 1998. What are the firm's major strengths and weaknesses?

h. Use the following simplified 1998 balance sheet to show, in general terms, how an improvement in the DSO would tend to affect the stock price. For example, if the company could improve its collection procedures and thereby lower its DSO from 44.9 days to the 32-day industry average without affecting sales, how would that change "ripple through" the financial statements (shown in thousands below) and influence the stock price?

Accounts receivable	$ 878	Debt	$1,945
Other current assets	1,802		
Net fixed assets	817	Equity	1,552
Total assets	$3,497	Liabilities plus equity	$3,497

I. Does it appear that inventories could be adjusted, and, if so, how should that adjustment affect D'Leon's profitability and stock price.

j. In 1997, the company paid its suppliers much later than the due dates, and it was not maintaining financial ratios at levels called for in its bank loan agreements. Therefore, suppliers could cut the company off, and its bank could refuse to renew the loan when it comes due in 90 days. On the basis of data provided, would you, as a credit manager, continue to sell to D'Leon on credit? (You could demand cash on delivery, that is, sell on terms of COD, but that might cause D'Leon to stop buying from your company.) Similarly, if you were the bank loan officer, would you recommend renewing the loan or demand its repayment? Would your actions be influenced if, in early 1998, D'Leon showed you its 1998 projections plus proof that it was going to raise over $1.2 million of new equity capital?

k. In hindsight, what should D'Leon have done back in 1996?

l. What are some potential problems and limitations of financial ratio analysis?

m.   What are some qualitative factors analysts should consider when evaluating a company's likely future financial performance?

3 - 1

CHAPTER 3
Analysis of Financial Statements

- Ratio analysis
- Du Pont system
- Effects of improving ratios
- Limitations of ratio analysis
- Qualitative factors

Handwritten notes (right side):

Altman's Z score for bankruptcy

$$Z = a x_1 + b x_2 + c x_3 + d x_4 + e x_5$$

with coefficients 1.2, 1.4, 3.3, 0.64, 1.0

- working capital $(CA - CL)$ / total assets
- retained earnings / total assets
- EBIT / total assets
- MV equity / BV of debt
- sales / total assets

---

3 - 2

Balance Sheet: Assets

	1998E	1997
Cash	85,632	7,282
AR	878,000	632,160
Inventories	1,716,480	1,287,360
Total CA	2,680,112	1,926,802
Gross FA	1,197,160	1,202,950
Less: Deprec.	380,120	263,160
Net FA	817,040	939,790
Total assets	3,497,152	2,866,592

---

3 - 3

Liabilities and Equity

	1998E	1997
Accounts payable	436,800	524,160
Notes payable	600,000	720,000
Accruals	408,000	489,600
Total CL	1,444,800	1,733,760
Long-term debt	500,000	1,000,000
Common stock	1,680,936	460,000
Retained earnings	(128,584)	(327,168)
Total equity	1,552,352	132,832
Total L & E	3,497,152	2,866,592

Income Statement

	1998E	1997
Sales	7,035,600	5,834,400
COGS	5,728,000	5,728,000
Other expenses	680,000	680,000
Depreciation	116,960	116,960
Tot. op. costs	6,524,960	6,524,960
EBIT	510,640	(690,560)
Interest exp.	88,000	176,000
EBT	422,640	(866,560)
Taxes (40%)	169,056	(346,624)
Net income	253,584	(519,936)

Other Data

	1998E	1997
Shares out.	250,000	100,000
EPS	$1.014	($5.199)
DPS	$0.220	$0.110
Stock price	$12.17	$2.25
Lease pmts	$40,000	$40,000

Why are ratios useful?

- Standardize numbers; facilitate comparisons
- Used to highlight weaknesses and strengths

What are the five major categories of ratios, and what questions do they answer?

- **Liquidity: Can we make required payments?** ~Solvency

- **Asset management: Right amount of assets vs. sales?**

- **Debt management: Right mix of debt and equity?**

- **Profitability: Do sales prices exceed unit costs, and are sales high enough as reflected in PM, ROE, and ROA?**

- **Market value: Do investors like what they see as reflected in P/E and M/B ratios?**

Calculate D'Leon's forecasted current and quick ratios for 1998.

$$CR_{98} = \frac{CA}{CL} = \frac{\$2,680}{\$1,445} = 1.85x.$$

$$QR_{98} = \frac{CA - Inv.}{CL}$$

$$= \frac{\$2,680 - \$1,716}{\$1,445} = 0.67x.$$

Comments on CR and QR

	1998	1997	1996	Ind.
CR	1.85x	1.1x	2.3x	2.7x
QR	0.67x	0.4x	0.8x	1.0x

- Expected to improve but still below the industry average.
- Liquidity position is weak.

What is the inventory turnover ratio vs. the industry average?

$$\text{Inv. turnover} = \frac{\text{Sales}}{\text{Inventories}}$$

$$= \frac{\$7,036}{\$1,716} = 4.10x.$$

	1998	1997	1996	Ind.
Inv. T.	4.1x	4.5x	4.8x	6.1x

Comments on Inventory Turnover

- Inventory turnover is below industry average.
- D'Leon might have old inventory, or its control might be poor.
- No improvement is currently forecasted.

DSO is the average number of days after making a sale before receiving cash.

$$\text{DSO} = \frac{\text{Receivables}}{\text{Average sales per day}}$$

$$= \frac{\text{Receivables}}{\text{Sales}/360} = \frac{\$878}{\$7,036/360} = 44.9.$$

Appraisal of DSO

	1998	1997	1996	Ind.
DSO	44.9	39.0	36.8	32.0

■ D'Leon collects too slowly, and is getting worse.

Poor credit policy.

F.A. and T.A. turnover vs. industry average

$$\frac{\text{Fixed assets}}{\text{turnover}} = \frac{\text{Sales}}{\text{Net fixed assets}}$$

$$= \frac{\$7,036}{\$817} = 8.61x.$$

$$\frac{\text{Total assets}}{\text{turnover}} = \frac{\text{Sales}}{\text{Total assets}}$$

$$= \frac{\$7,036}{\$3,497} = 2.01x.$$

	1998	1997	1996	Ind.
FA TO	8.6x	6.2x	10.0x	7.0x
TA TO	2.0x	2.0x	2.3x	2.6x

- FA turnover project to exceed industry average. Good.
- TA turnover not up to industry average. Caused by excessive current assets (A/R and inv.)

Calculate the debt, TIE, and fixed charge coverage ratios.

$$\text{Debt ratio} = \frac{\text{Total debt}}{\text{Total assets}}$$

$$= \frac{\$1,445 + \$500}{\$3,497} = 55.6\%.$$

$$\text{TIE} = \frac{\text{EBIT}}{\text{Int. expense}}$$

$$= \frac{\$510.6}{\$88} = 5.8x.$$

$$\text{Fixed charge coverage} = \text{FCC}$$

$$= \frac{\text{EBIT} + \text{Lease payments}}{\text{Interest expense} + \text{Lease pmt.} + \frac{\text{Sinking fund pmt.}}{(1 - T)}}$$

$$= \frac{\$510.6 + \$40}{\$88 + \$40 + \$0} = 4.3x.$$

All three ratios reflect use of debt, but focus on different aspects.

How do the debt management ratios compare with industry averages?

	1998	1997	1996	Ind.
D/A	55.6%	95.4%	54.8%	50.0%
TIE	5.8x	-3.9x	3.3x	6.2x
FCC	4.3x	-3.0x	2.4x	5.1x

Too much debt, but projected to improve.

Profit margin vs. industry average?

$$P.M. = \frac{NI}{Sales} = \frac{\$253.6}{\$7,036} = 3.6\%.$$

	1998	1997	1996	Ind.
P.M.	3.6%	-8.9%	2.6%	3.5%

Very bad in 1997, but projected to exceed industry average in 1998. Looking good.

BEP vs. Industry Average?

$$BEP = \frac{EBIT}{Total\ assets}$$

$$= \frac{\$510.6}{\$3,497} = 14.6\%.$$

3 - 22

	1998	1997	1996	Ind.
BEP	14.6%	-24.1%	14.2%	19.1%

- BEP removes effect of taxes and financial leverage. Useful for comparison.
- Projected to be below average.
- Room for improvement.

---

3 - 23

Return on Assets

$$ROA = \frac{\text{Net income}}{\text{Total assets}}$$

$$= \frac{\$253.6}{\$3,497} = 7.3\%.$$

---

3 - 24

$$ROE = \frac{\text{Net income}}{\text{Common equity}}$$

$$= \frac{\$253.6}{\$1,552} = 16.3\%.$$

	1998	1997	1996	Ind.
ROA	7.3%	-18.1%	6.0%	9.1%
ROE	16.3%	-391.0%	13.3%	18.2%

Both below average but improving.

Effects of Debt on ROA and ROE

- ROA is lowered by debt--interest lowers NI, which also lowers ROA = NI/Assets.

- But use of debt lowers equity, hence could raise ROE = NI/Equity.

Calculate and appraise the P/E and M/B ratios.

Price = $12.17.

$$EPS = \frac{NI}{Shares\ out.} = \frac{\$253.6}{250} = \$1.01.$$

$$P/E = \frac{Price\ per\ share}{EPS} = \frac{\$12.17}{\$1.01} = 12x.$$

$$BVPS = \frac{Com.\ equity}{Shares\ out.}$$

$$= \frac{\$1,552}{250} = \$6.21.$$

$$M/B = \frac{Mkt.\ price\ per\ share}{Book\ value\ per\ share}$$

$$= \frac{\$12.17}{\$6.21} = 1.96x.$$

	1998	1997	1996	Ind.
P/E	12.0x	-0.4x	9.7x	14.2x
M/B	1.96x	1.7x	1.3x	2.4x

- **P/E: How much investors will pay for $1 of earnings. High is good.**
- **M/B: How much paid for $1 of BV. Higher is good.**
- **P/E and M/B are high if ROE is high, risk is low.**

$$\left(\begin{array}{c}\text{Profit}\\\text{margin}\end{array}\right)\left(\begin{array}{c}\text{TA}\\\text{turnover}\end{array}\right)\left(\begin{array}{c}\text{Equity}\\\text{multiplier}\end{array}\right) = \text{ROE}$$

$$\frac{NI}{Sales} \times \frac{Sales}{TA} \times \frac{TA}{CE} = ROE.$$

1996	2.6%	x	2.3	x	2.2	=	13.2%
1997	-8.9%	x	2.0	x	21.9	=	-391.0%
1998	3.6%	x	2.0	x	2.3	=	16.3%
Ind.	3.5%	x	2.6	x	2.0	=	18.2%

The Du Pont system focuses on:

- **Expense control (P.M.)**
- **Asset utilization (TATO)**
- **Debt utilization (Eq. Mult.)**

It shows how these factors combine to determine the ROE.

Simplified D'Leon Data

A/R	878	Debt	1,945
Other CA	1,802	Equity	1,552
Net FA	817		
Total assets	$3,497	L&E	$3,497

$$\text{Sales} \bigg/ \text{day} = \frac{\$7,035,600}{360} = \$19,543.$$

Q. How would reducing DSO to 32 days affect the company?

Effect of reducing DSO from 44.9 days to 32 days:

Old A/R = 19,543 x 44.9 = 878,000

New A/R = 19,543 x 32.0 = 625,376

Cash freed up: 252,624

Initially shows up as additional cash.

New Balance Sheet

Added cash	$ 253	Debt	$1,945
A/R	625	Equity	1,552
Other CA	1,802		
Net FA	817		
Total assets	$3,497	Total L&E	$3,497

What could be done with the new cash? Effect on stock price and risk?

3 - 34

Potential use of freed up cash

- Repurchase stock. Higher ROE, higher EPS.
- Expand business. Higher profits.
- Reduce debt. Better debt ratio; lower interest, hence higher NI.
- All these actions would improve stock price.

---

3 - 35

Inventories are also too high.

Could analyze the effect of an inventory reduction on freeing up cash and increasing the quick ratio and asset management ratios--similar to what was done with DSO in slides #31 - #33.

---

3 - 36

Q. Would you lend money to the company?

A. Maybe. Things could get better. In business, one has to take some chances!

Company should not have relied exclusively on debt to finance its expansion.

What are some potential problems and limitations of financial ratio analysis?

■ Comparison with industry averages is difficult if the firm operates many different divisions.

■ "Average" performance not necessarily good.

■ Seasonal factors can distort ratios.

■ "Window dressing" techniques can make statements and ratios look better.

- Different operating and accounting practices distort comparisons.

- Sometimes hard to tell if a ratio is "good" or "bad."

- Difficult to tell whether company is, on balance, in strong or weak position.

What are some qualitative factors analysts should consider when evaluating a company's likely future financial performance?

- Are the company's revenues tied to 1 key customer?

- To what extent are the company's revenues tied to 1 key product?

- To what extent does the company rely on a single supplier? (Cont...)

- What percentage of the company's business is generated overseas?

- Competition

- Future prospects

- Legal and regulatory environment

EXAM-TYPE PROBLEMS

3-1.   Automotive Supply's ROE last year was only 2 percent, but its new owner has developed an operating plan designed to improve things. The new plan calls for a total debt ratio of 70 percent, which will result in interest charges of $500 per year. Management projects an EBIT of $2,000 on sales of $20,000, and it expects to have a total assets turnover ratio of 2.5. Under these conditions, the average tax rate will be 30 percent. If the changes are made, what return on equity will Automotive earn? (43.75%)

3-2.   Capital Garden Supply (CGS) recently hired a new chief financial officer, Louise Johnston, who was brought in and charged with raising the firm's profitability. CGS has sales of $5 million, a profit margin of 5%, and the following balance sheet:

Cash	$ 250,000	A/P	$ 750,000
Receivables	2,250,000	Other C.L.	500,000
Inventories	1,750,000	Long-term debt	2,250,000
Net fixed assets	3,250,000	Common equity	4,000,000
Total assets	$7,500,000	Total L/E	$7,500,000

a.   Ms. Johnston thinks that receivables are too high, and that they can be lowered to the point where the firm's DSO is equal to the industry average, 60 days, without affecting either sales or net income. If receivables are reduced so as to lower the DSO to 60 days (360-day basis), and if the funds generated are used to reduce common equity (stock can be repurchased at book value), and if no other changes occur, by how much will the ROE change? (3.43%)

b.   Suppose we wanted to modify this problem and use it on an exam, i.e., to create a new problem which you have not seen to test your knowledge of this general type of problem. How would your answer change under each of the following conditions:

(1) Double all dollar amounts. (3.43%)

(2) Set the target DSO at 70 days. (2.93%)

(3) State that the target is to achieve a receivables turnover of 6x rather than a DSO of 60. (3.43%)

(4) State that the company has 250,000 shares of stock outstanding, and ask how much the original change would increase EPS. ($0.55)

(5) Change part 4 to state that the stock was selling for twice book value, so common equity would not be reduced on a dollar-for-dollar basis. ($0.22)

c.   Now explain how we could have set the problem up to have you focus on changing inventory or fixed assets, or using the funds generated to retire debt, or how the original problem could have stated that the company needed *more* inventory and would finance them with new common equity, or with new debt.

3-3.   Which of the following statements is most correct?

a.   If two firms pay the same interest rate on their debt and have the same rate of return on assets, and if that ROA is positive, the firm with the *higher* debt ratio will also have a higher rate of return on common equity.

b.   One of the problems of ratio analysis is that the relationships are subject to manipulation. For example, we know that if we use some of our cash to pay off some of our current liabilities, the current ratio will always increase, especially if the current ratio is weak initially.

c.   Generally, firms with high profit margins have high asset turnover ratios, and firms with low profit margins have low turnover ratios; this result is exactly as predicted by the extended Du Pont equation.

d.   Firms A and B have identical earnings and identical dividend payout ratios. If Firm A's growth rate is higher than that of Firm B, Firm A's P/E ratio must be greater than Firm B's P/E ratio.

e.   None of the above statements is correct.

3-4.   Alumbat Corporation has $800,000 of debt outstanding, and it pays an interest rate of 10 percent annually on its bank loan. Alumbat's annual sales are $3,200,000; its average tax rate is 40 percent; and its net profit margin on sales is 6 percent. If the company does not maintain a TIE ratio of at least 4 times, its bank will refuse to renew its loan, and bankruptcy will result. What is Alumbat's current TIE ratio? (5x)

3-5.   Austin & Company has a debt ratio of 0.5, a total assets turnover ratio of 0.25, and a profit margin of 10 percent. The Board of Directors is unhappy with the current return on equity (ROE), and they think it could be doubled. This could be accomplished (1) by increasing the profit margin to 12 percent, and (2) by increasing debt utilization. Total assets turnover will not change. What new debt ratio, along with the new 12 percent profit margin, would be required to double the ROE? (70%)

3-6   Jecko Enterprises has an ROA of 12.5 percent, a 3 percent profit margin, and a return on equity equal to 16 percent.

a.   What is the company's total assets turnover? (4.167x)

b.   What is the firm's equity multiplier? (1.28)

c.   What is the firm's debt ratio? Assume the firm has no preferred stock. (22%)

4-15   Assume that you recently graduated with a degree in finance and have just reported to work as an investment advisor at the brokerage firm of Smyth Barry & Co. Your first assignment is to explain the nature of the U.S. financial markets to Michelle Varga, a professional tennis player who has just come to the United States from Mexico. Varga is a highly ranked tennis player who expects to invest substantial amounts of money through Smyth Barry. She is also very bright, and, therefore, she would like to understand in general terms what will happen to her money. Your boss has developed the following set of questions which you must ask and answer to explain the U.S. financial system to Varga.

a.   What is a *market*? How are physical asset markets differentiated from financial markets?

b.   Differentiate between *money markets* and *capital markets*.

c.   Differentiate between a *primary market* and a *secondary market*. If Apple Computer decided to issue additional common stock, and Varga purchased 100 shares of this stock from Merrill Lynch, the underwriter, would this transaction be a primary market transaction or a secondary market transaction? Would it make a difference if Varga purchased previously outstanding Apple stock in the over-the-counter market?

d.   Describe the three primary ways in which capital is transferred between savers and borrowers.

e.   Securities can be traded on *organized exchanges* or in the *over-the-counter market*. Define each of these markets, and describe how stocks are traded in each of them.

f.   What do we call the *price* that a borrower must pay for debt capital? What is the price of equity capital? What are the *four* most fundamental factors that affect the cost of money, or the general level of interest rates, in the economy?

g.   What is the *real risk-free rate of interest (k^*)* and the *nominal risk-free rate (k_{RF})*? How are these two rates measured?

h. Define the terms *inflation premium (IP)*, *default risk premium (DRP)*, *liquidity premium (LP)*, and *maturity risk premium (MRP)*. Which of these premiums is included when determining the interest rate on (1) short-term U.S. Treasury securities, (2) long-term U.S. Treasury securities, (3) short-term corporate securities, and (4) long-term corporate securities? Explain how the premiums would vary over time and among the different securities listed above.

I. Varga is also interested in investing in countries other than the United States. Describe the various types of risks that arise when investing overseas.

j. What is the *term structure* of interest rates? What is a *yield curve*? At any given time, how would the yield curve facing an AAA-rated company compare with the yield curve for U.S. Treasury securities? At any given time, how would the yield curve facing a BB-rated company compare with the yield curve for U.S. Treasury securities? Draw a graph to illustrate your answer.

k. Two main theories have been advanced to explain the shape of the yield curve: (1) the expectations theory and (2) the *liquidity preference theory*. Briefly describe each of these theories. Do economists regard one as being "true"?

l. Suppose most investors expect the rate of inflation to be 5 percent next year, 6 percent the following year, and 8 percent thereafter. The real risk-free rate is 3 percent. The maturity risk premium is zero for bonds that mature in 1 year or less, 0.1 percent for 2-year bonds, and then the MRP increases by 0.1 percent per year thereafter for 20 years, after which it is stable. What is the interest rate on 1-year, 10-year, and 20-year Treasury bonds? Draw a yield curve with these data. Is your yield curve consistent with the expectations theory or with the liquidity preference theory?

Federal Reserve — supervisory; regulator
Comptroller of Currency } chartering agency for banks
State Regulators
Federal Deposit } insurance for depositors
Insurance Corporation
Office of Thrift Supervision — chartering agency for S&L

---

4 - 1

CHAPTER 4
The Financial Environment: Markets, Institutions, and Interest Rates

- ■ **Financial markets**
- ■ **Types of financial institutions**
- ■ **Determinants of interest rates**
- ■ **Yield curves**

Financial Markets
I. Real versus financial assets
II. The Role of financial markets
III. Classification of financial markets
  A. primary vs. secondary institutions — direct to investors
  B. Spot vs. futures markets
  C. World, regional and local markets
  D. Some major types:
    1. money markets — today's rates
    2. capital markets
    3. mortgage markets
    4. consumer credit markets

Assets	Claims
Cash	Accounts payable
Accounts receivable	Notes payable
Inventories	Bonds
Plant	Common Equity

---

4 - 2

Define these markets

- ■ **Markets in general** — a place to buy & sell
- ■ **Physical assets**
- ■ **Financial assets** < 1 yr   > 1 yr
- ■ **Money vs. capital**
- ■ **Primary vs. secondary** → intermediary seller → buyer e.g.
- ■ **Spot vs. future** → commodities

issuer to buyer

p. 114 Figure 4-1

commodity market — corn, porkbellies future prices
money market < 1 yr e.g. CDs
commercial banks → short term commercial paper
capital markets > 1 yr e.g. stocks & bonds, long term commercial paper
NYSE
mortgage markets — S&L
mortgage backed securities

syndicated loans — libor rate
creditors collectively   London Int'n'l
decide rate & amount   Bank offer rate

---

4 - 3

Three Primary Ways Capital Is Transferred Between Savers and Borrowers

higher risk & return

- ■ **Direct transfer**
- ■ **Investment banking house**
- ■ **Financial intermediary**
  - A. Commercial banks — Industry loans
  - B. Savings and Loans — Mortgage loans
  - C. Mutual Savings banks
  - D. Credit unions — owned by depositors, lower rates for borrowing, higher rates for deposits
  - E. Life insurance
  - F. Mutual funds — pooled money from depositors
    1. Money — T bills
    2. Bond
    3. Stock
  - G. Pension funds

(@ 10,000 nation-wide)
investment banks — security firms
largest 3 firms — 40% market share
5 - 60%, 10 - 88%
offerings —
• best effort — investment bank takes to market; does not assume risk
• firm commitment — IB assumes risk
arbitrage — source of revenue
consultant during mergers & acquisitions, cash management
IPO — initial public offering issuance of stock to public

Organized Exchanges vs. Over-the-Counter Market

- Auction market vs. dealer market (exchanges vs. OTC)
- NYSE vs. NASDAQ system
- Differences are narrowing

NASDAQ- no exchange floor, computers
NYSE- requirement $2.5 PY earnings,
$6 mil 3yrs PY earnings, $18M outstanding
shares

- What do we call the price, or cost, of debt capital?

  The interest rate

- What do we call the price, or cost, of equity capital?

$$\text{Required return} = \text{Dividend yield} + \text{Capital gain}$$

What four factors affect the cost of money?

- Production opportunities
- Time preferences for consumption
- Risk
- Expected inflation

"Real" Versus "Nominal" Rates

k^* = **Real risk-free rate. T-bond rate if no inflation; 1% to 4%.**

k = **Any nominal rate.**

k_{RF} = **Rate on Treasury securities.**

real rate =

nominal rate = real rate + expected inflation

$$k = k^* + IP + DRP + LP + MRP.$$

Here:

k = **Required rate of return on a debt security.**

k^* = **Real risk-free rate.**

IP = **Inflation premium.**

DRP = **Default risk premium.**

LP = **Liquidity premium.**

MRP = **Maturity risk premium.**

Premiums Added to k^* for Different Types of Debt

- **S-T Treasury: only IP for S-T inflation**
- **L-T Treasury: IP for L-T inflation, MRP**
- **S-T corporate: S-T IP, DRP, LP**
- **L-T corporate: IP, DRP, MRP, LP**

What various types of risks arise when investing overseas?

Country risk: Arises from investing or doing business in a particular country. It depends on the country's economic, political, and social environment.

Exchange rate risk: If investment is denominated in a currency other than the dollar, the investment's value will depend on what happens to exchange rate.

Two Factors Lead to Exchange Rate Fluctuations

1. Changes in relative inflation will lead to changes in exchange rates.

2. An increase in country risk will also cause that country's currency to fall.

What is the "term structure of interest rates"? What is a "yield curve"?

- Term structure: the relationship between interest rates (or yields) and maturities.

- A graph of the term structure is called the yield curve.

T-Bond Yield Curve

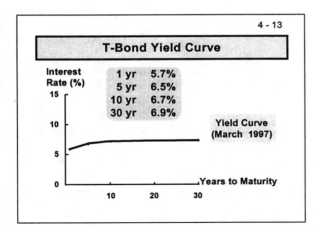

Interest Rate (%)

1 yr	5.7%
5 yr	6.5%
10 yr	6.7%
30 yr	6.9%

Yield Curve (March 1997)

Years to Maturity

What are the 2 main factors that explain the shape of the yield curve?

1. Expectations

■ Shape of the yield curve depends on the investors' expectations about future interest rates.

■ If interest rates are expected to increase, L-T rates will be higher than S-T rates and vice versa. Thus, the yield curve can slope up or down.

The Pure Expectations Hypothesis (PEH)

- MRP = 0.

- Long-term rates are an average of current and future short-term rates.

- If PEH is correct, you can use the yield curve to back out expected future interest rates.

An Example

- Assume that 1-year securities yield 6% today, and the market expects that 1-year securities will yield 7% in 1 year, and that 1-year securities will yield 8% in 2 years.

- If the PEH is correct, the 2-year rate today should be 6.5% = (6% + 7%)/2.

- If the PEH is correct, the 3-year rate today should be 7% = (6% + 7% + 8%)/3.

2. Risk

- Some argue that the PEH isn't correct, because securities of different maturities have different risk.

- General view (supported by most evidence) is that lenders prefer S-T securities, and view L-T securities as riskier.

- Thus, investors demand a MRP to get them to hold L-T securities (i.e., MRP > 0).

Example data:

■ **Inflation for Yr 1 is 5%.**

■ **Inflation for Yr 2 is 6%.**

■ **Inflation for Yr 3 and beyond is 8%.**

$$k^* = 3\%$$

$$MRP_t = 0.1\%(t - 1).$$

Yield Curve Construction

Step 1: Find the average expected inflation rate over years 1 to n:

$$IP_n = \frac{\sum\limits_{t=1}^{n} INFL_t}{n}.$$

$$IP_1 = 5\%/1.0 = 5.00\%.$$

$$IP_{10} = [5 + 6 + 8(8)]/10 = 7.5\%.$$

$$IP_{20} = [5 + 6 + 8(18)]/20 = 7.75\%.$$

Must earn these IPs to break even vs. inflation; these IPs would permit you to earn k* (before taxes).

Step 2: Find MRP based on this equation:

$$MRP_t = 0.1\%(t - 1).$$

$MRP_1 = 0.1\% \times 0 = 0.0\%.$

$MRP_{10} = 0.1\% \times 9 = 0.9\%.$

$MRP_{20} = 0.1\% \times 19 = 1.9\%.$

Step 3: Add the IPs and MRPs to k*:

$$k_{RF_t} = k^* + IP_t + MRP_t.$$

k_{RF} = **Quoted market interest rate on treasury securities.**

Assume k* = 3%:

$k_{RF1} = 3\% + 5\% + 0.0\% = 8.0\%.$

$k_{RF10} = 3\% + 7.5\% + 0.9\% = 11.4\%.$

$k_{RF20} = 3\% + 7.75\% + 1.9\% = 12.7\%.$

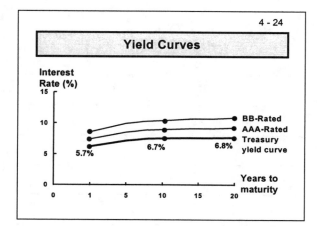

Yield Curves

EXAM-TYPE PROBLEMS

4-1. Which of the following statements is most correct?

a. Since the default risk premium (DRP) and the liquidity premium (LP) are both essentially zero for U.S. Treasury securities, the Treasury yield curve is influenced more heavily by expected inflation than corporate bonds' yield curves, i.e., we can be sure that a given amount of expected inflation will have more effect on the slope of the Treasury yield curve than on the corporate yield curve.

b. It is theoretically possible for the yield curve to have a downward slope, and there have been times when such a slope existed. That situation was probably caused by investors' liquidity preferences, i.e., by the factors which underlie the liquidity preference theory.

c. Yield curves for government and corporate bonds can be constructed from data that exist in the marketplace. If the yield curves for several companies were plotted on a graph, along with the yield curve for U.S. Treasury securities, the company with the largest total of DRP plus LP would have the highest yield curve.

d. An upward-sloping yield curve is the normal situation, because long-term securities have less interest rate risk than shorter-term securities, hence smaller MRPs. Therefore, long-term rates are normally lower than short-term rates.

e. All of the above statements are false.

4-2. Assume that the real risk-free rate, k*, is 4 percent, and that inflation is expected to be 9% in Year 1, 6% in Year 2, and 4% thereafter. Assume also that all Treasury bonds are highly liquid and free of default risk. If 2-year and 5-year Treasury bonds both yield 12%, what is the difference in the maturity risk premiums (MRPs) on the two bonds, i.e., what is $MRP_5 - MRP_2$? (2.1%)

4-3. A Treasury bond which matures in 8 years has a yield of 6.6 percent. An 8-year corporate bond has a yield of 9.3 percent. Assume that the liquidity premium on the corporate bond is 0.6 percent. What is the default risk premium on the corporate bond? (2.1%)

5-17 Assume that you recently graduated with a major in finance, and you just landed a job as a financial planner with Merrill Finch Inc., a large financial services corporation. Your first assignment is to invest $100,000 for a client. Because the funds are to be invested in a business at the end of one year, you have been instructed to plan for a one-year holding period. Further, your boss has restricted you to the following investment alternatives, shown with their probabilities and associated outcomes. (Disregard for now the items at the bottom of the data; you will fill in the blanks later.)

| | | | Returns on Alternative Investments | | | | |
| | | | Estimated Rate of Return | | | | |
State of the Economy	Prob.	T-Bills	High Tech	Collec-tions	U.S. Rubber	Market Portfolio	2-stock Portfolio
Recession	0.1	8.0%	-22.0%	28.0%	10.0%*	-13.0%	3.0%
Below avg	0.2	8.0	-2.0	14.7	-10.0	1.0	
Average	0.4	8.0	20.0	0.0	7.0	15.0	10.0%
Above avg	0.2	8.0	35.0	-10.0	45.0	29.0	
Boom	0.1	8.0	50.0	-20.0	30.0	43.0	15.0
k-Hat ($\hat{k}$)				1.7%	13.8%	15.0%	
Std dev (σ)		0.0		13.4	18.8	15.3	3.3
Coef of var (CV)				7.9	1.4	1.0	0.3
Beta (b)				-0.86	0.68		

* Note that the estimated returns of U.S. Rubber do not always move in the same direction as the overall economy. For example, when the economy is below average, consumers purchase fewer tires than they would if the economy was stronger. However, if the economy is in a flat-out recession, a large number of consumers who were planning to purchase a new car may choose to wait and instead purchase new tires for the car they currently own. Under these circumstances, we would expect U.S. Rubber's stock price to be higher if there is a recession than if the economy was just below average.

Merrill Finch's economic forecasting staff has developed probability estimates for the state of the economy, and its security analysts have developed a sophisticated computer program which was used to estimate the rate of return on each alternative under each state of the economy. High Tech Inc. is an electronics firm; Collections Inc. collects past-due debts; and U.S. Rubber manufactures tires and various other rubber and plastics products. Merrill Finch also maintains an "index fund" which owns a market-weighted fraction of all publicly traded stocks; you can invest in that fund, and thus obtain average stock market results. Given the situation as described, answer the following questions.

a. (1) Why is the T-bill's return independent of the state of the economy? Do T-bills promise a completely risk-free return?

   (2) Why are High Tech's returns expected to move with the economy whereas Collections' are expected to move counter to the economy?

b. Calculate the expected rate of return on each alternative and fill in the blanks on the row for $\hat{k}$ in the table above.

c. You should recognize that basing a decision solely on expected returns is only appropriate for risk-neutral individuals. Since your client, like virtually everyone, is risk averse, the riskiness of each alternative is an important aspect of the decision. One possible measure of risk is the *standard deviation* of returns.

   (1) Calculate this value for each alternative, and fill in the blank on the row for σ in the table above.

   (2) What type of risk is measured by the standard deviation?

   (3) Draw a graph which shows *roughly* the shape of the probability distributions for High Tech, U.S. Rubber, and T-bills.

d. Suppose you suddenly remembered that the *coefficient of variation (CV)* is generally regarded as being a better measure of stand-alone risk than the standard deviation when the alternatives being considered have widely differing expected returns. Calculate the missing CVs and fill in the blanks on the row for CV in the table above. Does the CV produce the same risk rankings as the standard deviation?

e. Suppose you created a 2-stock portfolio by investing $50,000 in High Tech and $50,000 in Collections.

   (1) Calculate the expected return ($\hat{k}_p$), the standard deviation (σ_p), and the coefficient of variation (CV_p) for this portfolio and fill in the appropriate blanks in the table above.

   (2) How does the riskiness of this 2-stock portfolio compare with the riskiness of the individual stocks if they were held in isolation?

f.   Suppose an investor starts with a portfolio consisting of one randomly selected stock. What would happen (1) to the riskiness and (2) to the expected return of the portfolio as more and more randomly selected stocks were added to the portfolio? What is the implication for investors? Draw a graph of the two portfolios to illustrate your answer.

g. (1) Should portfolio effects impact the way investors think about the riskiness of individual stocks?

   (2) If you decided to hold a 1-stock portfolio, and consequently were exposed to more risk than diversified investors, could you expect to be compensated for all of your risk; that is, could you earn a risk premium on that part of your risk that you could have eliminated by diversifying?

h.   The expected rates of return and the beta coefficients of the alternatives as supplied by Merrill Finch's computer program are as follows:

Security	Return ($\hat{k}$)	Risk (Beta)
High Tech	17.4%	1.29
Market	15.0	1.00
U.S. Rubber	13.8	0.68
T-bills	8.0	0.00
Collections	1.7	(0.86)

   (1) What is a *beta coefficient*, and how are betas used in risk analysis?

   (2) Do the expected returns appear to be related to each alternative's market risk?

   (3) Is it possible to choose among the alternatives on the basis of the information developed thus far? Use the data given at the start of the problem to construct a graph which shows how the T-bill's, High Tech's, and Collections' beta coefficients are calculated. Then discuss what betas measure and how they are used in risk analysis.

I. (1) Write out the Security Market Line (SML) equation, use it to calculate the required rate of return on each alternative, and then graph the relationship between the expected and required rates of return.

   (2) How do the expected rates of return compare with the required rates of return?

(3) Does the fact that Collections has an expected return which is less than the T-bill rate make any sense?

(4) What would be the market risk and the required return of a 50-50 portfolio of High Tech and Collections? Of High Tech and U.S. Rubber?

j. (1) Suppose investors raised their inflation expectations by 3 percentage points over current estimates as reflected in the 8 percent T-bill rate. What effect would higher inflation have on the SML and on the returns required on high- and low-risk securities?

(2) Suppose instead that investors' risk aversion increased enough to cause the market risk premium to increase by 3 percentage points. (Inflation remains constant.) What effect would this have on the SML and on returns of high- and low-risk securities?

CHAPTER 5
Risk and Rates of Return

- Stand-alone risk
- Portfolio risk
- Risk & return: CAPM/SML

What is investment risk?

Investment risk pertains to the probability of earning less than the expected return.

The greater the chance of low or negative returns, the riskier the investment.

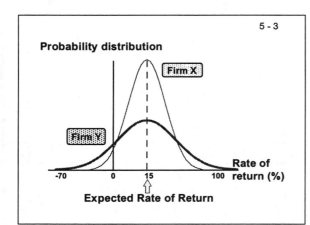

Probability distribution

Firm X

Firm Y

Rate of return (%)

-70   0   15   100

Expected Rate of Return

CAPM   beta

$E(R)$

market return

$$K_S = R_f + \beta [E(R_m) - R_f]$$

Risk-free rate   diversifiable risk

X undervalued line

security market line

X overvalued

R_f

β

Investment Alternatives
(Given in the problem)

Economy	Prob.	T-Bill	HT	Coll	USR	MP
Recession	0.1	8.0%	-22.0%	28.0%	10.0%	-13.0%
Below avg.	0.2	8.0	-2.0	14.7	-10.0	1.0
Average	0.4	8.0	20.0	0.0	7.0	15.0
Above avg.	0.2	8.0	35.0	-10.0	45.0	29.0
Boom	0.1	8.0	50.0	-20.0	30.0	43.0
	1.0					

Why is the T-bill return independent of the economy?

Will return the promised 8% regardless of the economy.

Do T-bills promise a completely risk-free return?

No, T-bills are still exposed to the risk of inflation.

However, not much unexpected inflation is likely to occur over a relatively short period.

Do the returns of HT and Coll. move with or counter to the economy?

- **HT: With. Positive correlation. Typical.**
- **Coll: Countercyclical. Negative correlation. Unusual.**

Calculate the expected rate of return on each alternative:

$\hat{k}$ = expected rate of return.

$$\hat{k} = \sum_{i=1}^{n} k P_i.$$

$\hat{k}_{HT}$ = (-22%)0.1 + (-2%)0.20
+ (20%)0.40 + (35%)0.20
+ (50%)0.1 = 17.4%.

	$\hat{k}$
HT	17.4%
Market	15.0
USR	13.8
T-bill	8.0
Coll.	1.7

HT appears to be the best, but is it really?

What's the standard deviation of returns for each alternative?

σ = Standard deviation.

$$\sigma = \sqrt{\text{Variance}} = \sqrt{\sigma^2}$$

$$= \sqrt{\sum_{i=1}^{n}(k_i - \hat{k})^2 P_i}.$$

$$\sigma = \sqrt{\sum_{i=1}^{n}(k_i - \hat{k})^2 P_i}.$$

$$\sigma_{\text{T-bills}} = \begin{bmatrix} (8.0 - 8.0)^2\,0.1 + (8.0 - 8.0)^2\,0.2 \\ + (8.0 - 8.0)^2\,0.4 + (8.0 - 8.0)^2\,0.2 \\ + (8.0 - 8.0)^2\,0.1 \end{bmatrix}^{.5}$$

$\sigma_{\text{T-bills}} = $ **0.0%.** $\qquad \sigma_{\text{Coll}} = $ **13.4%.**

$\sigma_{\text{HT}} = $ **20.0%.** $\qquad \sigma_{\text{USR}} = $ **18.8%.**

$\qquad\qquad\qquad\qquad \sigma_{M} = $ **15.3%.**

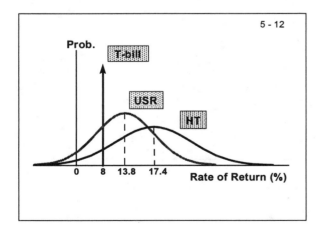

BLUEPRINTS: CHAPTER 5

- Standard deviation (σ_i) measures total, or stand-alone, risk.

- The larger the σ_i, the lower the probability that actual returns will be close to the expected return.

Expected Returns vs. Risk

Security	Expected return	Risk, σ
HT	17.4%	20.0%
Market	15.0	15.3
USR	13.8*	18.8*
T-bills	8.0	0.0
Coll.	1.7*	13.4*

*Seems misplaced.

Coefficient of Variation (CV)

Standardized measure of dispersion about the expected value:

$$CV = \frac{\text{Std dev}}{\text{Mean}} = \frac{\sigma}{\hat{k}}.$$

Shows risk per unit of return.

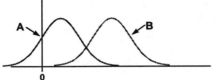

$\sigma_A = \sigma_B$, but A is riskier because larger probability of losses.

$$\frac{\sigma}{\hat{k}} = CV_A > CV_B.$$

Portfolio Risk and Return

Assume a two-stock portfolio with $50,000 in HT and $50,000 in Collections.

Calculate $\hat{k}_p$ and σ_p.

Portfolio Return, $\hat{k}_p$

$\hat{k}_p$ is a weighted average:

$$\hat{k}_p = \sum_{i=1}^{n} w_i \hat{k}_w.$$

$\hat{k}_p = 0.5(17.4\%) + 0.5(1.7\%) = 9.6\%.$

$\hat{k}_p$ is between $\hat{k}_{HT}$ and $\hat{k}_{COLL}$.

Alternative Method

Estimated Return

Economy	Prob.	HT	Coll.	Port.
Recession	0.10	-22.0%	28.0%	3.0%
Below avg.	0.20	-2.0	14.7	6.4
Average	0.40	20.0	0.0	10.0
Above avg.	0.20	35.0	-10.0	12.5
Boom	0.10	50.0	-20.0	15.0

$$\hat{k}_p = (3.0\%)0.10 + (6.4\%)0.20 + (10.0\%)0.40$$
$$+ (12.5\%)0.20 + (15.0\%)0.10 = 9.6\%.$$

$$\sigma_p = \left[\begin{array}{l} (3.0 - 9.6)^2 0.10 \\ +(6.4 - 9.6)^2 0.20 \\ +(10.0 - 9.6)^2 0.40 \\ +(12.5 - 9.6)^2 0.20 \\ +(15.0 - 9.6)^2 0.10 \end{array} \right]^{1/2} = 3.3\%.$$

$$CV_p = \frac{3.3\%}{9.6\%} = 0.34.$$

- $\sigma_p = 3.3\%$ is much lower than that of either stock (20% and 13.4%).

- $\sigma_p = 3.3\%$ is lower than average of HT and Coll = 16.7%.

- ∴ Portfolio provides average $\hat{k}$ but lower risk.

- Reason: negative correlation.

General statements about risk

- Most stocks are positively correlated. $r_{k,m} \approx 0.65$.
- $\sigma \approx 35\%$ for an average stock.
- Combining stocks generally lowers risk.

Returns Distribution for Two Perfectly Negatively Correlated Stocks (r = -1.0) and for Portfolio WM

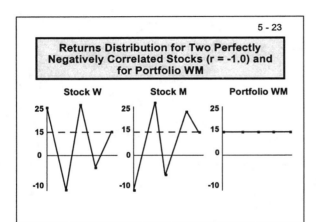

Returns Distributions for Two Perfectly Positively Correlated Stocks (r = +1.0) and for Portfolio MM'

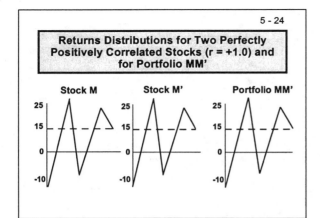

What would happen to the riskiness of an average 1-stock portfolio as more randomly selected stocks were added?

■ σ_p would decrease because the added stocks would not be perfectly correlated but $\hat{k}_p$ would remain relatively constant.

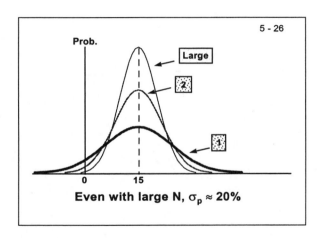

Even with large N, $\sigma_p \approx 20\%$

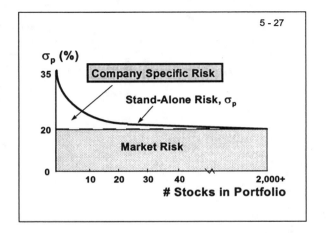

- As more stocks are added, each new stock has a smaller risk-reducing impact.

- σ_p falls very slowly after about 40 stocks are included. The lower limit for σ_p is about 20% = σ_M.

$$\text{Stand-alone risk} = \text{Market risk} + \text{Firm-specific risk}$$

Market risk is that part of a security's stand-alone risk that *cannot* be eliminated by diversification.

Firm-specific risk is that part of a security's stand-alone risk which can be eliminated by proper diversification.

- By forming portfolios, we can eliminate about half the riskiness of individual stocks (35% vs. 20%).

BLUEPRINTS: CHAPTER 5

If you chose to hold a one-stock portfolio and thus are exposed to more risk than diversified investors, would you be compensated for all the risk you bear?

- **NO!**
- **Stand-alone risk as measured by a stock's σ or CV is not important to a well-diversified investor.**
- **Rational, risk averse investors are concerned with σ_p, which is based on market risk.**

- **There can only be one price, hence market return, for a given security. Therefore, no compensation can be earned for the additional risk of a one-stock portfolio.**

- Beta measures a stock's market risk. It shows a stock's volatility relative to the market.

- Beta shows how risky a stock is if the stock is held in a well-diversified portfolio.

How are betas calculated?

- Run a regression of past returns on Stock *i* versus returns on the market. Returns = D/P + g.

- The slope of the regression line is defined as the beta coefficient.

Illustration of beta calculation:

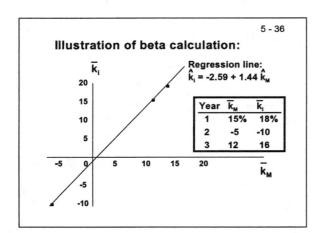

Regression line:
$\hat{k_I} = -2.59 + 1.44\ \hat{k_M}$

Year	$\overline{k_M}$	$\overline{k_I}$
1	15%	18%
2	-5	-10
3	12	16

Find beta

- "By Eye." Plot points, draw in regression line, set slope as b = Rise/Run. The "rise" is the difference in k_i, the "run" is the difference in k_M. For example, how much does k_i increase or decrease when k_M increases from 0% to 10%?

- Calculator. Enter data points, and calculator does least squares regression: $k_i = a + bk_M = -2.59 + 1.44k_M$. r = corr. coefficient = 0.997.

- In the real world, we would use weekly or monthly returns, with at least a year of data, and would always use a computer or calculator.

- If beta = 1.0, average stock.

- If beta > 1.0, stock riskier than average.

- If beta < 1.0, stock less risky than average.

- Most stocks have betas in the range of 0.5 to 1.5.

Can a beta be negative?

Answer: Yes, if r₍ᵢ,ₘ₎ is negative. Then in a "beta graph" the regression line will slope downward.

Answer: Yes, if $r_{i,m}$ is negative. Then in a "beta graph" the regression line will slope downward.

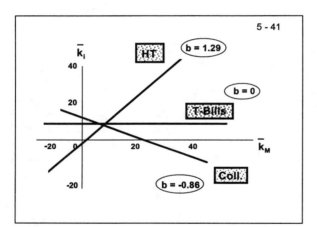

Security	Expected Return	Risk (Beta)
HT	17.4%	1.29
Market	15.0	1.00
USR	13.8	0.68
T-bills	8.0	0.00
Coll.	1.7	-0.86

Riskier securities have higher returns, so the rank order is OK.

Use the SML to calculate the required returns.

SML: $k_I = k_{RF} + (k_M - k_{RF})b_I$.

- Assume $k_{RF} = 8\%$.
- Note that $k_M = \hat{k}_M$ is 15%. (Equil.)
- $RP_M = k_M - k_{RF} = 15\% - 8\% = 7\%$.

Required Rates of Return

$$
\begin{aligned}
k_{HT} &= 8.0\% + (15.0\% - 8.0\%)(1.29) \\
&= 8.0\% + (7\%)(1.29) \\
&= 8.0\% + 9.0\% = \boxed{17.0\%}. \\
k_M &= 8.0\% + (7\%)(1.00) = \boxed{15.0\%}. \\
k_{USR} &= 8.0\% + (7\%)(0.68) = \boxed{12.8\%}. \\
k_{T\text{-bill}} &= 8.0\% + (7\%)(0.00) = \boxed{8.0\%}. \\
k_{Coll} &= 8.0\% + (7\%)(-0.86) = \boxed{2.0\%}.
\end{aligned}
$$

Expected vs. Required Returns

	$\hat{k}$	k	
HT	17.4%	17.0%	Undervalued: $\hat{k} > k$
Market	15.0	15.0	Fairly valued
USR	13.8	12.8	Undervalued: $\hat{k} > k$
T-bills	8.0	8.0	Fairly valued
Coll.	1.7	2.0	Overvalued: $\hat{k} < k$

SML: $k_I = 8\% + (15\% - 8\%) b_I$.

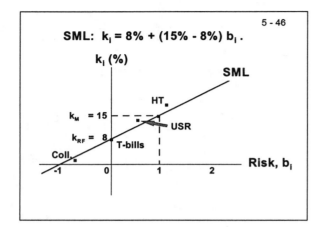

Calculate beta for a portfolio with 50% HT and 50% Collections

b_p = Weighted average
   = $0.5(b_{HT}) + 0.5(b_{Coll})$
   = $0.5(1.29) + 0.5(-0.86)$
   = 0.22.

The required return on the HT/Coll. portfolio is:

k_p = Weighted average k
   = $0.5(17\%) + 0.5(2\%) = 9.5\%$.

Or use SML:

$k_p = k_{RF} + (k_M - k_{RF}) b_p$
   = $8.0\% + (15.0\% - 8.0\%)(0.22)$
   = $8.0\% + 7\%(0.22)$ = 9.5%.

If investors raise inflation expectations by 3%, what would happen to the SML?

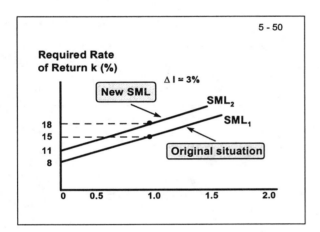

Required Rate of Return k (%)

Δ I ≈ 3%

New SML

SML₂

SML₁

18
15
11
8

Original situation

0   0.5   1.0   1.5   2.0

If inflation did not change but risk aversion increased enough to cause the market risk premium to increase by 3 percentage points, what would happen to the SML?

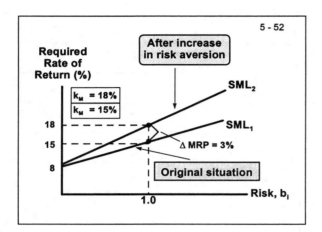

Required
Rate of
Return (%)

**After increase
in risk aversion**

SML₂

k_M = 18%
k_M = 15%

SML₁

18
15
8

△ MRP = 3%

Original situation

Risk, b_i

1.0

**Has the CAPM been verified through
empirical tests?**

■ Not completely. Those statistical
tests have problems which make
verification almost impossible.

■ Investors seem to be concerned
with both market risk and total risk.
Therefore, the SML may not
produce a correct estimate of k_i:

$$k_i = k_{RF} + (k_M - k_{RF})b + ?$$

■ Also, CAPM/SML concepts are based on expectations, yet betas are calculated using historical data. A company's historical data may not reflect investors' expectations about future riskiness.

EXAM-TYPE PROBLEMS

5-1.   For markets to be in equilibrium (that is, for there to be no strong pressure for prices to depart from their current levels),

a.   The expected rate of return must be equal to the required rate of return; that is, $\hat{k} = k$.

b.   The past realized rate of return must be equal to the expected rate of return; that is, $\overline{k} = \hat{k}$.

c.   The required rate of return must equal the realized rate of return; that is, $k = \overline{k}$.

d.   All three of the above statements must hold for equilibrium to exist; that is, $\hat{k} = k = \overline{k}$.

e.   None of the above statements is correct.

5-2.   Which of the following statements is most correct?

a.   According to CAPM theory, the required rate of return on a given stock can be found by use of the SML equation:

$$k_i = k_{RF} + (k_M - k_{RF})b_i.$$

Expectations for inflation are not reflected anywhere in this equation, even indirectly, and because of that the text notes that the CAPM may not be strictly correct.

b.   If the required rate of return is given by the SML equation as set forth in *answer a*, there is nothing a financial manager can do to change his or her company's cost of capital, because each of the elements in the equation is determined exclusively by the market, not by the type of actions a company's management can take, even in the long run.

c.   Assume that the required rate of return on the market is currently k_M = 15%, and that k_M remains fixed at that level. If the yield curve has a steep upward slope, the calculated market risk premium would be larger if the 30-day T-bill rate were used as the risk-free rate than if the 30-year T-bond rate were used as k_{RF}.

d.   Statements a and b are both true.

e.   Statements a and c are both true.

5-3.   You hold a diversified portfolio consisting of a $5,000 investment in each of 20 different common stocks. The portfolio beta is equal to 1.15. You have decided to sell one of your stocks, a lead mining stock whose b = 1.0, for $5,000 net and to use the proceeds to buy $5,000 of stock in a steel company whose b = 2.0. What will be the new beta of the portfolio? (1.20)

5-4   Electro Inc. has a beta of 1.7, Flowers Galore has a beta of 0.6, the expected rate of return on an average stock is 14 percent, and the risk-free rate of return is 7.8 percent. By how much does the required return on the riskier stock exceed the required return on the less risky stock? (6.82%)

6-46   Assume that you are nearing graduation and that you have applied for a job with a local bank, First National Bank. As part of the bank's evaluation process, you have been asked to take an examination which covers several financial analysis techniques. The first section of the test addresses time value of money analysis. See how you would do by answering the following questions.

a.   Draw time lines for (1) a $100 lump sum cash flow at the end of year 2, (2) an ordinary annuity of $100 per year for 3 years, and (3) an uneven cash flow stream of -$50, $100, $75, and $50 at the end of Years 0 through 3.

b. (1) What is the future value of an initial $100 after 3 years if it is invested in an account paying 10 percent, annual compounding?

    (2) What is the present value of $100 to be received in 3 years if the appropriate interest rate is 10 percent, annual compounding?

c.   We sometimes need to find how long it will take a sum of money (or anything else) to grow to some specified amount. For example, if a company's sales are growing at a rate of 20 percent per year, how long will it take sales to double?

d.   What is the difference between an ordinary annuity and an annuity due? What type of annuity is shown below? How would you change it to the other type of annuity?

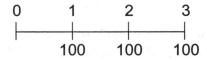

e. (1) What is the future value of a 3-year ordinary annuity of $100 if the appropriate interest rate is 10 percent, annual compounding?

    (2) What is the present value of the annuity?

    (3) What would the future and present values be if the annuity were an annuity due?

f.   What is the present value of the following uneven cash flow stream? The appropriate interest rate is 10 percent, compounded annually.

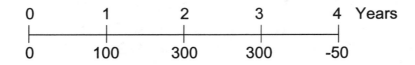

g.   What annual interest rate will cause $100 to grow to $125.97 in 3 years?

h. (1) Will the future value be larger or smaller if we compound an initial amount more often than annually, for example, every 6 months, or *semiannually*, holding the stated interest rate constant? Why?

(2) Define (a) the *stated, or quoted, or nominal, rate*, (b) the periodic rate, and (c) the *effective annual rate (EAR)*.

(3) What is the effective annual rate corresponding to a nominal rate of 10 percent, compounded semiannually? Compounded quarterly? Compounded daily?

(4) What is the future value of $100 after 3 years under 10 percent semiannual compounding? Quarterly compounding?

I.   When will the effective annual rate be equal to the nominal (quoted) rate?

j. (1) What is the value at the end of Year 3 of the following cash flow stream if the quoted interest rate is 10 percent, compounded semiannually?

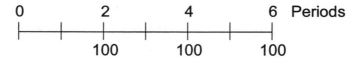

(2) What is the PV of the same stream?

(3) Is the stream an annuity?

(4) An important rule is that you should *never* show a nominal rate on a time line or use it in calculations unless what condition holds? (Hint: Think of annual compounding, when $i_{Nom} = EAR = i_{PER}$.) What would be wrong with your answer to questions j(1) and j(2) if you used the nominal rate, 10 percent, rather than the periodic rate $i_{Nom}/2$ = 10%/2 = 5%?

k. (1) Construct an amortization schedule for a $1,000, 10 percent, annual compounding, loan with 3 equal installments.

(2) What is the annual interest expense for the borrower, and the annual interest income for the lender, during Year 2?

l. Suppose on January 1, 1997, you deposit $100 in an account that pays a nominal, or quoted, interest rate of 10 percent, with interest added (compounded) 365 times per year. How much would you have in your account on October 1, or after 9 months (273 days)?

m. Now, suppose you left your money in the bank for 21 months. Thus, on January 1, 1997, you deposit $100 in an account that pays 10 percent, daily compounding, with a 365-day year. How much would be in your account on October 1, 1998, or 273 + 365 = 638 days later?

n. Suppose someone offered to sell you a note calling for the payment of $1,000 15 months from today (456 days). They offer to sell it to you for $850. You have $850 in a bank time deposit which pays a 7 percent nominal rate with daily (365 days per year) compounding, and you plan to leave the money in the bank unless you buy the note. The note is not risky--you are sure it will be paid on schedule. Should you buy the note? Check the decision in three ways: (1) by comparing your future value if you buy the note versus leaving your money in the bank, (2) by comparing the PV of the note with your current bank account, and (3) by comparing the EAR on the note versus that of the bank account.

o. Suppose the note discussed in Part n had a cost of $850, but called for 5 quarterly payments of $190 each, with the first payment due in 3 months rather than $1,000 at the end of 15 months. Would it be a good investment for you? (Assume that today is January 1, 1997, and that the first payment will be due April 1, 1997.)

6 - 1

CHAPTER 6
Time Value of Money

- ■ Future value
- ■ Present value
- ■ Rates of return
- ■ Amortization

$FV_1 = PV(1+i)$

$FV_2 = FV_1 + FV_1 * i$

$\quad = PV(1+i) + PV(1+i) * i$

$\quad = PV(1+i)^2$

$\quad = 1 + 2i + i^2$

$FV = PV(1+i)^n$

---

6 - 2

Time lines show timing of cash flows.

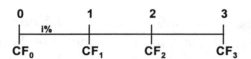

Tick marks at ends of periods, so Time 0 is today; Time 1 is the end of Period 1; or the beginning of Period 2.

Tables $\quad$ n↓ i ⟶

$PVF_{i,n}$

$FVF_{i,n}$

$FVIF_{i,n}$

$PVIF_{i,n}$

---

6 - 3

Time line for a $100 lump sum due at the end of Year 2.

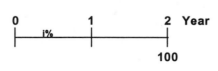

annuity = equal payments

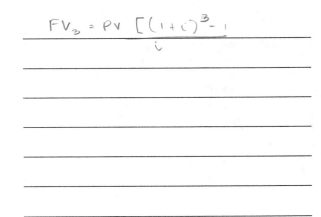

$$FV_3 = PV \left[\frac{(1+i)^3 - 1}{i} \right.$$

Time line for an ordinary annuity of $100 for 3 years.

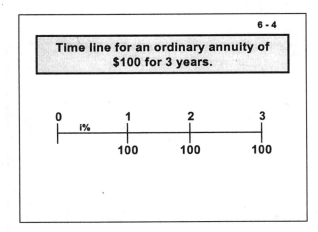

Time line for uneven CFs -$50 at t = 0 and $100, $75, and $50 at the end of Years 1 through 3.

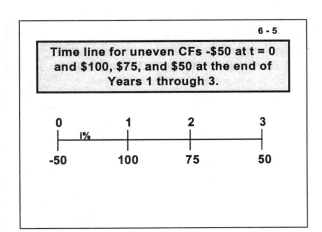

What's the FV of an initial $100 after 3 years if i = 10%?

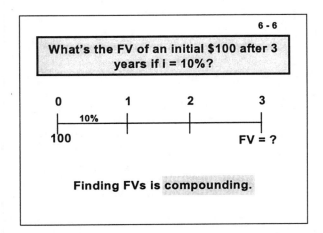

Finding FVs is compounding.

After 1 year:

$$FV_1 = PV + INT_1 = PV + PV\,(i)$$
$$= PV(1 + i)$$
$$= \$100(1.10)$$
$$= \$110.00.$$

After 2 years:

$$FV_2 = PV(1 + i)^2$$
$$= \$100(1.10)^2$$
$$= \$121.00.$$

After 3 years:

$$FV_3 = PV(1 + i)^3$$
$$= 100(1.10)^3$$
$$= \$133.10.$$

In general,

$$FV_n = PV(1 + i)^n$$

Three Ways to Find FVs

- Solve the equation with a regular calculator.
- Use tables.
- Use a financial calculator.

Financial Calculator Solution

Financial calculators solve this equation:

$$FV_n = PV(1 + i)^n.$$

There are 4 variables. If 3 are known, the calculator will solve for the 4th.

Here's the setup to find FV:

INPUTS	3	10	-100	0		
	N	I/YR	PV	PMT		FV
OUTPUT						133.10

Clearing automatically sets everything to 0, but for safety enter PMT = 0.

Set: P/YR = 1, END

What's the PV of $100 due in 3 years if i = 10%?

Finding PVs is <u>discounting</u>, and it's the reverse of compounding.

```
      0         1         2         3
      |---------|---------|---------|
         10%
PV = ? <- - - - - - - - - - - 100
```

$$PV = \frac{FV}{(1+i)^n}$$

Solve $FV_n = PV(1 + i)^n$ for PV:

$$PV = \frac{FV_n}{(1+i)^n} = FV_n\left(\frac{1}{1+i}\right)^n$$

$$PV = \$100\left(\frac{1}{1.10}\right)^3 = \$100\left(PVIF_{i,n}\right)$$
$$= \$100(0.7513) = \$75.13.$$

Handwritten notes:

$PV = FV (PVF_{i,n})$

$PV_A = A(PVIFA_{i,n})$

$FV = PV (FVF_{i,n})$

$FV_A = A(FVIFA_{i,n})$

Financial Calculator Solution

INPUTS	3	10		0	100
	N	I/YR	PV	PMT	FV
OUTPUT			-75.13		

Either PV or FV must be negative. Here PV = -75.13. Put in \$75.13 today, take out \$100 after 3 years.

Handwritten notes:

compounded monthly

$FV = PV\left(1 + \frac{y}{m}\right)^{mn}$

If sales grow at 20% per year, how long before sales double?

Solve for n:

$$FV_n = 1(1 + i)^n;$$
$$2 = 1(1.20)^n$$

Use calculator to solve, see next slide.

Handwritten notes:

EAR - effective annual rate

$\left[1 + \frac{\text{Quoted rate}}{m}\right]^m - 1$

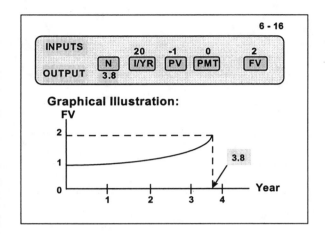

Graphical Illustration:

What's the difference between an ordinary annuity and an annuity due?

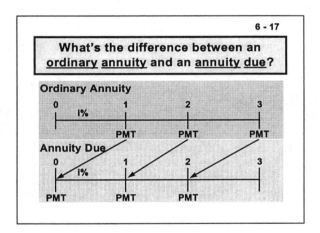

What's the FV of a 3-year ordinary annuity of $100 at 10%?

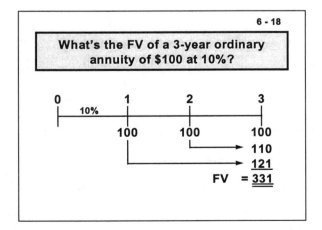

Financial Calculator Solution

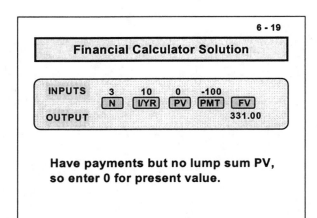

```
INPUTS    3      10     0     -100
         [N]   [I/YR]  [PV]  [PMT]  [FV]
OUTPUT                               331.00
```

Have payments but no lump sum PV,
so enter 0 for present value.

What's the PV of this ordinary annuity?

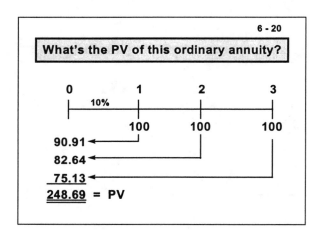

```
    0        1        2        3
    |--------|--------|--------|
        10%
            100      100      100
90.91 ◄------┘        |        |
82.64 ◄---------------┘        |
 75.13 ◄----------------------┘
248.69 = PV
```

```
INPUTS    3      10          100    0
         [N]   [I/YR]  [PV]  [PMT]  [FV]
OUTPUT                -248.69
```

Have payments but no lump sum FV,
so enter 0 for future value.

Find the FV and PV if the annuity were an annuity due.

```
0        1        2        3
|--------|--------|--------|
   10%
100      100      100
```

Switch from "End" to "Begin".
Then enter variables to find PVA_3 =
$273.55.

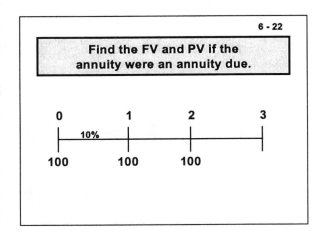

INPUTS	3	10		100	0
	N	I/YR	PV	PMT	FV
OUTPUT			-273.55		

Then enter PV = 0 and press FV to find
FV = $364.10.

What is the PV of this uneven cash flow stream?

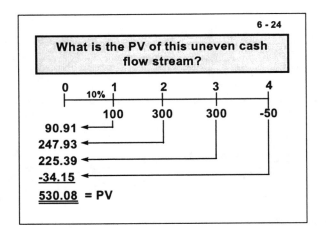

```
0    10%  1        2        3        4
|--------|--------|--------|--------|
         100      300      300      -50
90.91 ◄──
247.93 ◄─────────
225.39 ◄──────────────────
-34.15 ◄───────────────────────────
530.08  = PV
```

6 - 25

■ Input in "CFLO" register:

$CF_0 = 0$

$CF_1 = 100$

$CF_2 = 300$

$CF_3 = 300$

$CF_4 = -50$

■ Enter I = 10%, then press NPV button to get NPV = 530.09. (Here NPV = PV.)

---

6 - 26

What interest rate would cause $100 to grow to $125.97 in 3 years?

$$\$100 (1 + i)^3 = \$125.97.$$

INPUTS	3		-100	0	125.97
	N	I/YR	PV	PMT	FV
OUTPUT		8%			

---

6 - 27

Will the FV of a lump sum be larger or smaller if we compound more often, holding the stated I% constant? Why?

LARGER! If compounding is more frequent than once a year--for example, semiannually, quarterly, or daily--interest is earned on interest more often.

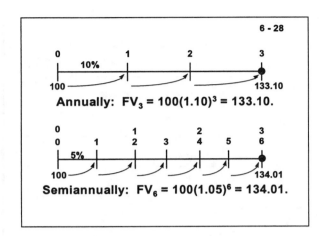

Annually: $FV_3 = 100(1.10)^3 = 133.10$.

Semiannually: $FV_6 = 100(1.05)^6 = 134.01$.

We will deal with 3 different rates:

i_{Nom} = nominal, or stated, or quoted, rate per year.

i_{Per} = periodic rate.

EAR = EFF% = effective annual rate

- i_{Nom} is stated in contracts. Periods per year (m) must also be given.
- Examples:
  - 8%; Quarterly
  - 8%, Daily interest (365 days)

- Periodic rate = i_{Per} = i_{Nom}/m, where m is number of compounding periods per year. m = 4 for quarterly, 12 for monthly, and 360 or 365 for daily compounding.
- Examples:

  8% quarterly: i_{per} = 8%/4 = 2%.

  8% daily (365): i_{per} = 8%/365 = 0.021918%.

- Effective Annual Rate (EAR = EFF%): The annual rate which causes PV to grow to the same FV as under multi-period compounding.

  Example: EFF% for 10%, semiannual:

  $$FV = (1 + i_{Nom}/m)^m$$
  $$= (1.05)^2 = 1.1025.$$

  EFF% = 10.25% because

  $$(1.1025)^1 = 1.1025.$$

  Any PV would grow to same FV at 10.25% annually or 10% semiannually.

- An investment with monthly payments is different from one with quarterly payments. Must put on EFF% basis to compare rates of return. Use EFF% only for comparisons.
- Banks say "interest paid daily." Same as compounded daily.

How do we find EFF% for a nominal rate of 10%, compounded semi-annually?

$$EFF\% = \left(1 + \frac{i_{nom}}{m}\right)^m - 1$$

$$= \left(1 + \frac{0.10}{2}\right)^2 - 1.0$$

$$= (1.05)^2 - 1.0$$

$$= 0.1025 = 10.25\%.$$

Or use a financial calculator.

EAR = EFF% of 10%

EAR_{Annual} = 10%.

EAR_Q = $(1 + 0.10/4)^4 - 1$ = 10.38%.

EAR_M = $(1 + 0.10/12)^{12} - 1$ = 10.47%.

$EAR_{D(360)}$ = $(1 + 0.10/360)^{360} - 1$ = 10.52%.

Can the effective rate ever be equal to the nominal rate?

■ **Yes, but only if annual compounding is used, i.e., if m = 1.**

■ **If m > 1, EFF% will always be greater than the nominal rate.**

When is each rate used?

i_{nom}: Written into contracts, quoted by banks and brokers. <u>Not</u> used in calculations or shown on time lines.

---

i_{Per}: Used in calculations, shown on time lines.

If i_{Nom} has annual compounding, then $i_{Per} = i_{Nom}/1 = i_{Nom}$.

EAR = EFF%: Used to compare returns on investments with different payments per year.

(Used for calculations if and only if dealing with annuities where payments don't match interest compounding periods.)

BLUEPRINTS: CHAPTER 6

FV of $100 after 3 years under 10% semiannual compounding? Quarterly?

$$FV_n = PV\left(1 + \frac{i_{Nom}}{m}\right)^{mn}.$$

$$FV_{3S} = \$100\left(1 + \frac{0.10}{2}\right)^{2 \times 3}$$

$$= \$100(1.05)^6 = \$134.01.$$

$$FV_{3Q} = \$100(1.025)^{12} = \$134.49.$$

What's the value at the end of Year 3 of the following CF stream if the quoted interest rate is 10%, compounded semi-annually?

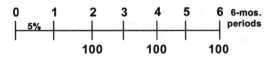

```
0      1      2      3      4      5      6   6-mos.
   5%                                          periods
            100           100          100
```

- Payments occur annually, but compounding occurs each 6 months.
- So we can't use normal annuity valuation techniques.

1st Method: Compound Each CF

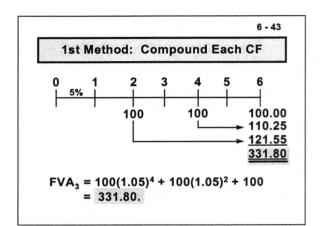

$$FVA_3 = 100(1.05)^4 + 100(1.05)^2 + 100$$
$$= \boxed{331.80.}$$

2nd Method: Treat as an Annuity

Could you find FV with a financial calculator?

Yes, by following these steps:

a. Find the EAR for the quoted rate:

$$EAR = \left(1 + \frac{0.10}{2}\right)^2 - 1 = 10.25\%.$$

Or, to find EAR with a calculator:

NOM% = 10
P/YR = 2
EFF% = 10.25

---

b. The cash flow stream is an annual annuity. Find k_{Nom} (annual) whose EFF% = 10.25%. In calculator,

EFF% = 10.25
P/YR = 1
NOM% = 10.25

c.

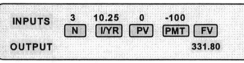

INPUTS	3	10.25	0	-100	
	N	I/YR	PV	PMT	FV
OUTPUT					331.80

What's the PV of this stream?

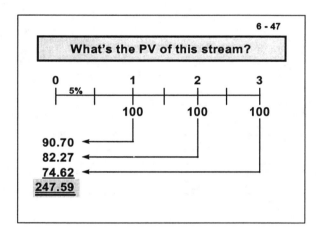

90.70
82.27
74.62
247.59

Amortization

Construct an amortization schedule for a $1,000, 10% annual rate loan with 3 equal payments.

Step 1: Find the required payments.

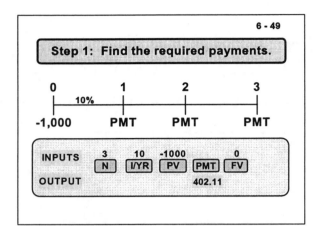

```
   0         1         2         3
   ├───10%───┼─────────┼─────────┤
-1,000      PMT       PMT       PMT
```

INPUTS	3	10	-1000		0
	N	I/YR	PV	PMT	FV
OUTPUT				402.11	

Step 2: Find interest charge for Year 1.

INT_t = Beg bal$_t$ (i)
INT_1 = $1,000(0.10) = $100.

Step 3: Find repayment of principal in Year 1.

Repmt = PMT - INT
    = $402.11 - $100
    = $302.11.

Step 4: Find ending balance after Year 1.

End bal = Beg bal - Repmt
     = $1,000 - $302.11 = $697.89.

Repeat these steps for Years 2 and 3 to complete the amortization table.

YR	BEG BAL	PMT	INT	PRIN PMT	END BAL
1	$1,000	$402	$100	$302	$698
2	698	402	70	332	366
3	366	402	37	366	0
TOT		1,206.34	206.34	1,000	

Interest declines. Tax implications.

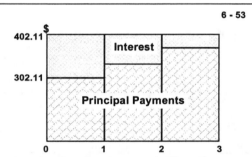

Level payments. Interest declines because outstanding balance declines. Lender earns 10% on loan outstanding, which is falling.

- Amortization tables are widely used-- for home mortgages, auto loans, business loans, retirement plans, etc. They are very important!

- Financial calculators (and spreadsheets) are great for setting up amortization tables.

On January 1 you deposit $100 in an account that pays a nominal interest rate of 10%, with daily compounding (365 days).

How much will you have on October 1, or after 9 months (273 days)? (Days given.)

---

i_{Per} = 10.0% / 365
= 0.027397% per day.

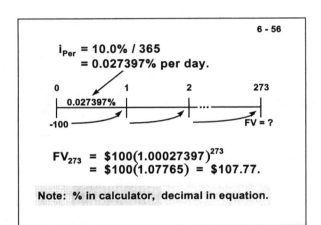

$$FV_{273} = \$100(1.00027397)^{273}$$
$$= \$100(1.07765) = \$107.77.$$

Note: % in calculator, decimal in equation.

---

i_{Per} = i_{Nom}/m
= 10.0/365
= 0.027397% per day.

INPUTS	273		-100	0	
	N	I/YR	PV	PMT	FV
OUTPUT					107.77

Enter i in one step.
Leave data in calculator.

Now suppose you leave your money in the bank for 21 months, which is 1.75 years or 273 + 365 = 638 days.

How much will be in your account at maturity?

Answer: Override N = 273 with N = 638. FV = $119.10.

---

i_{Per} = 0.027397% per day.

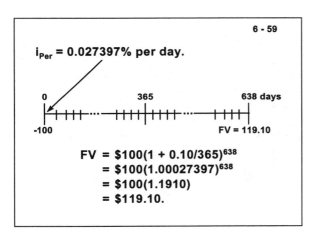

FV = $100(1 + 0.10/365)^{638}$
= $100(1.00027397)^{638}$
= $100(1.1910)$
= $119.10.

You are offered a note which pays $1,000 in 15 months (or 456 days) for $850. You have $850 in a bank which pays a 7.0% nominal rate, with 365 daily compounding, which is a daily rate of 0.019178% and an EAR of 7.25%. You plan to leave the money in the bank if you don't buy the note. The note is riskless.

Should you buy it?

$i_{Per} = 0.019178\%$ per day.

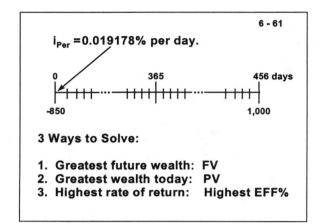

```
0              365           456 days
|++++++···+++++|+++++···+++|
-850                      1,000
```

3 Ways to Solve:

1. **Greatest future wealth: FV**
2. **Greatest wealth today: PV**
3. **Highest rate of return: Highest EFF%**

---

1. Greatest Future Wealth

Find FV of $850 left in bank for 15 months and compare with note's FV = $1000.

$$FV_{Bank} = \$850(1.00019178)^{456}$$
$$= \$927.67 \text{ in bank.}$$

Buy the note: $1000 > $927.67.

Calculator Solution to FV:

$$i_{Per} = i_{Nom}/m$$
$$= 7.0/365$$
$$= 0.019178\% \text{ per day.}$$

INPUTS	456		-850	0	
	N	I/YR	PV	PMT	FV
OUTPUT					927.67

Enter i_{Per} in one step.

---

2. Greatest Present Wealth

Find PV of note, and compare
with its $850 cost:

$$PV = \$1000(1.00019178)^{456}$$
$$= \$916.27.$$

	7/365 =			
INPUTS	456	.019178	0	1000
	N	I/YR	PV	PMT	FV
OUTPUT		-916.27			

PV of note is greater than its $850
cost, so buy the note. Raises your
wealth.

---

3. Rate of Return

Find the EFF% on note and
compare with 7.25% bank pays,
which is your opportunity cost of
capital:

$$FV_n = PV(1 + i)^n$$

$$1000 = \$850(1 + i)^{456}$$

Now we must solve for i.

---

6 - 67

INPUTS   456   -850   0   1000
     [N] [I/YR] [PV] [PMT] [FV]

OUTPUT   0.035646% per day

Convert % to decimal:

Decimal = 0.035646/100 = 0.00035646.

$$\text{EAR} = \text{EFF\%} = (1.00035646)^{365} - 1$$
$$= 13.89\%.$$

---

6 - 68

Using interest conversion:

  P/YR = 365
NOM% = 0.035646(365) = 13.01
 EFF% = 13.89

Since 13.89% > 7.25% opportunity cost, buy the note.

EXAM-TYPE PROBLEMS

6-1. Which of the following statements is most correct?

a. The first payment under a 3-year, annual payment, amortized loan for $1,000 will include a *smaller* percentage (or fraction) of the payment as interest if the interest rate is 5% than if it is 10%.

b. If you are lending money, then, based on effective interest rates, you should prefer to lend at a 10% nominal, or quoted, rate but with semiannual payments, rather than at a 10.1% nominal rate with annual payments. However, as a borrower you should prefer the annual payment loan.

c. The value of a perpetuity (say for $100 per year) will approach infinity as the interest rate used to evaluate the perpetuity approaches zero.

d. Statements a, b, and c are all true.

e. Only statements b and c are true.

6-2. You want to buy a new Nissan sports car on your 27th birthday. You have priced these cars and found that they currently sell for $25,000. You believe that the price will increase by 10 percent per year until you are ready to buy. You can presently invest to earn 14 percent. If you just turned 20 years old, how much must you invest at the end of each of the next 7 years to be able to purchase the Nissan in 7 years? ($4,540.15)

6-3. On January 1, 1997, a graduate student developed a 5-year financial plan which would provide enough money at the end of her graduate work (January 1, 2002) to open a business of her own. Her plan was to deposit $8,000 per year for 5 years, starting immediately, into an account paying 10 percent compounded annually. Her activities proceeded according to plan except that at the end of her third year (1/1/00) she withdrew $5,000 to take a Caribbean cruise, at the end of the fourth year (1/1/01) she withdrew $5,000 to buy a used Prelude, and at the end of the fifth year (1/1/02) she had to withdraw $5,000 to pay to have her dissertation typed. Her account, at the end of the fifth year, was less than the amount she had originally planned on by how much? ($16,550)

6-4. You have just taken out a 30-year, $120,000 mortgage on your new home. This mortgage is to be repaid in 360 equal end-of-month installments. If each of the monthly installments is $1,500, what is the effective annual interest rate on this mortgage? (15.87%)

6-5.   Assume that your father is now 50 years old, that he plans to retire in 10 years, and that he expects to live for 25 years after he retires, that is, until he is 85. He wants a fixed retirement income that has the same purchasing power at the time he retires as $40,000 has today (he realizes that the real value of his retirement income will decline year-by-year after he retires). His retirement income will begin the day he retires, 10 years from today, and he will then get 24 additional annual payments. Inflation is expected to be 5 percent per year from today forward; he currently has $100,000 saved up; and he expects to earn a return on his savings of 8 percent per year, annual compounding. To the nearest dollar, how much must he save during each of the next 10 years (with deposits being made at the end of each year) to meet his retirement goal? ($36,950)

6-6.   An investment pays you 10 percent interest, compounded quarterly.

a.   What is the periodic rate of interest? (2.5%)

b.   What is the nominal rate of interest? (10%)

c.   What is the effective rate of interest? (10.38%)

7-19 Robert Black and Carol Alvarez are vice-presidents of Western Money Management and codirectors of the company's pension fund management division. A major new client, the California League of Cities, has requested that Western present an investment seminar to the mayors of the represented cities, and Black and Alvarez, who will make the actual presentation, have asked you to help them by answering the following questions. Because the Walt Disney Company operates in one of the league's cities, you are to work Disney into the presentation. (See the vignette which opened the chapter for information on Disney.)

a.   What are the key features of a bond?

b.   What are call provisions and sinking fund provisions? Do these provisions make bonds more or less risky?

c.   How is the value of any asset whose value is based on expected future cash flows determined?

d.   How is the value of a bond determined? What is the value of a 10-year, $1,000 par value bond with a 10 percent annual coupon if its required rate of return is 10 percent?

e. (1) What would be the value of the bond described in Part d if, just after it had been issued, the expected inflation rate rose by 3 percentage points, causing investors to require a 13 percent return? Would we now have a discount or a premium bond? (If you do not have a financial calculator, $PVIF_{13\%,10} = 0.2946$; $PVIFA_{13\%,10} = 5.4262$.)

   (2) What would happen to the bonds' value if inflation fell, and k_d declined to 7 percent? Would we now have a premium or a discount bond?

   (3) What would happen to the value of the 10-year bond over time if the required rate of return remained at 13 percent, or if it remained at 7 percent? (Hint: With a financial calculator, enter N, I, PMT, and FV, and then change (override) N to see what happens to the PV as the bond approaches maturity.)

f. (1) What is the yield to maturity on a 10-year, 9 percent annual coupon, $1,000 par value bond that sells for $887.00? That sells for $1,134.20? What does the fact that a bond sells at a discount or at a premium tell you about the relationship between k_d and the bond's coupon rate?

    (2) What are the total return, the current yield, and the capital gains yield for the discount bond? (Assume the bond is held to maturity and the company does not default on the bonds.)

g.   What is *interest rate (or price) risk*? Which bond has more interest rate risk, an annual payment 1-year bond or a 30-year bond? Why?

h.   What is *reinvestment rate risk*? Which has more reinvestment rate risk, a 1-year bond or a 10-year bond?

I.   How does the equation for valuing a bond change if semiannual payments are made? Find the value of a 10-year, semiannual payment, 10 percent coupon bond if nominal k_d = 13%. (Hint: $PVIF_{6.5\%,20}$ = 0.2838 and $PVIFA_{6.5\%,20}$ = 11.0185.)

j.   Suppose you could buy, for $1,000, either a 10 percent, 10-year, annual payment bond or a 10 percent, 10-year, semiannual payment bond. They are equally risky. Which would you prefer? If $1,000 is the proper price for the semiannual bond, what is the equilibrium price for the annual payment bond?

k.   Suppose a 10-year, 10 percent, semiannual coupon bond with a par value of $1,000 is currently selling for $1,135.90, producing a nominal yield to maturity of 8 percent. However, the bond can be called after 5 years for a price of $1,050.

    (1) What is the bond's *nominal yield to call (YTC)*?

    (2) If you bought this bond, do you think you would be more likely to earn the YTM or the YTC? Why?

l.   Disney's bonds were issued with a yield to maturity of 7.5 percent. Does the yield to maturity represent the promised or expected return on the bond?

m.   Disney's bonds were rated AA- by S&P. Would you consider these bonds investment grade or junk bonds?

n.   What factors determine a company's bond rating?

o.   If Disney were to default on the bonds, would the company be immediately liquidated? Would the bondholders be assured of receiving all of their promised payments?

CHAPTER 7
Bonds and Their Valuation

- Key features of bonds
- Bond valuation
- Measuring yield
- Assessing risk

bonds are more frequently
issued than stocks; debt increases
company value

1) treasury - risk free
2) corporate - risky → depends on the
    financial condition of the co.
3) municipal
4) foreign

Key Features of a Bond

1. **Par value:** Face amount; paid at maturity. Assume $1,000.

2. **Coupon interest rate:** Stated interest rate. Multiply by par to get $ of interest. Generally fixed.

$$B_c = CP + Mt$$

Coupon payment - Coupon rate × face value
Floating rate bond - adjustable interest rates to maintain bond price
zero coupon bond - no interest payments

3. **Maturity:** Years until bond must be repaid. Declines.

4. **Issue date:** Date when bond was issued.

If int. rate ↑ bond prices ↓
required rate of return > mkt rate
∴ borrow rate > mkt rate

How does adding a "call provision" affect a bond?

- Issuer can refund if rates decline. That helps the issuer but hurts the investor.
- Therefore, borrowers are willing to pay more, and lenders require more, on callable bonds.
- Most bonds have a deferred call and a declining call premium. → compensation to investors for call

call protection- cannot call bond beyond certain point

What's a sinking fund?

- Provision to pay off a loan over its life rather than all at maturity.
- Similar to amortization on a term loan.
- Reduces risk to investor, shortens average maturity.
- But not good for investors if rates decline after issuance.

stockholders approve
(convertible)
bond issuances

floating rate bonds vs. index bonds
depends not only inflation, co. risk

convertible bond- at end of term investor can convert to equity
warrant- option attached to convertible bond - to convert to equity
income bond- int payments based on co.'s income
index bond- adjustable based on inflation rates

Sinking funds are generally handled in 2 ways

1. Call x% at par per year for sinking fund purposes.
2. Buy bonds on open market.

Company would call if k_d is below the coupon rate and bond sells at a premium. Use open market purchase if k_d is above coupon rate and bond sells at a discount.

Financial Asset Values

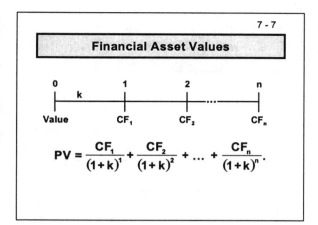

$$PV = \frac{CF_1}{(1+k)^1} + \frac{CF_2}{(1+k)^2} + \dots + \frac{CF_n}{(1+k)^n}.$$

- The discount rate (k_l) is the **opportunity cost of capital**, i.e., the rate that could be earned on alternative investments of equal risk.

$$k_l = k^* + IP + LP + MRP + DRP.$$

What's the value of a 10-year, 10% coupon bond if k_d = 10%?

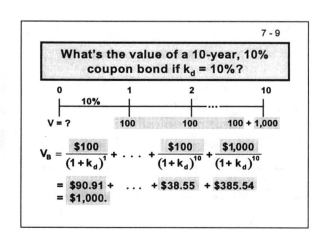

$$V_B = \frac{\$100}{(1+k_d)^1} + \dots + \frac{\$100}{(1+k_d)^{10}} + \frac{\$1,000}{(1+k_d)^{10}}$$

$$= \$90.91 + \dots + \$38.55 + \$385.54$$
$$= \$1,000.$$

The bond consists of a 10-yr, 10%
annuity of $100/yr plus a $1,000 lump
sum at t = 10:

PV annuity	= $ 614.46
PV maturity value	= 385.54
PV annuity	= $1,000.00

INPUTS					
	10	10		100	1000
	N	I/YR	PV	PMT	FV
OUTPUT			-1,000		

**What would happen if expected
inflation rose by 3%, causing k = 13%?**

INPUTS					
	10	13		100	1000
	N	I/YR	PV	PMT	FV
OUTPUT			-837.21		

When k_d rises, <u>above</u> the coupon rate,
the bond's value falls <u>below</u> par, so it
sells at a <u>discount</u>.

**What would happen if inflation fell, and
k_d declined to 7%?**

INPUTS					
	10	7		100	1000
	N	I/YR	PV	PMT	FV
OUTPUT			-1,210.71		

**Price rises above par, and bond sells
at a premium, if coupon > k_d.**

The bond was issued 20 years ago and now has 10 years to maturity. What would happen to its value over time if the required rate of return remained at 10%, or at 13%, or at 7%?

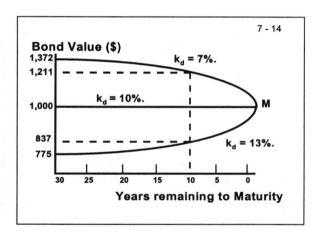

Bond Value ($)

1,372 — $k_d = 7\%$.
1,211
$k_d = 10\%$. — M
1,000
837
775 — $k_d = 13\%$.

30 25 20 15 10 5 0

Years remaining to Maturity

- At maturity, the value of any bond must equal its par value.
- The value of a premium bond would decrease to $1,000.
- The value of a discount bond would increase to $1,000.
- A par bond stays at $1,000 if k_d remains constant.

What's "yield to maturity"?

■ **YTM** is the rate of return earned on a bond held to maturity. Also called "promised yield."

What's the YTM on a 10-year, 9% annual coupon, $1,000 par value bond that sells for $887?

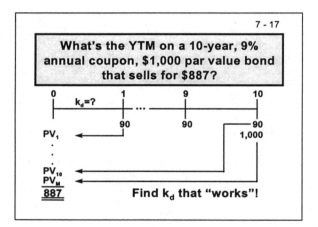

```
0       1        9      10
   k_d=?    ...
        90      90      90
PV_1  ←                1,000
 .
 .
 .
PV_10 ←
PV_M  ←
887        Find k_d that "works"!
```

Find k_d

$$V_B = \frac{INT}{(1+k_d)^1} + \cdots + \frac{INT}{(1+k_d)^N} + \frac{M}{(1+k_d)^N}$$

$$887 = \frac{90}{(1+k_d)^1} + \quad + \frac{90}{(1+k_d)^{10}} + \frac{1,000}{(1+k_d)^{10}}$$

INPUTS	10		-887	90	1000
	N	I/YR	PV	PMT	FV
OUTPUT		10.91			

- If coupon rate < k_d, discount.

- If coupon rate = k_d, par bond.

- If coupon rate > k_d, premium.

- If k_d rises, price falls.

- Price = par at maturity.

Find YTM if price were $1,134.20.

INPUTS	10		-1134.2	90	1000
	N	I/YR	PV	PMT	FV
OUTPUT		7.08			

Sells at a premium. Because coupon = 9% > k_d = 7.08%, bond's value > par.

Definitions

Current yield = $\dfrac{\text{Annual coupon pmt}}{\text{Current price}}$

Capital gains yield = $\dfrac{\text{Change in price}}{\text{Beginning price}}$

$\begin{matrix}\text{Exp total} \\ \text{return}\end{matrix}$ = YTM = $\begin{matrix}\text{Exp} \\ \text{Curr yld}\end{matrix}$ + $\begin{matrix}\text{Exp cap} \\ \text{gains yld}\end{matrix}$

Find current yield and capital gains yield for a 9%, 10-year bond when the bond sells for $887 and YTM = 10.91%.

Current yield $= \dfrac{\$90}{\$887}$

$= 0.1015 = \boxed{10.15\%.}$

YTM = Current yield + Capital gains yield.

Cap gains yield = YTM - Current yield
$= 10.91\% - 10.15\%$
$= \boxed{0.76\%.}$

Could also find value in Years 1 and 2, get difference, and divide by value in Year 1. Same answer.

What's <u>interest rate</u> (or price) <u>risk</u>? Does a 1-yr or 10-yr 10% bond have more risk?

<u>Interest rate risk:</u> Rising k_d causes bond's price to fall.

k_d	1-year	Change	10-year	Change
5%	$1,048		$1,386	
10%	1,000	4.8%	1,000	38.6%
15%	956	4.4%	749	25.1%

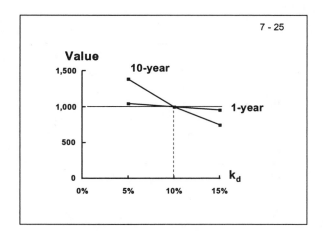

What is reinvestment rate risk?

The risk that CFs will have to be reinvested in the future at lower rates, reducing income.

Illustration: Suppose you just won $500,000 playing the lottery. You'll invest the money and live off the interest. You buy a 1-year bond with a YTM of 10%.

Year 1 income = $50,000. At year-end get back $500,000 to reinvest.

If rates fall to 3%, income will drop from $50,000 to $15,000. Had you bought 30-year bonds, income would have remained constant.

- **Long-term bonds: High interest rate risk, low reinvestment rate risk.**
- **Short-term bonds: Low interest rate risk, high reinvestment rate risk.**
- **Nothing is riskless!**

True or False: "All 10-year bonds have the same price and reinvestment rate risk."

False! Low coupon bonds have less reinvestment rate risk but more price risk than high coupon bonds.

Semiannual Bonds

1. **Multiply years by 2 to get periods = 2n.**
2. **Divide nominal rate by 2 to get periodic rate = $k_d/2$.**
3. **Divide annual INT by 2 to get PMT = INT/2.**

INPUTS	2n	k_d/2	OK	INT/2	OK
	[N]	[I/YR]	[PV]	[PMT]	[FV]
OUTPUT					

Find the value of 10-year, 10% coupon, semiannual bond if k_d = 13%.

```
              2(10)   13/2        100/2
    INPUTS     20     6.5           50      1000
              [N]    [I/YR]  [PV]  [PMT]   [FV]
    OUTPUT                 -834.72
```

You could buy, for $1,000, either a 10%, 10-year, annual payment bond or an equally risky 10%, 10-year semiannual bond. Which would you prefer?

The semiannual bond's EFF% is:

$$EFF\% = \left(1 + \frac{i_{Nom}}{m}\right)^m - 1 = \left(1 + \frac{0.10}{2}\right)^2 - 1 = 10.25\% .$$

10.25% > 10% EFF% on annual bond, so buy semiannual bond.

If $1,000 is the proper price for the semiannual bond, what is the proper price for the annual payment bond?

■ Semiannual bond has k_{Nom} = 10%, with EFF% = 10.25%. Should earn same EFF% on annual payment bond, so:

```
    INPUTS     10    10.25         100    1000
              [N]   [I/YR]  [PV]  [PMT]  [FV]
    OUTPUT                -984.80
```

■ At a price of $984.80, the annual and semiannual bonds would be in equilibrium, because investors would earn EFF% = 10.25% on either bond.

A 10-year, 10% semiannual coupon, $1,000 par value bond is selling for $1,135.90 with an 8% yield to maturity. It can be called after 5 years at $1,050.

What's the bond's nominal yield to call (YTC)?

INPUTS	10		-1135.9	50	1050
	N	I/YR	PV	PMT	FV
OUTPUT		3.765 x 2 = 7.53%			

k_{Nom} = 7.53% is the rate brokers would quote. Could also calculate EFF% to call:

EFF% = $(1.03765)^2$ - 1 = 7.672%.

This rate could be compared to monthly mortgages, etc.

If you bought bonds, would you be more likely to earn YTM or YTC?

- Coupon rate = 10% vs. YTC = k_d = 7.53%. Could raise money by selling new bonds which pay 7.53%.
- Could thus replace bonds which pay $100/year with bonds that pay only $75.30/year.
- Investors should expect a call, hence YTC = 7.5%, not YTM = 8%.

- In general, if a bond sells at a premium, then (1) coupon > k_d, so (2) a call is likely.
- So, expect to earn:
  - YTC on premium bonds.
  - YTM on par & discount bonds.

- Disney recently issued 100-year bonds with a YTM of 7.5%--this represents the promised return. The expected return was less than 7.5% when the bonds were issued.
- If issuer defaults, investors receive less than the promised return. Therefore, the expected return on corporate and municipal bonds is less than the promised return.

7 - 40

Bond Ratings Provide One Measure of Default Risk

	Investment Grade				Junk Bonds			
Moody's	Aaa	Aa	A	Baa	Ba	B	Caa	C
S&P	AAA	AA	A	BBB	BB	B	CCC	D

---

7 - 41

What factors affect default risk and bond ratings?

- **Financial performance**
  - **Debt ratio**
  - **TIE, FCC ratios**
  - **Current ratios**

---

7 - 42

- **Provisions in the bond contract**
  - **Secured vs. unsecured debt**
  - **Senior vs. subordinated debt**
  - **Guarantee provisions**
  - **Sinking fund provisions**
  - **Debt maturity**

Impact bond ratings

① Ratios → D/E, TIE

② Mortgage provision

③ Subordinated debt

④ Guarantee

⑤ Sinking fund

⑥ Maturity

⑦ Stability

⑧ Regulation

⑨ Antitrust

⑩ Overseas operations

⑪ Environmental costs

⑫ Product liability

⑬ Pension liability

⑭ Labor unrest

⑮ Accounting policy

■ **Other factors**
- ●**Earnings stability**
- ●**Regulatory environment**
- ●**Potential product liability**
- ●**Accounting policies**

---

7 - 44

Bankruptcy

■ **Two main chapters of Federal Bankruptcy Act:**
- ●**Chapter 11, Reorganization**
- ●**Chapter 7, Liquidation**

■ **Typically, company wants Chapter 11, creditors may prefer Chapter 7.**

banks - debtor imposition financing after Ch. 11 will prevent liquidation

---

7 - 45

■ **If company can't meet its obligations, it files under Chapter 11. That stops creditors from foreclosing, taking assets, and shutting down the business.**
- ●**Company has 120 days to file a reorganization plan.**
- ●**Court appoints a "trustee" to supervise reorganization.**
- ●**Management usually stays in control.**

7 - 46

- Company must demonstrate in its reorganization plan that it is "worth more alive than dead."

  Otherwise, judge will order liquidation under Chapter 7.

---

7 - 47

- If the company is liquidated, here's the payment priority:
  1. Secured creditors from sales of secured assets.
  2. Trustee's costs
  3. Wages, subject to limits
  4. Taxes
  5. Unfunded pension liabilities
  6. Unsecured creditors
  7. Preferred stock
  8. Common stock

---

7 - 48

- In a liquidation, unsecured creditors generally get zero. This makes them more willing to participate in reorganization even though their claims are greatly scaled back.
- Various groups of creditors vote on the reorganization plan. If both the majority of the creditors and the judge approve, company "emerges" from bankruptcy with lower debts, reduced interest charges, and a chance for success.

EXAM-TYPE PROBLEMS

7-1. Gator Services Unlimited (GSU) needs to raise $25 million in new debt capital. GSU's currently outstanding bonds have a $1,000 par value, an 8% coupon rate, pay interest semiannually, and have 30 years remaining to maturity. The bonds are callable after 5 years at a price of $1,080, and currently sell at a price of $676.77. Right now, the yield curve is flat and is expected to remain flat for a while. The risk on GSU's new bonds is the same as for its old bonds. Based on these data, what is the best estimate of GSU's nominal interest rate on new bonds? (12%)

7-2. Florida Financial Corporation (FFC) purchases packages of guaranteed student loans from banks for its portfolio. FFC is considering a package with the following characteristics. The securities, which are similar to bonds, have a $1,000 par value, pay 8% interest semiannually for 5 years and then pay a stepped-up interest rate of 10% semiannually for the next 7 years. The maturity value is $1,000, paid at the end of 12 years. FFC's alternative to this investment are 9% coupon bonds, selling at par of $1,000, which pay interest quarterly. Assuming that the investments are of similar risk, how much should FFC be willing to pay for the student loan package? ($985.97)

7-3. Trickle Corporation's 12% coupon rate, semiannual payment, $1,000 par value bonds which mature in 25 years, are callable at a price of $1,080 five years from now. The bonds currently sell for $1,230.51 in the market, and the yield curve is flat. Assuming that the yield curve is expected to remain flat, what is Trickle's most likely *before-tax cost* of debt if it issues new bonds today? (7.70%)

7-4. Recycler Battery Corporation (RBC) issued zero coupon bonds 5 years ago at a price of $214.50 per bond. RBC's zeros had a 20-year original maturity, and a $1,000 par value. The bonds were callable 10 years after the issue date at a price 7% over their accrued value on the call date. If the bonds sell for $239.39 in the market today, what annual rate of return should an investor who buys the bonds today expect to earn on them? (Hint: Material covered in Appendix 7A.) (10%)

7-5. Suppose a new company decides to raise its initial $200 million of capital as $100 million of common equity and $100 million of long-term debt. By an iron-clad provision in its charter, the company can never borrow any more money. Which of the following statements is most correct?

a. If the debt were raised by issuing $50 million of debentures and $50 million of first mortgage bonds, we could be absolutely certain that the firm's total interest expense would be lower than if the debt were raised by issuing $100 million of debentures.

b. If the debt were raised by issuing $50 million of debentures and $50 million of first mortgage bonds, we could be absolutely certain that the firm's total interest expense would be lower than if the debt were raised by issuing $100 million of first mortgage bonds.

c. The higher the percentage of total debt represented by debentures, the greater the risk of, and hence the interest rate on, the debentures.

d. The higher the percentage of total debt represented by mortgage bonds, the riskier both types of bonds will be, and, consequently, the higher the firms' total dollar interest charges will be.

e. In this situation, we cannot tell for sure how, or whether, the firm's total interest expense on the $100 million of debt would be affected by the mix of debentures versus first mortgage bonds. Interest rates on the two types of bonds would vary as their percentages were changed, but the result might well be such that the firm's total interest charges would not be affected materially by the mix between the two.

7-6. Which of the following statements is most correct?

a. Because bonds can generally be called only at a premium, meaning that the bondholder will enjoy a capital gain, including a call provision (other than a sinking fund call) in the indenture increases the value of the bond and lowers the bond's required rate of return.

b. You are considering two bonds. Both are rated AA, both mature in 20 years, both have a 10 percent coupon, and both are offered to you at their $1,000 par value. However, Bond X has a sinking fund while Bond Y does not. This is probably not an equilibrium situation, as Bond X, which has the sinking fund, would generally be expected to have a higher yield than Bond Y.

c. A sinking fund provides for the orderly retirement of a debt (or preferred stock) issue. Sinking funds generally force the firm to call a percentage of the issue each year. However, the call price for sinking fund purposes is generally higher than the call price for refunding purposes.

d. Zero coupon bonds are bought primarily by pension funds and other tax exempt investors because they avoid the tax that non-tax exempt investors must pay on the accrued value each year.

e. All of the above statements are false.

7-7   Research Technologies' noncallable bonds have 10 years remaining to maturity. The bonds have a face value of $1,000, a yield to maturity of 12 percent, pay interest semiannually, and have a 10 percent coupon rate. What is their current yield? (11.30%)

BLUEPRINTS: CHAPTER 8
STOCKS AND THEIR VALUATION

8-22 Robert Black and Carol Alvarez are vice-presidents of Western Money Management and codirectors of the company's pension fund management division. A major new client, the California League of Cities, has requested that Western present an investment seminar on common stock valuation to the mayors of the represented cities, and Black and Alvarez, who will make the actual presentation, have asked you to help them by answering the following questions. Because the Walt Disney Company operates in one of the league's cities, you are to work Disney into the presentation.

a. Describe briefly the legal rights and privileges of common stockholders.

b. (1) Write out and explain a formula that can be used to value any stock, regardless of its dividend pattern.

(2) What is a constant growth stock? How are constant growth stocks valued?

(3) What happens if the constant g exceeds k_s? Will many stocks have expected g > k_s in the short run? In the long run (i.e., forever)?

c. Assume that Disney has a beta coefficient of 1.2, that the risk-free rate (the yield on T-bonds) is 6 percent, and that the required rate of return on the market is 11 percent. What is the required rate of return on Disney's stock?

d. Assume that Disney is a constant growth company whose last dividend (D_0, which was paid yesterday) was $0.25, and whose dividend is expected to grow indefinitely at a 6 percent rate.

(1) What would Disney's expected dividend stream be over the next 3 years, and what is the PV of each dividend?

(2) Under these conditions, what would be Disney's current stock price? Note that g = 6%, k_s = 12%.

(3) What should the stock's expected value be 1 year from now?

(4) Calculate the expected dividend yield, the capital gains yield, and the total return during the first year.

e. Now assume that the stock is currently selling at $4.42. What is the expected rate of return on the stock?

f. What would the stock price be if Disney's dividends were expected to have zero growth?

g. Now assume that Disney is expected to experience supernormal dividend growth of 30 percent for the next 3 years, then to fall to a long-run constant growth rate of 10 percent. What would the stock's value be under these conditions? What would its expected dividend yield and capital gains yield be in Year 1? In Year 4?

h. Suppose Disney was expected to experience zero growth during the next 3 years and then to achieve a constant growth rate of 11 percent in the fourth year and thereafter. What would be the stock's value now? What is its expected dividend yield and its capital gains yield in Year 1? In Year 4?

I. Finally, assume that Disney's earnings and dividends are expected to decline by a constant 6 percent per year, that is, g = -6%. Would you or anyone else be willing to buy such a stock? At what price should it sell? What would be the dividend yield and capital gains yield in each year?

j. What does market equilibrium mean?

k. If equilibrium does not exist, how will it be established?

l. What are the various forms of market efficiency? What are the implications of market efficiency?

m. Taylor Company recently issued preferred stock with a constant dividend of $5 a year, at a share price of $50. What is the expected return on the company's preferred stock?

CHAPTER 8
Stocks and Their Valuation

- Features of common stock
- Determining common stock values
- Efficient markets
- Preferred stock

① Cashflow → timing

② Required rate of return
   interest rate

Stock
① dividends
② stock price appreciation

Facts about Common Stock

- Represents ownership.
- Ownership implies control.
- Stockholders elect directors.
- Directors elect management.
- Management's goal: Maximize stock price.

Stock valuation
- single period
- multiple period
perpetuity - uninterrupted
cash flow payments infinitely
$$P = \frac{CF}{i}$$

Social/Ethical Question

Should management be equally concerned about employees, customers, suppliers, "the public," or just the stockholders?

In enterprise economy, <u>work for stockholders</u> subject to <u>constraints</u> (environmental, fair hiring, etc.) and <u>competition</u>.

What's classified stock? How might classified stock be used?

- Classified stock has special provisions.
- Could classify existing stock as founders' shares, with voting rights but dividend restrictions.
- New shares might be called "Class A" shares, with voting restrictions but full dividend rights.

When is a stock sale an initial public offering (IPO)?

A firm "goes public" through an IPO when the stock is first offered to the public.

Stock Value = PV of Dividends

$$\hat{P}_0 = \frac{D_1}{(1+k_s)^1} + \frac{D_2}{(1+k_s)^2} + \frac{D_3}{(1+k_s)^3} + \ldots + \frac{D_\infty}{(1+k_s)^\infty}$$

What is a constant growth stock?

One whose dividends are expected to grow forever at a constant rate, g.

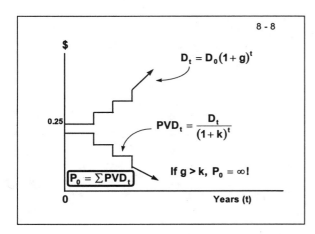

8 - 7

For a constant growth stock,

$$D_1 = D_0(1+g)^1$$
$$D_2 = D_0(1+g)^2$$
$$D_t = D_t(1+g)^t$$

If g is constant, then:

$$\hat{P}_0 = \frac{D_0(1+g)}{k_s - g} = \frac{D_1}{k_s - g}$$

8 - 8

$D_t = D_0(1+g)^t$

$PVD_t = \dfrac{D_t}{(1+k)^t}$

$P_0 = \Sigma PVD_t$

If g > k, $P_0 = \infty$!

Years (t)

8 - 9

What happens if g > k_s?

$$\hat{P}_0 = \frac{D_1}{k_s - g} \text{ requires } k_s > g.$$

- If $k_s < g$, get negative stock price, which is nonsense.
- We can't use model unless (1) $k_s > g$ and (2) g is expected to be constant forever. See slide #8-8.

Handwritten notes:

$P_0 = \dfrac{DIV_1}{k_s - g} = \dfrac{DIV_0(1+g)}{k_s - g}$

today's stock price = next period div / interest rate - growth rate

To find stock price:
1. dividend growth constant
2. infinite scenario
3. ks > g

A stock is expected to pay $2 dividend in years 1, 2 & 3 then it is expected to grow at a rate of 5%. Your rate of return (ks) = 8%. How much are you willing to pay for this stock?

$2 $2 $2 $2.10 2(1+.05)
0   1   2   3   4

$P_3 = \dfrac{DIV_4(1+g)}{k-g}$

$70 = \dfrac{2.10}{.08-.05}$

$P_0 = 2(PVFA_{.08,3})$ 2.5771
$+ 70(PVF_{.08,3})$ .7938

60.72

BLUEPRINTS: CHAPTER 8

Assume beta = 1.2, k_{RF} = 6%, and k_M = 11%. What is the required rate of return on the firm's stock?

Use the SML to calculate k_s:

$$k_s = k_{RF} + (k_M - k_{RF})b_{Firm}$$
$$= 6\% + (11\% - 6\%)(1.2)$$
$$= 12\%.$$

$$\frac{\$2}{1.05} + \frac{\$2}{(1.05)(1.06)} + \frac{\$72}{(1.05)(1.06)(1.08)}$$

$$05\%/1 \quad 6\%/2 \quad 8\%/3$$

$$P_3 = \$70$$
$$P_2 = \$166.67$$
$$P_1 = \$164.78$$
$$P_0 = \$163.70$$

$$2(PVF.05,1) + 2(PVF.06,1)(PVF.05,1) + 72(PVF.08,1)(PVF.06,1)$$
$$(PVF.05,1)$$

D_0 was \$0.25 and g is a constant 6%. Find the expected dividends for the next 3 years, and their PVs. k_s = 12%.

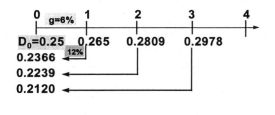

0	g=6%	1	2	3	4

D_0=0.25   0.265   0.2809   0.2978

0.2366   12%

0.2239

0.2120

What's the stock's market value?
D_0 = 0.25, k_s = 12%, g = 6%.

Constant growth model:

$$\hat{P}_0 = \frac{D_1}{k_s - g} = \frac{\$0.265}{0.12 - 0.06}$$

$$= \frac{\$0.265}{0.06} = \$4.42.$$

What is the stock's market value one year from now, $\hat{P}_1$?

■ D_1 will have been paid, so expected dividends are D_2, D_3, D_4 and so on. Thus,

$$\hat{P}_1 = \frac{D_2}{k_s - g} = \frac{\$0.2809}{0.12 - 0.06}$$

$$= \$4.68.$$

Could also find $\hat{P}_1$ as follows:

$$\hat{P}_1 = P_0(1 + g) = \$4.42(1.06) = \$4.68.$$

Find the expected dividend yield, capital gains yield, and total return during the first year.

$$\text{Dividend yld} = \frac{D_1}{P_0} = \frac{\$0.265}{\$4.42} = 6\%.$$

$$\text{Cap. gains yld} = \frac{\hat{P}_1 - P_0}{P_0} = k_s - \frac{D_1}{P_0} = 6\%.$$

$$\text{Total return} = 6\% + 6\% = 12\%.$$

Rearrange model to rate of return form:

$$\hat{P}_0 = \frac{D_1}{k_s - g} \quad \text{to} \quad \hat{k}_s = \frac{D_1}{P_0} + g.$$

Then, $\hat{k}_s = \$0.265/\$4.42 + 0.06$
$$= 0.06 + 0.06 = 12\%.$$

What would P_0 be if g = 0?

The dividend stream would be a perpetuity.

```
0        1        2        3
|--12%---|--------|--------|----...-->
         0.25     0.25     0.25
```

$$\hat{P}_0 = \frac{PMT}{k} = \frac{\$0.25}{0.12} = \$2.08.$$

If we have supernormal growth of 30% for 3 yrs, then a long-run constant g = 10%, what is $\hat{P}_0$? k is still 12%.

- Can no longer use constant growth model.
- However, growth becomes constant after 3 years.

Nonconstant growth followed by constant growth:

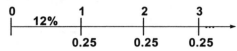

```
        0   k=12%  1         2         3         4
        |---------|---------|---------|---------|---...-->
          g = 30%   g = 30%   g = 30%   g = 10%
D₀ = 0.25   0.3250    0.4225    0.5493    0.6042
   0.2902 ←
   0.3368 ←
   0.3910 ←
  21.5029 ←
  22.52  = P̂₀
```

$$\hat{P}_3 = \frac{0.6042}{0.12 - 0.10} = \$30.21$$

BLUEPRINTS: CHAPTER 8

What is the expected dividend yield and capital gains yield at t = 0? At t = 4?

$$\text{Div. yield}_0 = \frac{\$0.3250}{\$22.52} = 1.44\%.$$

$$\text{Cap. gain}_0 = 12\% - 1.44\% = 10.56\%.$$

- During nonconstant growth, D/P and capital gains yield are not constant, and capital gains yield is less than g.

- After t = 3, g = constant = 10% = capital gains yield; k = 12%; so D/P = 12% - 10% = 2%.

Suppose g = 0 for t = 1 to 3, and then g is a constant 11%. What is $\hat{P}_0$?

```
0   k=12%   1        2        3         4
|           |        |        |         |
    g = 0%   g = 0%   g = 0%   g = 11%
          0.25     0.25     0.25      0.2775
0.2232 ←
0.1993 ←
0.1779 ←              ┌────── 0.2775
19.7519 ←      $\hat{P}_3 = \dfrac{0.2775}{0.01} = 27.75.$
20.3523
```

What is D/P and capital gains yield at t = 0 and at t = 3?

t = 0: $\dfrac{D_1}{P_0} = \dfrac{\$0.25}{\$20.35} = 1.23\%.$

$CGY = 12\% - 1.23\% = 10.77\%.$

t = 3: Now have constant growth with g = capital gains yield = 11% and D/P = 1%.

If g = -6%, would anyone buy the stock? If so, at what price?

Firm still has earnings and still pays dividends, so $P_0 > 0$:

$$\hat{P}_0 = \dfrac{D_1}{k_s - g} = \dfrac{D_0(1+g)}{k_s - g}.$$

$$= \dfrac{\$0.25(0.94)}{0.12 - (-0.06)} = \dfrac{\$0.235}{0.18} = \$1.31.$$

What is the annual D/P and capital gains yield?

Capital gains yield = g = -6.0%,

Dividend yield = 12.0% - (-6.0%)
= 18%.

D/P and cap. gains yield are constant, with high dividend yield (18%) offsetting negative capital gains yield.

What is market equilibrium?

In equilibrium, stock prices are stable. There is no general tendency for people to buy versus to sell.

In equilibrium, expected returns must equal required returns:

$$\hat{k}_s = D_1/P_0 + g = k_s = k_{RF} + (k_M - k_{RF})b.$$

How is equilibrium established?

If $\hat{k}_s = \dfrac{D_1}{P_0} + g > k_s$, then

P_0 is "too low" (a bargain).

Buy orders > sell orders;
P_0 bid up; D_1/P_0 falls until
$D_1/P_0 + g = \hat{k}_s = k_s.$

Why do stock prices change?

$$\hat{P}_0 = \frac{D_1}{k_I - g}$$

1. k_I could change:
   $k_I = k_{RF} + (k_M - k_{RF})b_I$
   $k_{RF} = k^* + IP$

2. g could change due to economic or firm situation.

What's the Efficient Market Hypothesis?

EMH: Securities are normally in equilibrium and are "fairly priced." One cannot "beat the market" except through good luck or better information.

1. Weak-form EMH:
   Can't profit by looking at past trends. A recent decline is no reason to think stocks will go up (or down) in the future. Evidence supports weak-form EMH, but "technical analysis" is still used.

2. Semistrong-form EMH:
   All publicly available information is reflected in stock prices, so doesn't pay to pore over annual reports looking for undervalued stocks. Largely true, but superior analysts can still profit by finding and using new information.

8 - 31

3. Strong-form EMH:
All information, even inside information, is embedded in stock prices. Not true--insiders can gain by trading on the basis of insider information, but that's illegal.

---

8 - 32

Markets are generally efficient because:

1. **15,000** or so trained analysts; MBAs, CFAs, Technical PhDs.
2. Work for firms like Merrill, Morgan, Prudential, which have **much money.**
3. Have **similar access** to data.
4. Thus, news is reflected in P_0 almost **instantaneously.**

---

8 - 33

Preferred Stock

- Hybrid security.
- Similar to bonds in that preferred stockholders receive a fixed dividend which must be paid before dividends can be paid on common stock.
- However, unlike interest payments on bonds, companies can omit dividend payments on preferred stock without fear of pushing the firm into bankruptcy.

What's the expected return of preferred stock with V_{ps} = $50 and annual dividend = $5?

$$V_{ps} = \$50 = \frac{\$5}{\hat{k}_{ps}}$$

$$\hat{k}_{ps} = \frac{\$5}{\$50} = 0.10 = 10.0\%.$$

EXAM-TYPE PROBLEMS

8-1. Carlson Products, a constant growth company, has a current market (and equilibrium) stock price of $20.00. Carlson's next dividend, D_1, is forecasted to be $2.00, and Carlson is growing at an annual rate of 6 percent. Carlson has a beta coefficient of 1.2, and the required rate of return on the market is 15 percent. As Carlson's financial manager, you have access to insider information concerning a switch in product lines which would not change the growth rate, but would cut Carlson's beta coefficient in half. If you buy the stock at the current market price, what is your expected percentage capital gain? (43%)

8-2. The Hart Mountain Company has recently discovered a new type of kitty litter which is extremely absorbent. It is expected that the firm will experience (beginning now) an unusually high growth rate of 20 percent during the 3-year period it has exclusive rights to the property where the raw material used to make this kitty litter is found. However, beginning with the fourth year the firm's competition will have access to the material, and from that time on the firm will achieve a normal growth rate of 8 percent annually. During the rapid growth period, the firm's dividend payout ratio will be a relatively low 20 percent in order to conserve funds for reinvestment. However, the decrease in growth in the fourth year will be accompanied by an increase in the dividend payout to 50 percent. Last year's earnings were $E_0 = 2.00 per share, and the firm's required return is 10 percent. What should be the current price of the common stock? ($71.54)

8-3. Which of the following statements is most correct?

a. One of the advantages of common stock financing is that there is no dilution of owner's equity, as there is with debt.

b. If the market price of a stock falls below its book value, the firm can be liquidated, with the book value proceeds then distributed to the shareholders. Thus, a stock's book value per share sets a floor below which the stock's market price is unlikely to fall.

c. The preemptive right gives a firm's preferred stockholders preference to assets over common stockholders in the event the firm is liquidated.

d. All of the above statements are true.

e. All of the above statements are false.

8-4.   Bosio Enterprises has preferred stock outstanding which pays a dividend of $8.75 at the end of each year. If the preferred stock's required return is 12.5 percent, for how much does each share of preferred stock sell? ($70)

9-21   During the last few years, Coleman Technologies has been too constrained by the high cost of capital to make many capital investments. Recently, though, capital costs have been declining, and the company has decided to look seriously at a major expansion program that had been proposed by the marketing department. Assume that you are an assistant to Jerry Lehman, the financial vice-president. Your first task is to estimate Coleman's cost of capital. Lehman has provided you with the following data, which he believes may be relevant to your task:

1. The firm's tax rate is 40 percent.

2. The current price of Coleman's 12 percent coupon, semiannual payment, noncallable bonds with 15 years remaining to maturity is $1,153.72. Coleman does not use short-term interest-bearing debt on a permanent basis. New bonds would be privately placed with no flotation cost.

3. The current price of the firm's 10 percent, $100 par value, quarterly dividend, perpetual preferred stock is $113.10. Coleman would incur flotation costs of $2.00 per share on a new issue.

4. Coleman's common stock is currently selling at $50 per share. Its last dividend (D_0) was $4.19, and dividends are expected to grow at a constant rate of 5 percent in the foreseeable future. Coleman's beta is 1.2, the yield on T-bonds is 7 percent, and the market risk premium is estimated to be 6 percent. For the bond-yield-plus-risk-premium approach, the firm uses a 4 percentage point risk premium.

5. New common stock can be sold at a flotation cost of 15 percent.

6. Coleman's target capital structure is 30 percent long-term debt, 10 percent preferred stock, and 60 percent common equity.

7. The firm is forecasting retained earnings of $300,000 for the coming year.

   To structure the task somewhat, Lehman has asked you to answer the following questions.

a. (1) What sources of capital should be included when you estimate Coleman's weighted average cost of capital (WACC)?

   (2) Should the component costs be figured on a before-tax or an after-tax basis?

(3) Should the costs be historical (embedded) costs or new (marginal) costs?

b.   What is the market interest rate on Coleman's debt and its component cost of debt?

c. (1) What is the firm's cost of preferred stock?

    (2) Coleman's preferred stock is riskier to investors than its debt, yet the preferred's yield to investors is lower than the yield to maturity on the debt. Does this suggest that you have made a mistake? (Hint: Think about taxes.)

d. (1) Why is there a cost associated with retained earnings?

    (2) What is Coleman's estimated cost of retained earnings using the CAPM approach?

    (3) Why is the T-bond rate a better estimate of the risk-free rate for cost of capital purposes than the T-bill rate?

e.   What is the estimated cost of retained earnings using the discounted cash flow (DCF) approach?

f.   What is the bond-yield-plus-risk-premium estimate for Coleman's cost of retained earnings?

g.   What is your final estimate for k_s?

h.   What is Coleman's cost for newly issued common stock, k_e?

I.   Explain in words why new common stock has a higher percentage cost than retained earnings.

j. (1) What is Coleman's overall, or weighted average, cost of capital (WACC) when retained earnings are used as the equity component?

    (2) What is the WACC after retained earnings have been exhausted and Coleman uses new common stock with a 15 percent flotation cost?

k. (1) At what amount of new investment would Coleman be forced to issue new common stock? Put another way, what is the largest capital budget the company could support without issuing new common stock? Assume that the 30/10/60 target capital structure will be maintained.

(2) What is a marginal cost of capital (MCC) schedule? Construct a graph which shows Coleman's MCC schedule.

I.   Coleman's director of capital budgeting has identified the three following potential projects:

Project	Cost	Rate of Return
A	$700,000	17.0%
B	500,000	15.0
C	800,000	11.5

All of the projects are equally risky, and they are all similar in risk to the company's existing assets.

(1) Plot the IOS schedule on the same graph that contains your MCC schedule. What is the firm's marginal cost of capital for capital budgeting purposes?

(2) What is the dollar size, and the included projects, in Coleman's optimal capital budget? Explain your answer fully.

(3) Would Coleman's MCC schedule remain constant at 12.1 percent beyond $2 million regardless of the amount of capital required?

CHAPTER 9
The Cost of Capital

■ Cost of Capital Components
  ● Debt
  ● Preferred
  ● Common Equity
■ WACC
■ MCC
■ IOS

What types of long-term capital do firms use?

Long-term debt
Preferred stock
Common equity:
  Retained earnings
  New common stock

Should we focus on before-tax or after-tax capital costs?

Stockholders focus on A-T CFs. Thus, focus on A-T capital costs, i.e., use A-T costs in WACC. Only k_d needs adjustment.

Should we focus on historical (embedded) costs or new (marginal) costs?

The cost of capital is used primarily to make decisions which involve raising new capital. So, focus on today's marginal costs (for WACC).

A 15-year, 12% semiannual bond sells for $1,153.72. What's k_d?

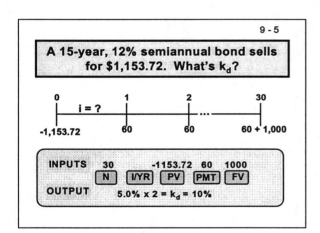

Component Cost of Debt

- Interest is tax deductible, so

  $k_{d\,AT}$ = $k_{d\,BT}(1 - T)$
  = 10%(1 - 0.40) = 6%.

- Use nominal rate.
- Flotation costs small. Ignore.

What's the cost of preferred stock?
$P_P = \$113.10$; 10%Q; Par = $100; F = $2.

Use this formula:

$$k_{ps} = \frac{D_{ps}}{P_{Net}} = \frac{0.1\,(\$100)}{\$113.10 - \$2.00}$$

$$= \frac{\$10}{\$111.10} = 0.090 = 9.0\%.$$

Picture of Preferred

0	$k_{ps} = ?$	1	2	∞
-111.1		2.50	2.50	2.50

$$111.10 = \frac{D_Q}{k_{Per}} = \frac{\$2.50}{k_{Per}}.$$

$$k_{Per} = \frac{\$2.50}{\$111.10} = 2.25; \; k_{ps(Nom)} = 2.25(4) = 9\%.$$

Note:

- Flotation costs for preferred are significant, so are reflected. Use net price.
- Preferred dividends are not deductible, so no tax adjustment. Just k_{ps}.
- Nominal k_{ps} is used.

Is preferred stock more or less risky to investors than debt?

- **More risky;** company not required to pay preferred dividend.
- However, firms try to pay preferred dividend. Otherwise, (1) cannot pay common dividend, (2) difficult to raise additional funds, (3) preferred stockholders may gain control of firm.

Why is yield on preferred lower than k_d?

- Corporations own most preferred stock, because 70% of preferred dividend are nontaxable to corporations.
- Therefore, preferred often has a lower B-T yield than the B-T yield on debt.
- The A-T yield to an investor, and the A-T cost to the issuer, are higher on preferred than on debt. Consistent with higher risk of preferred.

Example:

k_{ps} = 8.84% k_d = 10%   T = 40%

$k_{ps, AT}$ = k_{ps} - k_{ps} (1 - 0.7)(T)

= 8.84% - 8.84%(0.3)(0.4) = 7.78%

$k_{d, AT}$ = 10% - 10%(0.4)   = 6.00%

A-T Risk Premium on Preferred = 1.78%

Why is there a cost for retained earnings?

- Earnings can be reinvested or paid out as dividends.
- Investors could buy other securities, earn a return.
- Thus, there is an opportunity cost if earnings are retained.

- Opportunity cost: The return stockholders could earn on alternative investments of equal risk.
- They could buy similar stocks and earn k_s, or company could repurchase its own stock and earn k_s. So, k_s is the cost of retained earnings.

Three ways to determine cost of retained earnings, k_s:

1. CAPM: $k_s = k_{RF} + (k_M - k_{RF})b$.
2. DCF: $k_s = D_1/P_0 + g$.
3. Own-Bond-Yield-Plus-Risk Premium:

   $$k_s = k_d + RP.$$

What's the cost of retained earnings based on the CAPM?
$k_{RF} = 7\%$, MRP = 6%, b = 1.2.

$$k_s = k_{RF} + (k_M - k_{RF})b.$$

$$= 7.0\% + (6.0\%)1.2 = 14.2\%.$$

What's the DCF cost of retained earnings, k_s? Given: $D_0 = \$4.19$; $P_0 = \$50$; g = 5%.

$$k_s = \frac{D_1}{P_0} + g = \frac{D_0(1+g)}{P_0} + g$$

$$= \frac{\$4.19(1.05)}{\$50} + 0.05$$

$$= 0.088 + 0.05$$

$$= 13.8\%.$$

Suppose the company has been earning 15% on equity (ROE = 15%) and retaining 35% (dividend payout = 65%), and this situation is expected to continue.

What's the expected future g?

Retention growth rate:

$g = b(ROE) = 0.35(15\%) = 5.25\%$.

Here b = Fraction retained.

Close to g = 5% given earlier. Think of bank account paying 10% with b = 0, b = 1.0, and b = 0.5. What's g?

Could DCF methodology be applied if g is not constant?

- YES, nonconstant g stocks are expected to have constant g at some point, generally in 5 to 10 years.
- But calculations get complicated.

Find k_s using the own-bond-yield-plus-risk-premium method.
(k_d = 10%, RP = 4%.)

$k_s = k_d + RP$

$= 10.0\% + 4.0\% = 14.0\%$

- This RP $\neq$ CAPM RP.
- Produces ballpark estimate of k_s. Useful check.

What's a reasonable final estimate of k_s?

Method	Estimate
CAPM	14.2%
DCF	13.8%
k_d + RP	14.0%
Average	14.0%

How do we find the cost of new common stock, k_e?

Use DCF formula, but
adjust P_0 for flotation cost.
End up with $k_e > k_s$.

New common, F = 15%:

$$k_e = \frac{D_0(1+g)}{P_0(1-F)} + g$$

$$= \frac{\$4.19(1.05)}{\$50(1-0.15)} + 5.0\%$$

$$= \frac{\$4.40}{\$42.50} + 5.0\% = \boxed{15.4\%.}$$

Flotation adjustment:

$k_e - k_s = 15.4\% - 13.8\% = 1.6\%$.

Add the 1.6% flotation adjustment to average k_s = 14% to find average k_e :

$k_e = k_s$ + Floatation adjustment
$= 14\% + 1.6\% = \boxed{15.6\%.}$

Why is $k_e > k_s$?

1. Investors expect to earn k_s.
2. Company gets money as retained earnings; earns k_s; everything's O.K.
3. But investors put up money to buy new stock; F pulled out; so net money must earn > k_s to provide k_s on money investors put up.

Example

1. $k_s = D_1/P_0 + g = 10\%$; F = 20%.
2. Investors put up $100, expect EPS = DPS = 0.1($100) = $10.
3. But company nets only $80.
4. If earn k_s = 10% on $80, EPS = DPS = 0.10($80) = $8. Too low. Price falls.
5. Need to earn k_e = 10% /0.8 = 12.5%.
6. Then EPS = 0.125($80) = $10.
Conclusion: k_e = 12.5% > k_s = 10.0%.

What's WACC using only retained earnings for equity component of WACC$_1$?

$\text{WACC}_1 = w_d k_d (1 - T) + w_{ps} k_{ps} + w_{ce} k_s$

$\quad\quad = 0.3(10\%)(0.6) + 0.1(9\%) + 0.6(14\%)$

$\quad\quad = 1.8\% + 0.9\% + 8.4\% = 11.1\%.$

$\quad\quad =$ Cost per \$1 until retained earnings used up.

WACC with New CS

F = 15%

$\text{WACC}_2 = w_d k_d (1 - T) + w_{ps} k_{ps} + w_{ce} k_e$

$\quad\quad = 0.3(10\%)(0.6) + 0.1(9\%) + 0.6(15.6\%)$

$\quad\quad = 1.8\% + 0.9\% + 9.4\% = \boxed{12.1\%.}$

Summary to this Point

	k_e or k_s	WACC
Debt + Pfd + RE:	14.0%	11.1%
Debt + Pfd + F = 15%	15.6%	12.1%

WACC rises because equity cost is rising.

MCC Schedule Definition

- MCC shows cost of each dollar raised.

- Each dollar consists of $0.30 of debt, $0.10 of Preferred and $0.60 of equity (retained earnings or new common stock).

- First dollars cost $WACC_1 = 11.1\%$, then $WACC_2 = 12.1\%$.

How large will capital budget be before must issue new CS?

Capital Budget = Capital Raised

  Debt = 0.3 Capital Raised
Preferred = 0.1 Capital Raised
  Equity = 0.6 Capital Raised
       = 1.0 Total Capital

  Equity = RE = 0.6 Capital Raised, so
Capital Raised = RE/0.6.

Find Retained Earnings Break Point

$$BP_{RE} = \frac{\text{Dollars of RE}}{\text{Fraction of equity}}$$

$$= \frac{\$300,000}{0.60} = \$500,000.$$

$500,000 total can be financed with retained earnings, debt, and preferred.

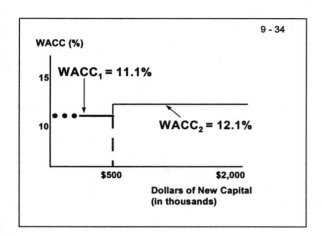

Investment Opportunities
(Capital Budgeting Projects)

A	$700,000	17.0%
B	500,000	15.0%
C	800,000	11.5%
	$2,000,000	

Which to accept?

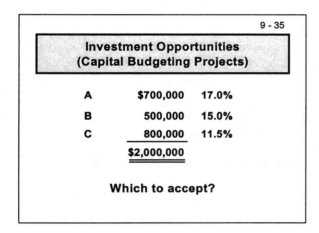

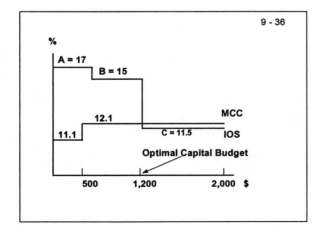

■ **Projects A and B would be accepted (IRR exceeds the MCC).**

■ **Project C would be rejected (IRR is less than the MCC).**

■ **Capital Budget = $1.2 million.**

Would the MCC remain constant beyond $2 million?

■ **No. WACC would eventually rise above 12.1%.**

■ **Costs of debt, preferred stock would rise.**

■ **Large increases in capital budget may also increase the perceived risk of the firm, increasing WACC.**

EXAM-TYPE PROBLEMS

9-1. Barak Company's 8% coupon rate, quarterly payment, $1,000 par value bond, which matures in 20 years, currently sells at a price of $686.86. The company's tax rate is 40%. Based on the nominal interest rate, not the EAR, what is the firm's component cost of debt for purposes of calculating the WACC? (7.32%)

9-2. Allison Engines Corporation has established a target capital structure of 40% debt and 60% common equity. The firm expects to earn $600 in after-tax income during the coming year, and it will retain 40% of those earnings. The current market price of the firm's stock is P_0 = $28; its last dividend was D_0 = $2.20, and its expected dividend growth rate is 6%. Allison can issue new common stock at a flotation cost of 15%. What will Allison's marginal cost of *equity capital* (not the WACC) be if it must fund a capital budget requiring $600 in total new capital? (15.8%)

9-3. Gator Services Unlimited's (GSU) financial analyst must determine the firm's WACC for use in capital budgeting. She has gathered the following relevant data:

(1) Target capital structure: Debt 55%, Common equity 45%.

(2) Net income = $50 million; payout ratio = 40%.

(3) Interest rate on new debt = 10%.

(4) Flotation cost on all new stock issued = 15%.

(5) GSU's current stock price = $50.00; its last dividend was $3.00.

(6) The firm's constant growth rate is 10%; its tax rate is 35%.

If GSU will raise $100 million, what will be its WACC? (11.57%)

9-4. The Hiers Company has a target capital structure of 42 percent debt and 58 percent equity. The yield to maturity on the company's bonds is 11 percent, and the company's tax rate is 40 percent. Hiers' treasurer has calculated the company's WACC as 10.53 percent. What is the company's cost of equity capital, according to the treasurer's calculation? (13.38%)

10-23 Assume that you recently went to work for Allied Components Company, a supplier of auto repair parts used in the after-market with products from Chrysler, Ford, and other auto makers. Your boss, the chief financial officer (CFO), has just handed you the estimated cash flows for two proposed projects. Project L involves adding a new item to the firm's ignition system line; it would take some time to build up the market for this product, so the cash inflows would increase over time. Project S involves an add-on to an existing line, and its cash flows would decrease over time. Both projects have 3-year lives, because Allied is planning to introduce entirely new models after 3 years.

Here are the projects' net cash flows (in thousands of dollars):

	Expected Net Cash Flow	
Year	Project L	Project S
0	($100)	($100)
1	10	70
2	60	50
3	80	20

Depreciation, salvage values, net working capital requirements, and tax effects are all included in these cash flows.

The CFO also made subjective risk assessments of each project, and he concluded that both projects have risk characteristics which are similar to the firm's average project. Allied's weighted average cost of capital is 10 percent. You must now determine whether one or both of the projects should be accepted.

a. What is capital budgeting? Are there any similarities between a firm's capital budgeting decisions and an individual's investment decisions?

b. What is the difference between independent and mutually exclusive projects? Between projects with normal and nonnormal cash flows?

c. (1) What is the payback period? Find the paybacks for Projects L and S.

(2) What is the rationale for the payback method? According to the payback criterion, which project or projects should be accepted if the firm's maximum acceptable

payback is 2 years, and if Projects L and S are independent? If they are mutually exclusive?

(3) What is the difference between the regular payback and the discounted payback periods?

(4) What is the main disadvantage of discounted payback? Is the payback method of any real usefulness in capital budgeting decisions?

d. (1) Define the term *net present value (NPV)*. What is each project's NPV?

(2) What is the rationale behind the NPV method? According to NPV, which project or projects should be accepted if they are independent? Mutually exclusive?

(3) Would the NPVs change if the cost of capital changed?

e. (1) Define the term *internal rate of return (IRR)*. What is each project's IRR?

(2) How is the IRR on a project related to the YTM on a bond?

(3) What is the logic behind the IRR method? According to IRR, which projects should be accepted if they are independent? Mutually exclusive?

(4) Would the projects' IRRs change if the cost of capital changed?

f. (1) Draw NPV profiles for Projects L and S. At what discount rate do the profiles cross?

(2) Look at your NPV profile graph without referring to the actual NPVs and IRRs. Which project or projects should be accepted if they are independent? Mutually exclusive? Explain. Are your answers correct at any cost of capital less than 23.6 percent?

g. (1) What is the underlying cause of ranking conflicts between NPV and IRR?

(2) What is the "reinvestment rate assumption," and how does it affect the NPV versus IRR conflict?

(3) Which method is the best? Why?

h. (1) Define the term *"modified IRR (MIRR)"*. Find the MIRRs for Projects L and S.

(2) What are the MIRR's advantages and disadvantages vis-a-vis the regular IRR? What are the MIRR's advantages and disadvantages vis-a-vis the NPV?

l. As a separate project (Project P), the firm is considering sponsoring a pavilion at the upcoming World's Fair. The pavilion would cost $800,000, and it is expected to result in $5 million of incremental cash inflows during its 1 year of operation. However, it would then take another year, and $5 million of costs, to demolish the site and return it to its original condition. Thus, Project P's expected net cash flows look like this (in millions of dollars):

Year	Net Cash Flows
0	($0.8)
1	5.0
2	(5.0)

The project is estimated to be of average risk, so its cost of capital is 10 percent.

(1) What is Project P's NPV? What is its IRR? Its MIRR?

(2) Draw Project P's NPV profile. Does Project P have normal or nonnormal cash flows? Should this project be accepted?

CHAPTER 10
The Basics of Capital Budgeting

Should we build this plant?

What is capital budgeting?

- Analysis of potential additions to fixed assets.
- Long-term decisions; involve large expenditures.
- Very important to firm's future.

Steps

1. Estimate CFs (inflows & outflows).
2. Assess riskiness of CFs.
3. Determine k = WACC (adj.).
4. Find NPV and/or IRR.
5. Accept if NPV > 0 and/or IRR > WACC.

An Example of Mutually Exclusive Projects

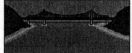 

BRIDGE vs. BOAT to get products across a river.

Normal Cash Flow Project:

Cost (negative CF) followed by a series of positive cash inflows. **One** change of signs.

Nonnormal Cash Flow Project:

Two or more changes of signs. Most common: Cost (negative CF), then string of positive CFs, then cost to close project. Nuclear power plant, strip mine.

Inflow (+) or Outflow (-) in Year

0	1	2	3	4	5	N	NN
-	+	+	+	+	+	N	
-	+	+	+	+	-		NN
-	-	-	+	+	+	N	
+	+	+	-	-	-	N	
-	+	+	-	+	-		NN

What is the payback period?

The number of years required to recover a project's cost,

or how long does it take to get our money back?

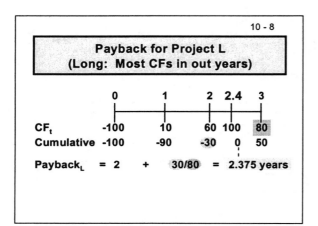

Payback for Project L
(Long: Most CFs in out years)

	0	1	2	2.4	3
CF$_t$	-100	10	60	100	80
Cumulative	-100	-90	-30	0	50

Payback$_L$ = 2 + 30/80 = 2.375 years

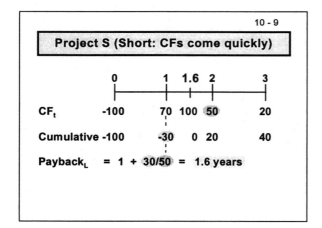

Project S (Short: CFs come quickly)

	0	1	1.6	2	3
CF$_t$	-100	70	100	50	20
Cumulative	-100	-30	0	20	40

Payback$_L$ = 1 + 30/50 = 1.6 years

Strengths of Payback:

1. Provides an indication of a project's risk and liquidity.
2. Easy to calculate and understand.

Weaknesses of Payback:

1. Ignores the TVM.
2. Ignores CFs occurring after the payback period.

Discounted Payback: Uses discounted rather than raw CFs.

	0	1	2	3
		10%		
CF_t	-100	10	60	80
$PVCF_t$	-100	9.09	49.59	60.11
Cumulative	-100	-90.91	-41.32	18.79

Discounted payback = 2 + 41.32/60.11 = 2.7 yrs

Recover invest. + cap. costs in 2.7 yrs.

NPV: Sum of the PVs of inflows and outflows.

$$NPV = \sum_{t=0}^{n} \frac{CF_t}{(1+k)^t}.$$

Cost often is CF_0 and is negative.

$$NPV = \sum_{t=0}^{n} \frac{CF_t}{(1+k)^t} - CF_0.$$

What's Project L's NPV?

Project L:

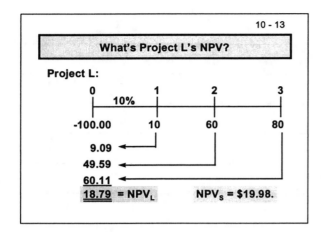

$18.79 = NPV_L$ $NPV_S = \$19.98.$

Calculator Solution

Enter in CFLO for L:

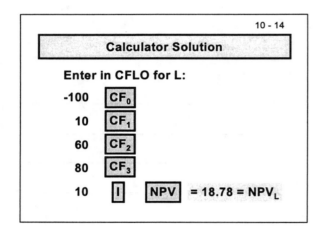

Rationale for the NPV Method

NPV = PV inflows - Cost
    = Net gain in wealth.

Accept project if NPV > 0.

Choose between mutually
exclusive projects on basis of
higher NPV. Adds most value.

Using NPV method, which project(s) should be accepted?

- If Projects S and L are mutually exclusive, accept S because $NPV_s > NPV_L$.

- If S & L are independent, accept both; NPV > 0.

Internal Rate of Return: IRR

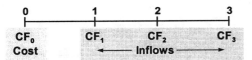

IRR is the discount rate that forces PV inflows = cost. This is the same as forcing NPV = 0.

NPV: Enter k, solve for NPV.

$$\sum_{t=0}^{n} \frac{CF_t}{(1+k)^t} = NPV.$$

IRR: Enter NPV = 0, solve for IRR.

$$\sum_{t=0}^{n} \frac{CF_t}{(1+IRR)^t} = 0.$$

What's Project L's IRR?

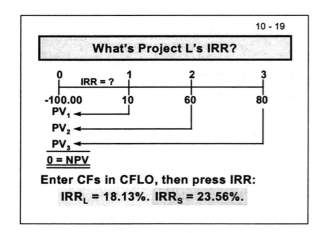

Enter CFs in CFLO, then press IRR:

IRR$_L$ = 18.13%. IRR$_S$ = 23.56%.

Find IRR if CFs are constant:

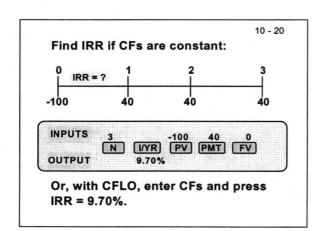

Or, with CFLO, enter CFs and press
IRR = 9.70%.

Q. How is a project's IRR
   related to a bond's YTM?

A. They are the same thing.
   A bond's YTM is the IRR
   if you invest in the bond.

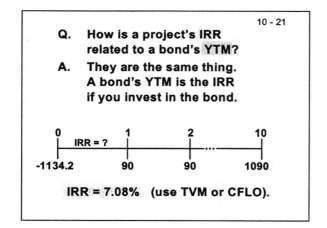

IRR = 7.08%   (use TVM or CFLO).

BLUEPRINTS: CHAPTER 10

Rationale for the IRR Method

If IRR > WACC, then the project's rate of return is greater than its cost-- some return is left over to boost stockholders' returns.

Example: WACC = 10%, IRR = 15%. Profitable.

IRR Acceptance Criteria

- If IRR > k, accept project.

- If IRR < k, reject project.

Decisions on Projects S and L per IRR

- If S and L are independent, accept both. IRRs > k = 10%.

- If S and L are mutually exclusive, accept S because $IRR_S > IRR_L$.

Construct NPV Profiles

Enter CFs in CFLO and find NPV$_L$ and NPV$_S$ at different discount rates:

k	NPV$_L$	NPV$_S$
0	50	40
5	33	29
10	19	20
15	7	12
20	(4)	5

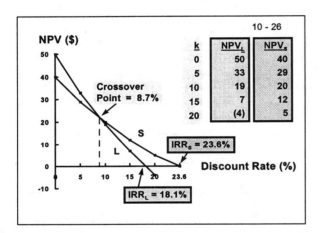

k	NPV$_L$	NPV$_s$
0	50	40
5	33	29
10	19	20
15	7	12
20	(4)	5

Crossover Point = 8.7%

IRR$_s$ = 23.6%

IRR$_L$ = 18.1%

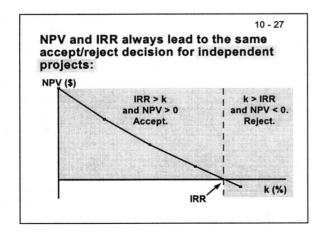

NPV and IRR always lead to the same accept/reject decision for independent projects:

NPV ($)

IRR > k and NPV > 0. Accept.

k > IRR and NPV < 0. Reject.

IRR

k (%)

Mutually Exclusive Projects

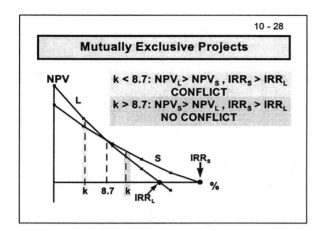

$k < 8.7$: $NPV_L > NPV_S$, $IRR_S > IRR_L$
CONFLICT
$k > 8.7$: $NPV_S > NPV_L$, $IRR_S > IRR_L$
NO CONFLICT

To Find the Crossover Rate

1. Find cash flow differences between the projects. See data at beginning of the case.
2. Enter these differences in CFLO register, then press IRR. Crossover rate = 8.68%, rounded to 8.7%.
3. Can subtract S from L or vice versa, but better to have first CF negative.
4. If profiles don't cross, one project dominates the other.

Two Reasons NPV Profiles Cross

1. Size (scale) differences. Smaller project frees up funds at $t = 0$ for investment. The higher the opportunity cost, the more valuable these funds, so high k favors small projects.

2. Timing differences. Project with faster payback provides more CF in early years for reinvestment. If k is high, early CF especially good, $NPV_S > NPV_L$.

10 - 31

Reinvestment Rate Assumptions

- NPV assumes reinvest at k (opportunity cost of capital).

- IRR assumes reinvest at IRR.

- Reinvest at opportunity cost, k, is more realistic, so NPV method is best. NPV should be used to choose between mutually exclusive projects.

---

10 - 32

Managers like rates--prefer IRR to NPV comparisons. Can we give them a better IRR?

Yes, MIRR is the discount rate which causes the PV of a project's terminal value (TV) to equal the PV of costs. TV is found by compounding inflows at WACC.

Thus, MIRR assumes cash inflows are reinvested at WACC.

---

10 - 33

MIRR for Project L (k = 10%)

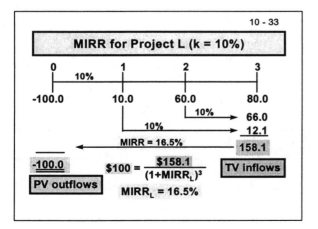

$$\$100 = \frac{\$158.1}{(1+MIRR_L)^3}$$

$MIRR_L = 16.5\%$

To find TV with 10B, enter in CFLO:

$CF_0 = 0$, $CF_1 = 10$, $CF_2 = 60$, $CF_3 = 80$
$I = 10$

NPV = 118.78 = PV of inflows.

Enter PV = -118.78, N = 3, I = 10, PMT = 0.
Press FV = 158.10 = FV of inflows.

Enter FV = 158.10, PV = -100, PMT = 0, N = 3.
Press I = 16.50% = MIRR.

Why use MIRR versus IRR?

MIRR correctly assumes reinvestment at opportunity cost = WACC. MIRR also avoids the problem of multiple IRRS.

Managers like rate of return comparisons, and MIRR is better for this than IRR.

Pavilion Project: NPV and IRR?

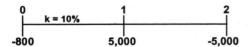

```
0        k = 10%       1              2
|------------------|--------------|
-800             5,000        -5,000
```

Enter CFs in CFLO, enter I = 10.
NPV = -386.78
IRR = ERROR. Why?

We got IRR = ERROR because there are 2 IRRs. Nonnormal CFs--two sign changes. Here's a picture:

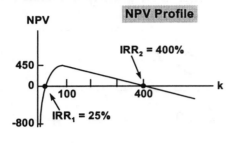

NPV

NPV Profile

$IRR_2 = 400\%$

450

0

100

400

k

-800

$IRR_1 = 25\%$

Logic of Multiple IRRs

1. **At very low discount rates, the PV of CF_2 is large & negative, so NPV < 0.**

2. **At very high discount rates, the PV of both CF_1 and CF_2 are low, so CF_0 dominates and again NPV < 0.**

3. **In between, the discount rate hits CF_2 harder than CF_1, so NPV > 0.**

4. **Result: 2 IRRs.**

Could find IRR with calculator:

1. **Enter CFs as before.**

2. **Enter a "guess" as to IRR by storing the guess. Try 10%:**

   10 ▆▆ STO

   ▆▆ IRR = 25% = lower IRR

   Now guess large IRR, say, 200:

   200 ▆▆ STO

   ▆▆ IRR = 400% = upper IRR

When there are nonnormal CFs and more than one IRR, use MIRR:

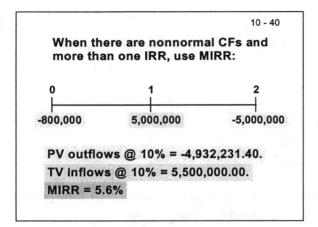

0	1	2
-800,000	5,000,000	-5,000,000

PV outflows @ 10% = -4,932,231.40.
TV inflows @ 10% = 5,500,000.00.
MIRR = 5.6%

Accept Project P?

NO. Reject because MIRR = 5.6% < k = 10%.

Also, if MIRR < k, NPV will be negative: NPV = -$386,777.

EXAM-TYPE PROBLEMS

10-1. A company is analyzing two mutually exclusive projects, S and L, whose cash flows are shown below:

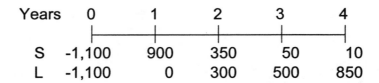

Years	0	1	2	3	4
S	-1,100	900	350	50	10
L	-1,100	0	300	500	850

The company's cost of capital is 12 percent, and it can get an unlimited amount of capital at that cost. What is the *regular IRR* (not MIRR) of the *better* project? (Hint: Note that the better project may or may not be the one with the higher IRR.) (13.09%)

10-2. As the director of capital budgeting for Lasser Company, you are evaluating two mutually exclusive projects with the following net cash flows:

Year	Project X	Project Z
0	-$100	-$100
1	50	10
2	40	30
3	30	40
4	10	60

Is there a crossover point in the relevant part of the NPV profile graph (the upper right quadrant) and, if there is, at what rate does it occur? (7.17%)

10-3. Below are the returns of Nulook Cosmetics and the "market" over a three-year period:

Year	Nulook	Market
1	9%	6%
2	15%	10%
3	36%	24%

Nulook finances internally using only retained earnings, and it uses the Capital Asset Pricing Model with a historical beta to determine its cost of equity. Currently, the risk-free rate is 7%, and the estimated market risk premium is 6%. Nulook is evaluating a project which has a cost today of $2,028 and will provide estimated after-tax cash inflows of $1,000 at the end of each of the next 3 years. What is this project's MIRR? (20.01%)

11-13 After seeing Snapple's success with noncola soft drinks and learning of Coke's and Pepsi's interest, Allied Food Products has decided to consider an expansion of its own in the fruit juice business. The product being considered is fresh lemon juice. Assume that you were recently hired as assistant to the director of capital budgeting, and you must evaluate the new project.

The lemon juice would be produced in an unused building adjacent to Allied's Fort Myers plant; Allied owns the building, which is fully depreciated. The required equipment would cost $200,000, plus an additional $40,000 for shipping and installation. In addition, inventories would rise by $25,000, while accounts payable would go up by $5,000. All of these costs would be incurred at t = 0. By a special ruling, the machinery could be depreciated under the MACRS system as 3-year property.

The project is expected to operate for 4 years, at which time it will be terminated. The cash inflows are assumed to begin 1 year after the project is undertaken, or at t = 1, and to continue out to t = 4. At the end of the project's life (t = 4), the equipment is expected to have a salvage value of $25,000.

Unit sales are expected to total 100,000 cans per year, and the expected sales price is $2.00 per can. Cash operating costs for the project (total operating costs less depreciation) are expected to total 60 percent of dollar sales. Allied's tax rate is 40 percent, and its weighted average cost of capital is 10 percent. Tentatively, the lemon juice project is assumed to be of equal risk to Allied's other assets.

You have been asked to evaluate the project and to make a recommendation as to whether it should be accepted or rejected. To guide you in your analysis, your boss gave you the following set of questions.

a. Draw a time line which shows when the net cash inflows and outflows will occur, and explain how the time line can be used to help structure the analysis.

b. Allied has a standard form which is used in the capital budgeting process; see Table IC11-1. Part of the table has been completed, but you must replace the blanks with the missing numbers.

Table IC11-1. Allied's Lemon Juice Project
(Total Cost in Thousands)

	0	1	2	3	4
End of Year:					
I. Investment Outlay					
Equipment cost					
Installation					
Increase in inventory					
Increase in accounts payable	_____				
Total net investment	======				
II. Operating Cash Flows					
Unit sales (thousands)			100		
Price/unit		$ 2.00	$ 2.00	_____	_____
Total revenues					$200.0
Operating costs,					
excluding depreciation			$120.0		
Depreciation		_____	_____	36.0	16.8
Total costs		$199.2	$228.0	_____	_____
Oper. income bef. taxes				$44.0	
Taxes on oper. income		0.3	_____	_____	25.3
Oper. income after taxes				$26.4	
Depreciation	_____	79.2	_____	36.0	_____
Operating cash flow	$ 0.0	$ 79.7	_____	_____	$ 54.7
III. Terminal Year Cash Flows					
Return of net working capital					
Salvage value					
Tax on salvage value					_____
Total termination cash flows					======
IV. Net Cash Flows					
Net cash flow	($260.0)	_____	_____	_____	$ 89.7
Cumulative cash flow					
for payback:	(260.0)	(180.3)			63.0
Compounded inflows for MIRR:		106.1			89.7
Terminal value of inflows:					
V. Results					
NPV =					
IRR =					
MIRR =					
Payback =					

Complete the table in the following steps:

(1) Fill in the blanks under Year 0 for the initial investment outlay.

(2) Complete the table for unit sales, sales price, total revenues, and operating costs excluding depreciation.

(3) Complete the depreciation data.

(4) Now complete the table down to operating income after taxes, and then down to net cash flows.

(5) Now fill in the blanks under Year 4 for the termination cash flows, and complete the net cash flow line. Discuss working capital. What would have happened if the machinery were sold for less than its book value?

c. (1) Allied uses debt in its capital structure, so some of the money used to finance the project will be debt. Given this fact, should the projected cash flows be revised to show projected interest charges? Explain.

(2) Suppose you learned that Allied had spent $50,000 to renovate the building last year, expensing these costs. Should this cost be reflected in the analysis? Explain.

(3) Now suppose you learned that Allied could lease its building to another party and earn $25,000 per year. Should that fact be reflected in the analysis? If so, how?

(4) Now assume that the lemon juice project would take away profitable sales from Allied's fresh orange juice business. Should that fact be reflected in your analysis? If so, how?

d. Disregard all the assumptions made in Part c, and assume there was no alternative use for the building over the next 4 years. Now calculate the project's NPV, IRR, MIRR, and regular payback. Do these indicators suggest that the project should be accepted?

e. If this project had been a replacement rather than an expansion project, how would the analysis have changed? Think about the changes that would have to occur in the cash flow table.

f.   Assume that inflation is expected to average 5 percent over the next 4 years; that this expectation is reflected in the WACC; and that inflation will increase variable costs and revenues by the same percentage, 5 percent. Does it appear that inflation has been dealt with properly in the analysis? If not, what should be done, and how would the required adjustment affect the decision? You can modify the numbers in the table to quantify your results.

g.   In an unrelated analysis, you have also been asked to choose between the following two mutually exclusive projects:

<u>Expected Net Cash Flows</u>

Year	Project S	Project L
0	($100,000)	($100,000)
1	60,000	33,500
2	60,000	33,500
3	--	33,500
4	--	33,500

The projects provide a necessary service, so whichever one is selected is expected to be repeated into the foreseeable future. Both projects are of average risk.

(1) What is each project's initial NPV without replication?

(2) Now construct a time line, and then apply the replacement chain approach to determine the projects' extended NPVs. Which project should be chosen?

(3) Repeat the analysis using the equivalent annual annuity approach.

(4) Now assume that the cost to repeat Project S in Year 2 will increase to $105,000 because of inflationary pressures. How should the analysis be handled now, and which project should be chosen?

CHAPTER 11
Cash Flow Estimation and Other Topics in Capital Budgeting

- Relevant cash flows
- Working capital in capital budgeting
- Unequal project lives
- Inflation

Proposed Project

- Cost: $200,000 + $10,000 shipping + $30,000 installation. Depreciable cost: $240,000.
- Inventories will rise by $25,000 and payables by $5,000.
- Economic life = 4 years.
- Salvage value = $25,000.
- MACRS 3-year class.

- Sales: 100,000 units/yr @ $2.
- Variable cost = 60% of sales.
- Tax rate = 40%.
- WACC = 10%.

Set up, without numbers, a time line for the project's cash flows.

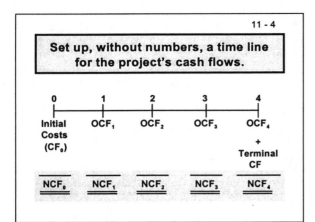

0	1	2	3	4
Initial Costs (CF$_0$)	OCF$_1$	OCF$_2$	OCF$_3$	OCF$_4$ + Terminal CF
NCF$_0$	NCF$_1$	NCF$_2$	NCF$_3$	NCF$_4$

Investment at t = 0:

Equipment	-$200
Installation & Shipping	-40
Increase in inventories	-25
Increase in A/P	5
Net CF$_0$	-$260

ΔNWC = $25 - $5 = $20.

What's the annual depreciation?

Year	Rate	x	Basis	Depreciation
1	0.33		$240	$ 79
2	0.45		240	108
3	0.15		240	36
4	0.07		240	17
	1.00			$240

Due to 1/2-year convention, a 3-year asset is depreciated over 4 years.

Operating cash flows:

	1	2	3	4
Revenues	$200	$200	$200	$200
Op. Cost, 60%	-120	-120	-120	-120
Depreciation	-79	-108	-36	-17
Oper. inc. (BT)	1	-28	44	63
Tax, 40%	--	-11	18	25
Oper. inc. (AT)	1	-17	26	38
Add. Depr'n	79	108	36	17
Op. CF	80	91	62	55

Net Terminal CF at t = 4:

Recovery of NWC	$20
Salvage Value	25
Tax on SV (40%)	-10
Net termination CF	$35

Q. Always a tax on SV? Ever a positive tax number?

Q. How is NWC recovered?

Should CFs include interest expense? Dividends?

■ No. The cost of capital is accounted for by discounting at the 10% WACC, so deducting interest and dividends would be "double counting" financing costs.

Suppose $50,000 had been spent last year to improve the building. Should this cost be included in the analysis?

No. This is a sunk cost.
Analyze incremental investment.

Suppose the plant could be leased out for $25,000 a year. Would this affect the analysis?

- Yes. Accepting the project means foregoing the $25,000. This is an opportunity cost, and it should be charged to the project.
- A.T. opportunity cost = $25,000(1 - T) = $25,000(0.6) = $15,000 annual cost.

If the new product line would decrease sales of the firm's other lines, would this affect the analysis?

- Yes. The effect on other projects' CFs is an "externality."
- Net CF loss per year on other lines would be a cost to this project.
- Externalities can be positive or negative, i.e., complements or substitutes.

Here are all the project's net CFs (in thousands) on a time line:

```
      0  k = 10%  1        2        3        4
      ├─────────┼────────┼────────┼────────┤
    -260       79.7     91.2     62.4     54.7
                              Terminal CF ──→  35.0
                                               89.7
```

Enter CFs in CF register, and I = 10%.

NPV = -$4.03
IRR = 9.3%

What's the project's MIRR?

```
      0        1        2        3        4
      ├────────┼────────┼────────┼────────┤
    -260      79.7     91.2     62.4     89.7
                                    10%   68.6
                              10%  ──→   110.4
                        10%   ────────→  106.1
    -260  ←──────────────────────────   374.8
              MIRR = ?
```

Can we solve using a calculator?

Yes. CF$_0$ = 0
CF$_1$ = 79.7
CF$_2$ = 91.2
CF$_3$ = 62.4
CF$_4$ = 89.7
  I = 10
■ NPV = 255.97

INPUTS	4	10	-255.97	0	
	N	I/YR	PV	PMT	FV
OUTPUT					TV = FV = 374.8

Use the FV = TV of inputs to find MIRR

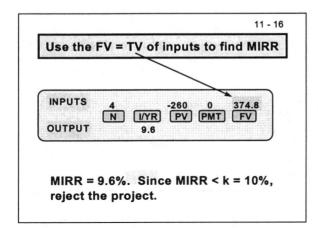

INPUTS	4		-260	0	374.8
	N	I/YR	PV	PMT	FV
OUTPUT		9.6			

MIRR = 9.6%. Since MIRR < k = 10%, reject the project.

What's the payback period?

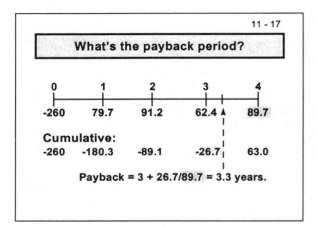

0	1	2	3	4
-260	79.7	91.2	62.4	89.7

Cumulative:

-260	-180.3	-89.1	-26.7	63.0

Payback = 3 + 26.7/89.7 = 3.3 years.

If this were a replacement rather than a new project, would the analysis change?

Yes. The old equipment would be sold, and the incremental CFs would be the changes from the old to the new situation.

■ The relevant depreciation would be the change with the new equipment.

■ Also, if the firm sold the old machine now, it would not receive the SV at the end of the machine's life. This is an opportunity cost for the replacement project.

Q. If E(INFL) = 5%, is NPV biased?

A. YES. $NPV = \sum_{t=0}^{n} \frac{CF_t}{(1+k)^t} = \frac{Rev_t - Cost_t}{(1+k)^t}$.

$k = k^* + IP + DRP + LP + MRP$.

Inflation is in denominator but not in numerator, so downward bias to NPV. Should build inflation into CF forecasts.

Consider project with 5% inflation. Investment remains same, $260. Terminal CF remains same, $35.

Operating cash flows:

	1	2	3	4
Revenues	$210	$220	$232	$243
Op. cost 60%	-126	-132	-139	-146
Depr'n	-79	-108	-36	-17
Oper. inc. (BT)	5	-20	57	80
Tax, 40%	2	-8	23	32
Oper. inc. (AT)	3	-12	34	48
Add Depr'n	79	108	36	17
Op. CF	82	96	70	65

Here are all the project's net CFs (in thousands) when inflation is considered.

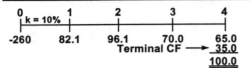

```
   0        1        2        3        4
   | k = 10% |        |        |        |
 -260      82.1     96.1     70.0     65.0
                   Terminal CF ──→     35.0
                                      100.0
```

Enter CFs in CF register, and I = 10%.

NPV = $15.0   Project should be accepted.
IRR = 12.6%

S and L are mutually exclusive and will be repeated. k = 10%. Which is better?

	Expected Net CFs	
Year	Project S	Project L
0	($100,000)	($100,000)
1	60,000	33,500
2	60,000	33,500
3	--	33,500
4	--	33,500

	S	L
CF_0	-100,000	-100,000
CF_1	60,000	33,500
N_j	2	4
I	10	10
NPV	4,132	6,190

Q. $NPV_L > NPV_S$. Is L better?

A. Can't say. Need replacement chain analysis.

- Note that Project S could be *repeated* after 2 years to generate additional profits.

- Use *replacement chain* to calculate *extended NPV$_S$* to a common life.

- Since S has a 2-year life and L has a 4-year life, the common life is 4 years.

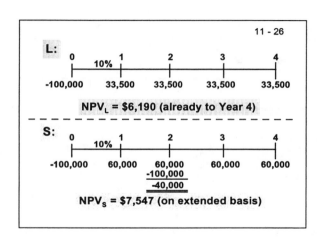

L:

0		1	2	3	4
-100,000		33,500	33,500	33,500	33,500

10%

NPV$_L$ = $6,190 (already to Year 4)

- -

S:

0		1	2	3	4
-100,000		60,000	60,000	60,000	60,000
			-100,000		
			-40,000		

10%

NPV$_S$ = $7,547 (on extended basis)

Equivalent Annual Annuity (EAA)

That annuity PMT whose PV equals the project's NPV.

S:

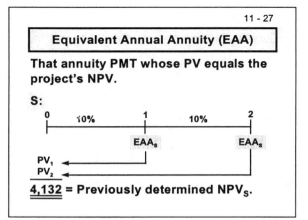

0	10%	1	10%	2
		EAA$_s$		EAA$_s$

PV$_1$

PV$_2$

4,132 = Previously determined NPV$_S$.

Project S (EAA):

```
INPUTS      2      10    -4132          0
           [N]   [I/YR]  [PV]  [PMT]  [FV]
OUTPUT                    EAA_S = 2380.82
```

Project L (EAA):

```
INPUTS      4      10    -6190          0
           [N]   [I/YR]  [PV]  [PMT]  [FV]
OUTPUT                    EAA_L = 1952.76
```

The higher annuity is better.

- ■ **The project, in effect, provides an annuity of EAA.**

- ■ **$EAA_S > EAA_L$, so pick S.**

- ■ **Replacement chains and EAA always lead to the same decision.**

If the cost to repeat S in two years rises to $105,000, which would be best?

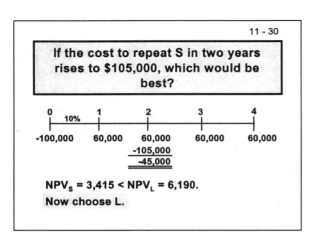

```
0      1         2         3         4
 10%
-100,000  60,000  60,000  60,000  60,000
                 -105,000
                 ─────────
                  -45,000
```

$NPV_S = 3{,}415 < NPV_L = 6{,}190.$
Now choose L.

EXAM-TYPE PROBLEMS

11-1. McQueen Corporation is considering two mutually exclusive projects which are expected to generate the following cash flows:

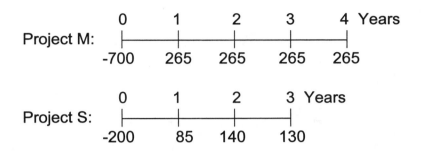

	0	1	2	3	4 Years
Project M:	-700	265	265	265	265

	0	1	2	3 Years
Project S:	-200	85	140	130

The two projects are not repeatable. McQueen evaluates investment projects with close to equal lives, such as these, only with the NPV method. At what cost of capital should McQueen be indifferent between the two projects? (14.19%)

11-2. Far West Airlines seeks to purchase one of two alternative jetliners. Jet A costs $2 million, has an expected life of 7 years, and will generate net cash flows of $520,000 per year. An identical Jet A can be purchased for the same price when the first jet's life is over. Jet B costs $6.2 million, has an expected life of 14 years, and is expected to produce net cash flows of $1,012,000 per year. Assume that inflation in operating costs, airplane expenditures, and fares will be zero, that the cash inflows occur at the end of the year, and that the firm's cost of capital is 12%. If the firm chooses the jet project that will add the most value to the firm, by how much will the company's value increase? ($541,949.05)

11-3. Envirotech Company issued $10,000,000 in $1,000 par value, 15% coupon bonds 10 years ago. When issued, the bonds had 30 years to maturity, paid interest semiannually, and were callable at a call premium of $100 each. Market interest rates are now 13.5%. Envirotech can issue new bonds at current market rates with a $1,000 par value, 20-year maturity, and semiannual payments which would replace the old issue, for flotation costs of $400,000. Assume that the firm has a marginal tax rate of zero percent and that all flotation costs will be treated as a lump sum cost incurred at time = 0 (i.e., there are no tax effects). What is the NPV of this refunding project? (Hint: See Appendix 11B.) (-$370,367)

12-14 The Chapter 11 Integrated Case contained the details of a capital budgeting evaluation being conducted by Allied Food Products. Although inflation was considered in the initial analysis, the riskiness of the project was not considered. The expected cash flows, considering inflation as they were estimated in Chapter 11 (in thousands of dollars), are given in the following table. Allied's overall cost of capital (WACC) is 10 percent.

You have been asked to answer the following questions.

a. (1) What are the three levels, or types, of project risk that are normally considered?

(2) Which type is most relevant?

(3) Which type is easiest to measure?

(4) Are the three types of risk generally highly correlated?

b. (1) What is sensitivity analysis?

(2) Discuss how one would perform a sensitivity analysis on the unit sales, salvage value, and cost of capital for the project. Assume that each of these variables deviates from its base-case, or expected, value by plus and minus 10, 20, and 30 percent. Explain how you would calculate the NPV, IRR, MIRR, and payback for each case. Include a sensitivity diagram, and discuss the results.

(3) What is the primary weakness of sensitivity analysis? What are its primary advantages?

c. Assume that you are confident about the estimates of all the variables that affect the cash flows except unit sales. If product acceptance is poor, sales would be only 75,000 units a year, while a strong consumer response would produce sales of 125,000 units. In either case, cash costs would still amount to 60 percent of revenues. You believe that there is a 25 percent chance of poor acceptance, a 25 percent chance of excellent acceptance, and a 50 percent chance of average acceptance (the base case).

Allied's Lemon Juice Project
(Total Cost in Thousands)

End of Year:	0	1	2	3	4
I. Investment Outlay					
Equipment cost	($200)				
Installation	(40)				
Increase in inventory	(25)				
Increase in accounts payable	5				
Total net investment	($260)				
II. Operating Cash Flows					
Unit sales (thousands)		100	100	100	100
Price/unit		$2.100	$2.205	$2.315	$2.431
Total revenues		$210.0	$220.5	$231.5	$243.1
Operating costs,					
excluding depreciation		126.0	132.3	138.9	145.9
Depreciation		79.2	108.0	36.0	16.8
Total costs		$205.2	$240.3	174.9	162.7
Oper. income bef. taxes		$ 4.8	($ 19.8)	$ 56.6	$ 80.4
Taxes on oper. income		1.9	(7.9)	22.6	32.1
Oper. income after taxes		$ 2.9	($ 11.9)	$ 34.0	$ 48.3
Depreciation		79.2	108.0	36.0	16.8
Operating cash flow	$ 0.0	$ 82.1	$ 96.1	$ 70.0	$ 65.1
III. Terminal Year Cash Flows					
Return of net working capital					20.0
Salvage value					25.0
Tax on salvage value					(10.0)
Total termination cash flows					$35.0
IV. Net Cash Flows					
Net cash flow	($260.0)	$ 82.1	$ 96.1	$ 70.0	$100.1
Cumulative cash flow					
for payback:	(260.0)	(177.9)	(81.8)	(11.8)	88.3
Compounded inflows for MIRR:		109.2	116.3	77.0	100.1
Terminal value of inflows:					402.6
V. Results					

- NPV = $15.0
- IRR = 12.6%
- MIRR = 11.6%

(1) What is the worst-case NPV? The best-case NPV?

(2) Use the worst-, most likely (or base), and best-case NPVs, with their probabilities of occurrence, to find the project's expected NPV, standard deviation, and coefficient of variation.

d. (1) Assume that Allied's average project has a coefficient of variation (CV) in the range of 1.25 to 1.75. Would the lemon juice project be classified as high risk, average risk, or low risk? What type of risk is being measured here?

(2) Based on common sense, how highly correlated do you think the project would be with the firm's other assets? (Give a correlation coefficient, or range of coefficients, based on your judgment.)

(3) How would this correlation coefficient and the previously calculated σ combine to affect the project's contribution to corporate, or within-firm, risk? Explain.

e. (1) Based on your judgment, what do you think the project's correlation coefficient would be with respect to the general economy and thus with returns on "the market"?

(2) How would correlation with the economy affect the project's market risk?

f. (1) Allied typically adds or subtracts 3 percentage points to the overall cost of capital to adjust for risk. Should the lemon juice project be accepted?

(2) What subjective risk factors should be considered before the final decision is made?

g. (1) Assume for purposes of this problem that Allied's target capital structure is 50 percent debt and 50 percent common equity, its cost of debt is 12 percent, the risk-free rate is 10 percent, the market risk premium is 6 percent, and the firm's tax rate is 40 percent. If your estimate of the new project's beta is 1.2, what is its weighted average cost of capital based on the CAPM?

(2) How does the project's market risk compare with the firm's overall market risk?

(3) How does the project's market risk compare with its stand-alone risk?

(4) Briefly describe two methods that you could conceivably have used to estimate the project's beta. How feasible do you think those procedures would actually be in this case?

(5) What are the advantages and disadvantages of focusing on a project's market risk?

h.　As a completely different project, Allied is also evaluating two different systems for disposing of wastes associated with another product, fresh grapefruit juice. Plan W requires more workers but less capital, while Plan C requires more capital but fewer workers. Both systems have 3-year lives. Since the production line choice has no impact on revenues, you will base your decision on the relative costs of the two systems as set forth below:

| | Expected Net Costs | |
Year	Plan W	Plan C
0	($500)	($1,000)
1	(500)	(300)
2	(500)	(300)
3	(500)	(300)

(1) Assume initially that the two systems are both of average risk. Which one should be chosen?

(2) Now assume that the worker-intensive plan (W) is judged to be riskier than average, because future wage rates are very difficult to forecast. Under this condition, which system should be chosen? Base your answer on the lowest reasonable PV of future costs. (Hint: This is a tricky question; risky *outflows* should be discounted at *low* rates.)

(3) Do the two plans have IRRs?

12-15 Ron Redwine, financial manager of Blum Industries, is developing the firm's optimal capital budget for the coming year. He has identified the five potential projects shown below; none of the projects can be repeated. Projects B and B* are mutually exclusive, while the remainder are independent.

Project	Cost	CF_{1-n}	Life (n)	IRR	NPV
A	$400,000	$119,326	5	15%	
B	200,000	56,863	5	13	
B*	200,000	35,397	10	12	
C	100,000	27,057	5	11	
D	300,000	79,139	5	10	

The following information was developed for use in determining Blum's weighted average cost of capital (WACC):

Interest rate on new debt	8.0%
Tax rate	40.0%
Debt ratio	60.0%
Current stock price, P_0	$20.00
Last dividend, D_0	$2.00
Expected growth rate, g	6.0%
Flotation cost on common, F	19.0%
Expected addition to retained earnings	$200,000.00

Blum adjusts for differential project risk by adding or subtracting 2 percentage points to the firm's marginal cost of capital.

a. Calculate the WACC, and then plot the company's IOS and MCC schedules. What is the firm's marginal cost of capital for capital budgeting purposes?

b. Assume initially that all five projects are of average risk. What is Blum's optimal capital budget? Explain your answer.

c. Now assume that the retained earnings break point occurred at $900,000 of new capital. What effect would this have on the firm's MCC schedule and on its optimal capital budget?

d. Return to the situation in Part a, with the $500,000 retained earnings break point. Suppose Project A is reexamined, and it is judged to be a high-risk project, while Projects C and D are, upon reexamination, judged to have low risk. Projects B and B* remain average-risk projects. How would these changes affect Blum's optimal capital budget?

e. In reality, companies like Blum have hundreds of projects to evaluate each year; hence it is generally not practical to draw the IOS and MCC schedules which include every potential project. Suppose this situation exists for Blum. Suppose also that the company has 3 divisions, L, A, and H, with low, average, and high risk, respectively, and that the projects within each division can also be grouped into three risk categories. Describe how Blum might go about structuring its capital budgeting decision process and choosing its optimal set of projects. For this purpose, assume that Blum's overall WACC is estimated to be 11 percent. As part of your answer, find appropriate divisional and project hurdle rates when differential risk is considered.

CHAPTER 12
Risk Analysis and the Optimal Capital Budget

- Types of risk: stand-alone, corporate, and market
- Risky outflows
- Optimal capital budget

What does "risk" mean in capital budgeting?

- Risk relates to uncertainty about a project's future profitability.
- Measured by σ_{NPV}, σ_{IRR}, beta.
- Will taking on the project increase the firm's and stockholders' risk?

Is risk analysis based on historical data or subjective judgment?

- Can sometimes use historical data, but generally cannot.
- So risk analysis in capital budgeting is usually based on subjective judgments.

What three types of risk are relevant in capital budgeting?

- Stand-alone risk
- Corporate risk
- Market risk

How is each type of risk measured, and how do they relate to one another?

1. Stand-Alone Risk:
   - The project's risk if it were the firm's only asset and there were no share-holders.
   - Ignores both firm and shareholder diversification.
   - Measured by the σ or CV of NPV, IRR, or MIRR.

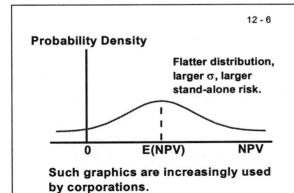

Probability Density

Flatter distribution, larger σ, larger stand-alone risk.

0   E(NPV)   NPV

Such graphics are increasingly used by corporations.

---

2. Corporate Risk:

- ■Reflects the project's effect on corporate earnings stability.
- ■Considers firm's other assets (diversification within firm).
- ■Depends on:
  - ●project's σ, and
  - ●its correlation with returns on firm's other assets.
- ■Measured by the project's corporate beta versus total corporate earnings.

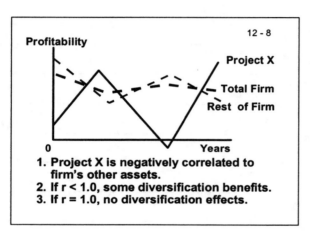

Profitability

Project X

Total Firm

Rest of Firm

0   Years

1. Project X is negatively correlated to firm's other assets.
2. If r < 1.0, some diversification benefits.
3. If r = 1.0, no diversification effects.

---

3. Market Risk:

- ■Reflects the project's effect on a well-diversified stock portfolio.
- ■Takes account of stockholders' other assets.
- ■Depends on project's σ and correlation with the stock market.
- ■Measured by the project's market beta.

How is each type of risk used?

- Market risk is theoretically best in most situations.

- However, creditors, customers, suppliers, and employees are more affected by corporate risk.

- Therefore, corporate risk is also relevant.

- Stand-alone risk is easiest to measure, more intuitive.

- Core projects are highly correlated with other assets, so stand-alone risk generally reflects corporate risk.

- If the project is highly correlated with the economy, stand-alone risk also reflects market risk.

What is sensitivity analysis?

- Shows how changes in a variable such as unit sales affect NPV or IRR.

- Each variable is fixed except one. Change this one variable to see the effect on NPV or IRR.

- Answers "what if" questions, e.g. "What if sales decline by 30%?"

Illustration

Change from	Resulting NPV (000s)		
Base Level	Unit Sales	Salvage	k
-30%	-$ 36	$12	$34
-20	-19	13	28
-10	-2	14	21
0 (base)	15	15	15
+10	32	16	9
+20	49	17	3
+30	66	18	-2

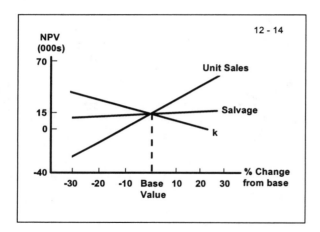

Results of Sensitivity Analysis

- Steeper sensitivity lines show greater risk. Small changes result in large declines in NPV.

- Unit sales line is steeper than salvage value or k, so NPV is more sensitive to changes in unit sales than in salvage value or k.

What are the weaknesses of sensitivity analysis?

- Does not reflect diversification.

- Says nothing about the likelihood of change in a variable, i.e., a steep sales line is not a problem if sales won't fall.

- Ignores relationships among variables.

Why is sensitivity analysis useful?

- Gives some idea of stand-alone risk.

- Identifies dangerous variables.

- Gives some breakeven information.

What is scenario analysis?

- Examines several possible situations, usually worst case, most likely case, and best case.

- Provides a range of possible outcomes.

Assume we know with certainty all variables except unit sales, which could range from 75,000 to 125,000.

Scenario	Probability	NPV(000)
Worst	0.25	-$27.8
Base	0.50	15.0
Best	0.25	57.8
	E(NPV) =	$15.0

Standard Deviation

$$\sigma_{NPV} = \$30.3.$$

Coefficient of Variation

$$CV_{NPV} = \frac{\sigma_{NPV}}{E(NPV)} = \frac{\$30.3}{\$15} = 2.0.$$

If the firm's average project has a CV of 1.25 to 1.75, is this a high-risk project? What type of risk is being measured?

■ Since CV = 2.0 > 1.75, this project has high risk.

■ CV measures a project's *stand-alone risk*. It does not reflect firm or stockholder diversification.

12 - 22

Based on common sense, should the lemon project be highly correlated with the firm's other assets?

- ■ Yes. Positively correlated. Economy and customer demand would affect all core products.
- ■ But each line could be more or less successful, so correlation less than +1.0.

---

12 - 23

Would correlation with the economy affect market risk?

- ■ Yes.
  - ● High correlation increases market risk (beta).
  - ● Low correlation lowers it.

---

12 - 24

With a 3% risk adjustment, should our project be accepted?

- ■ Project k = 10% + 3% = 13%.
- ■ That's 30% above base k.
- ■ NPV = -$2,200, so reject.

12 - 25

What is a simulation analysis?

- A computerized version of scenario analysis which uses continuous probability distributions of input variables.

- Computer selects values for each variable based on given probability distributions.

(Cont...)

---

12 - 26

- NPV and IRR are calculated.

- Process is repeated many times (1,000 or more).

- End result: Probability distribution of NPV and IRR based on sample of simulated values.

- Generally shown graphically.

---

12 - 27

Probability Density

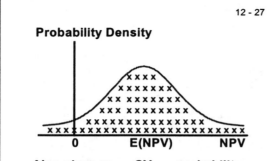

Also gives σ_{NPV}, CV_{NPV}, probability of NPV > 0.

What are the advantages of simulation analysis?

■ Reflects the probability distributions of each input.

■ Shows range of NPVs, the expected NPV, σ_{NPV}, and CV_{NPV}.

■ Gives an intuitive graph of the risk situation.

What are the disadvantages of simulation?

■ Difficult to specify probability distributions and correlations.

■ If inputs are bad, output will be bad: "Garbage in, garbage out."

■ May look more accurate than it really is. It is really a SWAG ("Scientific Wild A-- Guess"). (Cont...)

■ Sensitivity, scenario, and simulation analyses do not provide a decision rule. They do not indicate whether a project's expected return is sufficient to compensate for its risk.

■ Sensitivity, scenario, and simulation analyses all ignore diversification. Thus they measure only stand-alone risk, which may not be the most relevant risk in capital budgeting.

Find the project's market risk and cost of capital based on the CAPM, given these inputs:

- Target debt ratio = 50%.
- k_d = 12%.
- k_{RF} = 10%.
- Tax rate = 40%.
- $beta_{Project}$ = 1.2.
- Market risk premium = 6%.

- Beta = 1.2, so project has more market risk than average.
- Project's required return on equity:

$k_s = k_{RF} + (k_M - k_{RF})b_p$

$= 10\% + (6\%)1.2 = 17.2\%.$

$WACC_p = w_d k_d(1 - T) + w_{ce}k_s$

$= 0.5(12\%)(0.6) + 0.5(17.2\%)$

$= 12.2\%.$

How does the project's market risk compare with the firm's overall market risk?

- Project WACC = 12.2% versus company WACC = 10%.
- Indicates that project's market risk is greater than firm's average project.

---

12 - 34

Is the project's relative market risk consistent with its stand-alone risk?

- Yes. Project CV = 2.0 versus 1.5 for an average project, which is consistent with project's higher market risk.

12 - 35

Methods for Estimating a Project's Beta

1. Pure play. Find several publicly traded companies exclusively in project's business.

   Use average of their betas as proxy for project's beta.

   Hard to find such companies.

12 - 36

2. Accounting beta. Run regression between project's ROA and S&P index ROA.

   Accounting betas are correlated (0.5 - 0.6) with market betas.

   But normally can't get data on new projects' ROAs before the capital budgeting decision has been made.

Evaluating Risky Outflows

■ Company is evaluating two alternative waste disposal systems. Plan W requires more workers but less capital. Plan C requires more capital but fewer workers.

■ Both systems have 3-year lives.

■ The choice will have no impact on sales revenues, so the decision will be based on relative costs.

Year	Plan W	Plan C
0	($500)	($1,000)
1	(500)	(300)
2	(500)	(300)
3	(500)	(300)

The two systems are of average risk, so WACC = 10%. Which to accept?

PV_{COSTS_W} = -$1,743. PV_{COSTS_C} = -$1,746.

W's costs are slightly lower so pick W.

Now suppose Plan W is riskier than Plan C because future wage rates are difficult to forecast. Would this affect the choice?

If we add a 3% risk adjustment to the 10% to get $WACC_W$ = 13%, W's new PV would be:

$$PV_{COSTS_W} = -\$1,681,$$
which is < old PV_{COSTS_W} = -$1,743.

W now looks even better.

- Plan W now looks better, but since it is riskier, it should look worse!
- When costs are being discounted, we must use a lower discount rate to reflect higher risk. Thus, the appropriate discount rate would be

    10% - 3% = 7%, making
    PV_{COSTS_W} = -$1,812 > old -$1,743.

- With risk adjustment, PV_{COSTS_W} > PV_{COSTS_C}, so now choose Plan C.

- Note that neither plan has an IRR.
- IRR is the discount rate that equates the PV of inflows to the PV of outflows.
- Since there are only outflows, there can be no IRR (or MIRR).
- Similarly, a meaningful NPV can only be calculated if a project has both inflows and outflows.
- If CFs all have the same sign, the result is a PV, not an NPV.

Part 2: The Optimal Capital Budget

- We've seen how to evaluate projects.
- We need cost of capital for evaluation.
- But corporate cost of capital depends on size of capital budget.
- Must combine WACC and capital budget analysis.

Blum Industries has 5 potential projects:

Project	Cost	CF	Life (N)	IRR
A	$400,000	$119,326	5	15%
B	200,000	56,863	5	13
B*	200,000	35,397	10	12
C	100,000	27,057	5	11
D	300,000	79,139	5	10

Projects B & B* are mutually exclusive, the others are independent. Neither B nor B* will be repeated.

Additional Information

Interest rate on new debt	8.0%
Tax rate	40.0%
Debt ratio	60.0%
Current stock price, P_0	$20.00
Last dividend, D_0	$2.00
Expected growth rate, g	6.0%
Flotation cost on CS, F	19.0%
Expected addition to RE	$200,000
(NI = $500,000, Payout = 60%.)	

For differential project risk, add or subtract 2% to WACC.

Calculate WACC, then plot IOS and MCC schedules.

Step 1: Estimate the cost of equity

$$k_s = \frac{D_0(1 + g)}{P_0} + g = \frac{\$2(1.06)}{\$20} + 6\% = 16.6\%.$$

$$k_e = \frac{D_1}{P_0(1 - F)} + g = \frac{\$2(1.06)}{\$20(1 - 0.19)} + 6\%$$

$$= \frac{\$2.12}{\$16.2} + 6\% = 19.1\%.$$

Step 2: Estimate the WACCs

$WACC_1 = w_d k_d (1 - T) + w_{ce} k_s$
$\quad\quad\quad = (0.6)(8\%)(0.6) + 0.4(16.6\%) = 9.5\%.$

$WACC_2 = w_d k_d (1 - T) + w_{ce} k_e$
$\quad\quad\quad = (0.6)(8\%)(0.6) + 0.4(19.1\%) = 10.5\%.$

Step 3: Estimate the RE break point

$$BP_{RE} = \frac{\text{Retained earnings}}{\text{Equity fraction}}$$

$$= \frac{\$200,000}{0.4} = \$500,000.$$

Each dollar up to $500,000 has $0.40 of RE at cost of 16.6%, then WACC rises. Only 1 compensating cost increase, so only 1 break point.

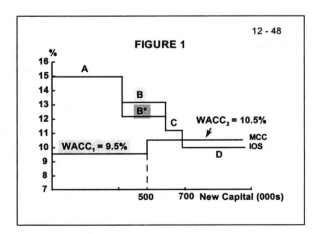

FIGURE 1

12 - 49

- The IOS schedule plots projects in descending order of IRR.

- Two potential IOS schedules--one with A, B, C, and D and another with A, B*, C, and D.

- The WACC has a break point at $500,000 of new capital.

---

12 - 50

What MCC do we use for capital budgeting, i.e., for calculating NPV?

- MCC: WACC that exists where IOS and MCC schedules intersect. In this case, MCC = 10.5%.

---

12 - 51

If all 5 projects are average risk, what's the optimal capital budget?

- MCC = 10.5%.

- IRR and NPV lead to same decisions for independent projects. Thus, all independent projects with IRRs above 10.5% should be accepted.

- Therefore, accept A and C, reject D, and accept B or B*.

12 - 52

- NPV and IRR can conflict for mutually exclusive projects.

- NPV method is better, so choose between B and B* based on NPV at WACC = 10.5%.

- $NPV_{B*} = \$12,905 > NPV_B = \$12,830$, so choose B* over B.

---

12 - 53

Suppose you aren't sure of WACC. At what WACC would B and B* have the same NPV?

Get differences:

$CF_0 = 200,000 - 2000,000 = 0$

$CF_{1-5} = 56,863 - 35,397 = 21,466$

$CF_{6-10} = 0 - 35,397 = -35,397$

Indifference WACC = IRR = 10.52%.

---

12 - 54

The risk-adjusted rates are as follows:

WACC = 10.5% ± 2%

Project Risk	Risk-Adjusted Hurdle Rate
Low: C, D	8.5%
Average: B, B*	10.5
High: A	12.5

	IRR	Hurdle Rate	
A	15%	12.5%	Accept
B	13	10.5	Accept ⎤—one
B*	12	10.5	Accept ⎦
C	11	8.5	Accept
D	10	8.5	Accept

Now the optimal capital budget consists of A, B (or B*), C, and D, for a total of $1,000,000.

Corporate k is still = 10.5%, so NPV_B. still larger than NPV_B.

EXAM-TYPE PROBLEMS

12-1. Alabama Pulp Company (APC) can control its environmental pollution using either "Project Old Tech" or "Project New Tech." Both will do the job, but the actual costs involved with Project New Tech, which uses unproven, new state-of-the-art technology, could be much higher than the expected cost levels. The cash outflows associated with Project Old Tech, which uses standard proven technology, are less risky--they are about as uncertain as the cash flows associated with an average project. APC's cost of capital for average risk projects is normally set at 12%, and the company adds 3% for high risk projects but subtracts 3% for low risk projects. The two projects in question meet the criteria for high and average risk, but the financial manager is concerned about applying the normal risk adjustment rule to such cost-only projects. You must decide which project to recommend, and you should recommend the one with the lower PV of costs. What is the PV of costs of the better project? (-$2,422.41)

Years:	Cash Outflows				
	0	1	2	3	4
Project New Tech	1,500	315	315	315	315
Project Old Tech	600	600	600	600	600

12-2. Career Training Associates (CTA) has a debt ratio of 20 percent. Management has concluded that this capital structure is optimal. CTA has analyzed its investment opportunities for the coming year and has identified four possible additions to assets which generate IRRs greater than zero.

Investment	Size	IRR
A	$ 3 Million	20.1%
B	6 Million	18.8
C	12 Million	19.2
D	9 Million	18.0

CTA is forecasting net income for the coming year of $10 million and expects to pay out 50 percent in dividends to the 1 million outstanding shares of common stock. The earnings have been growing at a constant rate of 10 percent over the past few years, and this rate is expected to continue indefinitely. If CTA has to sell new common stock, it will be faced with flotation costs of 15 percent. The current market price of the stock is $50 per share. Any debt that is raised, up to $5 million, will require a coupon rate of 8 percent. However, if the total debt required is greater than $5 million, the coupon rate will have to be 10 percent. The marginal tax rate is 34 percent. How large will CTA's capital budget be if all investments with an IRR greater than the MCC are accepted? ($21,000,000)

12-3. Which of the following statements is most correct?

a. A relatively risky future cash outflow should be evaluated using a relatively low discount rate.

b. If a firm's managers want to maximize the value of the stock, they should concentrate exclusively on projects' market, or beta, risk.

c. If a firm evaluates all projects using the same cost of capital to determine NPVs, then the riskiness of the firm as measured by its beta will probably decline over time.

d. If a firm has a beta which is less than 1.0, say 0.9, this would suggest that its assets' returns are negatively correlated with the returns of most other firms' assets.

e. The above statements are all false.

12-4. In theory, the decision maker should view market risk as being of primary importance. However, within-firm, or corporate, risk is relevant to a firm's

a. Well-diversified stockholders, because it may affect debt capacity and operating income.

b. Management, because it affects job stability.

c. Creditors, because it affects the firm's credit worthiness.

d. All of the above are correct.

e. Only answers a and c are correct.

12-5. If a typical U.S. company uses the same discount rate to evaluate all projects, the firm will most likely become

a. Riskier over time, and its value will decline.

b. Riskier over time, and its value will rise.

c. Less risky over time, and its value will rise.

d. Less risky over time, and its value will decline.

e. There is no reason to expect its risk position or value to change over time as a result of its use of a single discount rate.

12-6. Klott Company encounters significant uncertainty with its sales volume and the market price for its primary product. The firm uses scenario analysis in order to determine an expected NPV, which it then uses in its budget. The base case, best case, and worse case scenarios and their respective probabilities of occurrence are provided in the table below. What is Klott's expected NPV, standard deviation of NPV, and coefficient of variation of NPV? ($10,300; $12,083; 1.17)

	Probability of Outcome	Unit Sales Volume	Sales Price	NPV (In Thousands)
Worst case	0.30	6,000	$3,600	-$6,000
Base case	0.50	10,000	4,200	+13,000
Best case	0.20	13,000	4,400	+28,000

```
┌─────────────────────────────────────────────────────────────┐
│                                                             │
│                BLUEPRINTS: CHAPTER 13                       │
│              CAPITAL STRUCTURE AND LEVERAGE                  │
│                                                             │
└─────────────────────────────────────────────────────────────┘
```

13-14 Assume that you have just been hired as business manager of Campus Deli (CD), which is located adjacent to the campus. Sales were $1,350,000 last year; variable costs were 60 percent of sales; and fixed costs were $40,000. Therefore, EBIT totaled $500,000. Because the university's enrollment is capped, EBIT is expected to be constant over time. Since no expansion capital is required, CD pays out all earnings as dividends. Assets are $2 million, and 100,000 shares are outstanding. The management group owns about 50 percent of the stock, which is traded in the over-the-counter market.

CD currently has no debt—it is an all-equity firm—and its 100,000 shares outstanding sell at a price of $20 per share, which is also the book value. The firm's federal-plus-state tax rate is 40 percent. On the basis of statements made in your finance text, you believe that CD's shareholders would be better off if some debt financing were used. When you suggested this to your new boss, she encouraged you to pursue the idea, but to provide support for the suggestion.

You then obtained from a local investment banker the following estimates of the costs of debt and equity at different debt levels (in thousands of dollars):

Amount Borrowed	k_d	k_s
$ 0	10.0%	15.0%
250	10.0	15.5
500	11.0	16.5
750	13.0	18.0
1,000	16.0	20.0

If the firm were recapitalized, debt would be issued, and the borrowed funds would be used to repurchase stock. Stockholders, in turn, would use funds provided by the repurchase to buy equities in other fast-food companies similar to CD. You plan to complete your report by asking and then answering the following questions.

a. (1) What is business risk? What factors influence a firm's business risk?

   (2) What is operating leverage, and how does it affect a firm's business risk?

b. (1) What is meant by the terms "financial leverage" and "financial risk"?

(2) How does financial risk differ from business risk?

c. Now, to develop an example which can be presented to CD's management as an illustration, consider two hypothetical firms, Firm U, with zero debt financing, and Firm L, with $10,000 of 12 percent debt. Both firms have $20,000 in total assets and a 40 percent federal-plus-state tax rate, and they have the following EBIT probability distribution for next year:

Probability	EBIT
0.25	$2,000
0.50	3,000
0.25	4,000

(1) Complete the partial income statements and the firms' ratios in Table IC13-1.

Table IC13-1. Income Statements and Ratios

	Firm U			Firm L		
Assets	$20,000	$20,000	$20,000	$20,000	$20,000	$20,000
Equity	$20,000	$20,000	$20,000	$10,000	$10,000	$10,000
Probability	0.25	0.50	0.25	0.25	0.50	0.25
Sales	$ 6,000	$ 9,000	$12,000	$ 6,000	$ 9,000	$12,000
Oper. costs	4,000	6,000	8,000	4,000	6,000	8,000
EBIT	$ 2,000	$ 3,000	$ 4,000	$ 2,000	$ 3,000	$ 4,000
Int. (12%)	0	0	0	1,200		1,200
EBT	$ 2,000	$ 3,000	$ 4,000	$ 800	$	$ 2,800
Taxes (40%)	800	1,200	1,600	320		1,120
Net income	$ 1,200	$ 1,800	$ 2,400	$ 480	$	$ 1,680
BEP	10.0%	15.0%	20.0%	10.0%	%	20.0%
ROE	6.0%	9.0%	12.0%	4.8%	%	16.8%
TIE	∞	∞	∞	1.7×	×	3.3×
E(BEP)		15.0%			%	
E(ROE)		9.0%			10.8%	
E(TIE)		∞			2.5×	
σ(BEP)		3.5%			%	
σ(ROE)		2.1%			4.2%	
σ(TIE)		0			0.6×	

(2) Be prepared to discuss each entry in the table and to explain how this example illustrates the impact of financial leverage on expected rate of return and risk.

d.   With the above points in mind, now consider the optimal capital structure for CD.

(1) To begin, define the terms "optimal capital structure" and "target capital structure."

(2) Describe briefly, without using numbers, the sequence of events that would occur if CD decided to recapitalize and to increase its use of debt.

(3) Assume that shares could be repurchased at the current market price of $20 per share. Calculate CD's expected EPS and TIE at debt levels of $0, $250,000, $500,000, $750,000, and $1,000,000. How many shares would remain after recapitalization under each scenario?

(4) What would be the new stock price if CD recapitalizes with $250,000 of debt? $500,000? $750,000? $1,000,000? Recall that the payout ratio is 100 percent, so $g = 0$.

(5) Considering only the levels of debt discussed, what is CD's optimal capital structure?

(6) Is EPS maximized at the debt level which maximizes share price? Why?

(7) What is the WACC at the optimal capital structure?

e.   Suppose you discovered that CD had more business risk than you originally estimated. Describe how this would affect the analysis. What if the firm had less business risk than originally estimated?

f.   What are some factors a manager should consider when establishing his or her firm's target capital structure?

g.   Put labels on Figure IC13-1, and then discuss the graph as you might use it to explain to your boss why CD might want to use some debt.

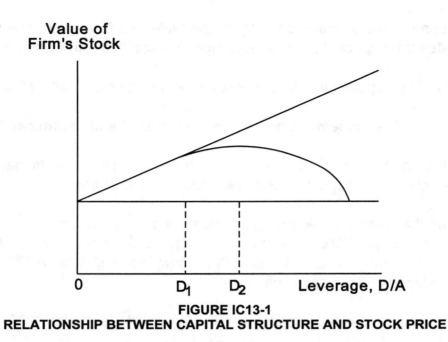

**Value of
Firm's Stock**

0   D₁   D₂   Leverage, D/A

FIGURE IC13-1
RELATIONSHIP BETWEEN CAPITAL STRUCTURE AND STOCK PRICE

h.   How does the existence of asymmetric information and signaling affect capital structure?

CHAPTER 13
Capital Structure and Leverage

- Business vs. financial risk
- Optimal capital structure
- Operating leverage
- Capital structure theory

What is business risk?

- Uncertainty about future operating income (EBIT), i.e., how well can we predict operating income?

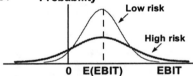

- Note that business risk does not include financing effects.

Business risk is affected primarily by:

- Uncertainty about demand (sales).
- Uncertainty about output prices.
- Uncertainty about costs.
- Product, other types of liability.
- Operating leverage.

What is operating leverage, and how does it affect a firm's business risk?

■ Operating leverage is the use of fixed costs rather than variable costs.

■ If most costs are fixed, hence do not decline when demand falls, then the firm has high operating leverage.

■ More operating leverage leads to more business risk, for then a small sales decline causes a big profit decline.

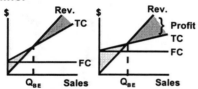

■ What happens if variable costs change?

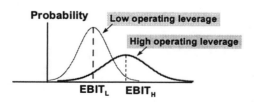

Typical situation: Can use operating leverage to get higher E(EBIT), but risk increases.

What is financial leverage? Financial risk?

- Financial leverage is the use of debt and preferred stock.

- Financial risk is the additional risk concentrated on common stockholders as a result of financial leverage.

Business Risk vs. Financial Risk

- Business risk depends on business factors such as competition, product liability, and operating leverage.

- Financial risk depends only on the types of securities issued: More debt, more financial risk. Concentrates business risk on stockholders.

Consider 2 Hypothetical Firms

Firm U	Firm L
No debt	$10,000 of 12% debt
$20,000 in assets	$20,000 in assets
40% tax rate	40% tax rate

Both firms have same operating leverage, business risk, and probability distribution of EBIT. Differ only with respect to use of debt (capital structure).

Firm U: Unleveraged

	Economy		
	Bad	Avg.	Good
Prob.	0.25	0.50	0.25
EBIT	$2,000	$3,000	$4,000
Interest	0	0	0
EBT	$2,000	$3,000	$4,000
Taxes (40%)	800	1,200	1,600
NI	$1,200	$1,800	$2,400

Firm L: Leveraged

	Economy		
	Bad	Avg.	Good
Prob.*	0.25	0.50	0.25
EBIT*	$2,000	$3,000	$4,000
Interest	1,200	1,200	1,200
EBT	$ 800	$1,800	$2,800
Taxes (40%)	320	720	1,120
NI	$ 480	$1,080	$1,680

*Same as for Firm U.

Firm U	Bad	Avg.	Good
BEP*	10.0%	15.0%	20.0%
ROE	6.0%	9.0%	12.0%
TIE	∞	∞	∞

Firm L	Bad	Avg.	Good
BEP*	10.0%	15.0%	20.0%
ROE	4.8%	10.8%	16.8%
TIE	1.67x	2.5x	3.3x

*BEP same for U and L.

Expected Values:

	U	L
E(BEP)	15.0%	15.0%
E(ROE)	9.0%	10.8%
E(TIE)	∞	2.5x

Risk Measures:

	U	L
σ_{ROE}	2.12%	4.24%
CV_{ROE}	0.24%	0.39%

- For leverage to raise expected ROE, must have BEP > k_d.

- Why? If k_d > BEP, then the interest expense will be higher than the operating income produced by debt-financed assets, so leverage will depress income.

Conclusions

- Basic earning power = BEP = EBIT/Total assets is unaffected by financial leverage.

- L has higher expected ROE because BEP > k_d.

- L has much wider ROE (and EPS) swings because of fixed interest charges. Its higher expected return is accompanied by higher risk.

If debt increases, TIE falls.

$$TIE = \frac{EBIT}{I}$$

EBIT is constant (unaffected by use of debt), and since I = k_dD, as D increases, TIE must fall.

Optimal Capital Structure

That capital structure (mix of debt, preferred, and common equity) at which P_0 is maximized. Trades off higher E(ROE) and EPS against higher risk.

What are "signaling" effects in capital structure?

Assumptions:

- **Managers have better information about a firm's long-run value than outside investors.**

- **Managers act in the best interests of current stockholders.**

13 - 19

Therefore, managers can be expected to:

- issue stock if they think stock is overvalued.

- issue debt if they think stock is undervalued.

  As a result, investors view a *common stock* offering as a negative signal-- managers think stock is overvalued.

---

13 - 20

Estimated costs of debt and equity for Campus Deli (see p. 1):

Amt. borrowed	k_d	k_s
$0	10.0%	15.0%
250	10.0	15.5
500	11.0	16.5
750	13.0	18.0
1,000	16.0	20.0

---

13 - 21

Describe the sequence of events in a recapitalization.

- Campus Deli *announces* the recapitalization.

- New debt is *issued*.

- Proceeds are used to *repurchase* stock.

$$\text{Shares bought} = \frac{\text{Debt issued}}{\text{Price per share}} .$$

What would the new stock price be if Campus Deli capitalized and used these amounts of debt: $0, $250,000, $500,000, $750,000? Assume EBIT = $500,000, T = 40%, and shares can be repurchased at P_0 = $20.

D = 0:

$$EPS_0 = \frac{(EBIT - k_d D)(1 - T)}{\text{Shares outstanding}}$$

$$= \frac{\$500,000(0.6)}{100,000} = \$3.00.$$

D = $250, k_d = 10%.

$$\text{Shares repurchased} = \frac{\$250,000}{\$20} = 12,500.$$

$$EPS_1 = \frac{[\$500 - 0.1(\$250)](0.6)}{100 - 12.5}$$

$$= \$3.26.$$

$$TIE = \frac{EBIT}{I} = \frac{\$500}{\$25} = 20x.$$

D = $500, k_d = 11%.

$$\text{Shares repurchased} = \frac{\$500}{\$20} = 25.$$

$$EPS_2 = \frac{[\$500 - 0.11(\$500)](0.6)}{100 - 25}$$

$$= \$3.56.$$

$$TIE = \frac{EBIT}{I} = \frac{\$500}{\$55} = 9.1x.$$

Stock Price (Zero Growth)

$$P_0 = \frac{D_1}{k_s - g} = \frac{EPS}{k_s} = \frac{DPS}{k_s} \; .$$

If payout = 100%, then EPS = DPS and E(g) = 0.

We just calculated EPS = DPS, and k_s was given on Page 1, so we can use the equation to find P_0 as shown on the next slide.

$P_0 = DPS/k_s$

Debt	DPS	k_s	P_0
$0	$3.00	15.0%	$20.00
250,000	3.26	15.5	21.03
500,000	3.56	16.5	21.58*
750,000	3.86	18.0	21.44
1,000,000	4.08	20.0	20.40

*Maximum: Since D = $500,000 and assets = $2,000,000, optimal D/A = 25%.

What debt ratio maximizes EPS?

See preceding slide. Maximum EPS = $4.08 at

D = $1,000,000, and D/A = 50%.

Risk is too high at D/A = 50%.

What is Campus Deli's optimal capital structure?

P_0 is maximized ($21.58) at D/A = $500,000/$2,000,000 = 25%, so optimal D/A = 25%.

EPS is maximized at 50%, but primary interest is stock price, not E(EPS).

The example shows that we can push up E(EPS) by using more debt, but the risk resulting from increased leverage more than offsets the benefit of higher E(EPS).

What's WACC at D = 0, D = $500, D = $1,000?

$$WACC = w_d k_d (1 - T) + w_{ce} k_s$$

D = 0:
WACC =   0   + 1.0(15%) = 15.0%.

D = 500:
WACC = .25(11)(.6) + .75(16.5) = 14.0%.

D = 1,000:
WACC = .50(16)(.6) + .50(20.0) = 14.8%.

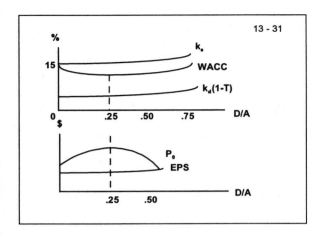

13 - 31

How would these factors affect the Target Capital Structure?

1. Sales stability?
2. High operating leverage?
3. Increase in the corporate tax rate?
4. Increase in the personal tax rate?
5. Increase in bankruptcy costs?
6. Management spending lots of money on lavish perks?

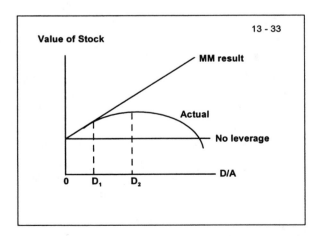

13 - 33

- The graph shows MM's tax benefit vs. bankruptcy cost theory.

- Logical, but doesn't tell whole capital structure story. Main problem--assumes investors have same information as managers.

Signaling theory, discussed earlier, suggests firms should use less debt than MM suggest.

This *unused debt capacity* helps avoid stock sales, which depress P_0 because of signaling effects.

Conclusions on Capital Structure

1. Need to make calculations as we did, but should also recognize inputs are "guesstimates."
2. As a result of imprecise numbers, capital structure decisions have a large judgmental content.
3. We end up with capital structures varying widely among firms, even similar ones in same industry.

EXAM-TYPE PROBLEMS

13-1. If a firm uses debt financing (debt ratio = 0.4) and sales change from the current level, which of the following statements is most correct?

a. The percentage change in net operating income (EBIT) resulting from the change in sales will exceed the percentage change in net income.

b. The percentage change in EBIT will equal the percentage change in net income.

c. The percentage change in net income relative to the percentage change in sales (and in EBIT) will not depend on the interest rate paid on the debt.

d. The percentage change in net operating income will be less than the percentage change in net income.

e. All of the above are false.

13-2. If you know that your firm is facing relatively poor prospects but needs new capital, and you know that investors do not have this information, signaling theory would predict that you would

a. Issue debt to maintain the returns of equity holders.

b. Issue equity to share the burden of decreased equity returns between old and new shareholders.

c. Be indifferent between issuing debt and equity.

d. Postpone going into the capital markets until your firm's prospects improve.

e. Convey your inside information to investors using the media to eliminate the information asymmetry.

13-3. Howell Enterprises is forecasting EPS of $4.00 per share for next year. The firm has 10,000 shares outstanding, it pays 12% interest on its debt, and it faces a 40% marginal tax rate. Its estimated fixed costs are $80,000 while its variable costs are estimated at 40% of revenue. The firm's target capital structure is 40% equity and 60% debt and it has total assets of $400,000. On what level of sales is Howell basing its EPS forecast? ($292,445)

13-4. A company estimates that its fixed operating costs are $900,000, and its variable costs are $3.25 per unit sold. Each unit produced sells for $4.75. What is the company's breakeven point? In other words, how many units must it sell before its operating income becomes positive? (600,000)

14-8   Southeastern Steel Company (SSC) was formed 5 years ago to exploit a new continuous-casting process. SSC's founders, Donald Brown and Margo Valencia, had been employed in the research department of a major integrated-steel company, but when that company decided against using the new process (which Brown and Valencia had developed), they decided to strike out on their own. One advantage of the new process was that it required relatively little capital in comparison with the typical steel company, so Brown and Valencia have been able to avoid issuing new stock, and thus they own all of the shares. However, SCC has now reached the stage where outside equity capital is necessary if the firm is to achieve its growth targets yet still maintain its target capital structure of 60 percent equity and 40 percent debt. Therefore, Brown and Valencia have decided to take the company public. Until now, Brown and Valencia have paid themselves reasonable salaries but routinely reinvested all after-tax earnings in the firm, so dividend policy has not been an issue. However, before talking with potential outside investors, they must decide on a dividend policy.

Assume that you were recently hired by Arthur Adamson & Company (AA), a national consulting firm, which has been asked to help SSC prepare for its public offering. Martha Millon, the senior AA consultant in your group, has asked you to make a presentation to Brown and Valencia in which you review the theory of dividend policy and discuss the following questions.

a. (1) What is meant by the term "dividend policy"?

   (2) The terms "irrelevance," "bird-in-the-hand," and "tax preference" have been used to describe three major theories regarding the way dividend policy affects a firm's value. Explain what these terms mean, and briefly describe each theory.

   (3) What do the three theories indicate regarding the actions management should take with respect to dividend policy?

   (4) Explain the relationships between dividend policy, stock price, and the cost of equity under each dividend policy theory by constructing two graphs such as those shown in Figure 14-1. Dividend payout should be placed on the X axis.

(5) What results have empirical studies of the dividend theories produced? How does all this affect what we can tell managers about dividend policy?

b.   Discuss (1) the information content, or signaling, hypothesis, (2) the clientele effect, and (3) their effects on dividend policy.

c. (1) Assume that SSC has an $800,000 capital budget planned for the coming year. You have determined that its present capital structure (60 percent equity and 40 percent debt) is optimal, and its net income is forecasted at $600,000. Use the residual dividend policy approach to determine SSC's total dollar dividend and payout ratio. In the process, explain what the residual dividend model is, and use a graph to illustrate your answer. Then, explain what would happen if net income were forecasted at $400,000, or at $800,000.

(2) In general terms, how would a change in investment opportunities affect the payout ratio under the residual payment policy?

(3) What are the advantages and disadvantages of the residual policy? (Hint: Don't neglect signaling and clientele effects.)

d.   What is a dividend reinvestment plan (DRIP), and how does it work?

e.   Describe the series of steps that most firms take in setting dividend policy in practice.

f.   What are stock repurchases? Discuss the advantages and disadvantages of a firm's repurchasing its own shares.

g.   What are stock dividends and stock splits? What are the advantages and disadvantages of stock dividends and stock splits?

CHAPTER 14
Dividend Policy

- Theories of investor preferences
- Signaling effects
- Residual model
- Dividend reinvestment plans
- Stock repurchases
- Stock dividends and stock splits

What is "dividend policy"?

- It's the decision to pay out earnings versus retaining and reinvesting them. Includes these elements:

  1. High or low payout?

  2. Stable or irregular dividends?

  3. How frequent?

  4. Do we announce the policy?

Do investors prefer high or low payouts? There are three theories:

- Dividends are irrelevant: Investors don't care about payout.

- Bird in the hand: Investors prefer a high payout.

- Tax preference: Investors prefer a low payout, hence growth.

Dividend Irrelevance Theory

- Investors are indifferent between dividends and retention-generated capital gains. If they want cash, they can sell stock. If they don't want cash, they can use dividends to buy stock.
- Modigliani-Miller support irrelevance.
- Theory is based on unrealistic assumptions (no taxes or brokerage costs), hence may not be true. Need empirical test.

Bird-in-the-Hand Theory

- Investors think dividends are less risky than potential future capital gains, hence they like dividends.

- If so, investors would value high payout firms more highly, i.e., a high payout would result in a high P_0.

Tax Preference Theory

- Retained earnings lead to capital gains, which are taxed at lower rates than dividends: 28% maximum vs. up to 39.6%. Capital gains taxes are also deferred.

- This could cause investors to prefer firms with low payouts, i.e., a high payout results in a low P_0.

Implications of 3 Theories for Managers

Theory	Implication
Irrelevance	Any payout OK
Bird in the hand	Set high payout
Tax preference	Set low payout

But which, if any, is correct???

Possible Stock Price Effects

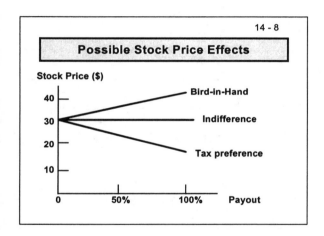

Possible Cost of Equity Effects

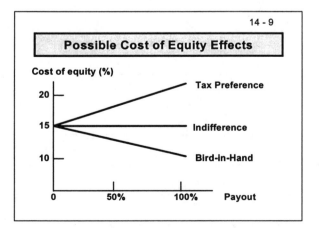

Which theory is most correct?

- Empirical testing has not been able to determine which theory, if any, is correct.
- Thus, managers use judgment when setting policy.
- Analysis is used, but it must be applied with judgment.

What's the "information content," or "signaling," hypothesis?

- Managers hate to cut dividends, so won't raise dividends unless they think raise is sustainable. So, investors view dividend increases as *signals* of management's view of the future.
- Therefore, a stock price increase at time of a dividend increase could reflect higher expectations for future EPS, not a desire for dividends.

What's the "clientele effect"?

- Different groups of investors, or clienteles, prefer different dividend policies.
- Firm's past dividend policy determines its current clientele of investors.
- Clientele effects impede changing dividend policy. Taxes & brokerage costs hurt investors who have to switch companies.

What's the "residual dividend model"?

- Find the retained earnings needed for the capital budget.
- Pay out any leftover earnings (the residual) as dividends.
- This policy minimizes flotation and equity signaling costs, hence minimizes the WACC.

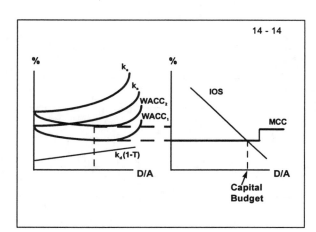

Data for SSC

- Capital budget: $800,000. Given.
- Target capital structure: 40% debt, 60% equity. Want to maintain.
- Forecasted net income: $600,000.
- How much of the $600,000 should we pay out as dividends?

Of the $800,000 capital budget, $0.6(\$800,000) = \$480,000$ must be equity to keep at target capital structure. $[0.4(\$800,000) = \$320,000$ will be debt.]

With $600,000 of net income, the residual is $600,000 - $480,000 = $120,000 = dividends paid.

Payout ratio = $120,000/$600,000
$$= 0.20 = 20\%.$$

How would a drop in NI to $400,000 affect the dividend? A rise to $800,000?

- NI = $400,000: Need $480,000 of equity, so should retain the whole $400,000. Dividends = 0.
- NI = $800,000: Dividends = $800,000 - $480,000 = $320,000. Payout = $320,000/$800,000 = 40%.

How would a change in investment opportunities affect dividend under the residual policy?

- Fewer good investments would lead to smaller capital budget, hence to a higher dividend payout.
- More good investments would lead to a lower dividend payout.

Advantages and Disadvantages of the Residual Dividend Policy

- **Advantages:** Minimizes new stock issues and flotation costs.
- **Disadvantages:** Results in variable dividends, sends conflicting signals, increases risk, and doesn't appeal to any specific clientele.
- **Conclusion:** Consider residual policy when setting target payout, but don't follow it rigidly.

What's a "dividend reinvestment plan (DRIP)"?

- Shareholders can automatically reinvest their dividends in shares of the company's common stock. Get more stock than cash.
- There are two types of plans:
  - Open market
  - New stock

Open Market Purchase Plan

- Dollars to be reinvested are turned over to trustee, who buys shares on the open market.
- Brokerage costs are reduced by volume purchases.
- Convenient, easy way to invest, thus useful for investors.

New Stock Plan

- Firm issues new stock to DRIP enrollees, keeps money and uses it to buy assets.

- No fees are charged, plus sells stock at discount of 5% from market price, which is about equal to flotation costs of underwritten stock offering.

Optional investments sometimes possible, up to $150,000 or so.

Firms that need new equity capital use new stock plans.

Firms with no need for new equity capital use open market purchase plans.

Most NYSE listed companies have a DRIP. Useful for investors.

Setting Dividend Policy

- Forecast capital needs over a planning horizon, often 5 years.
- Set a target capital structure.
- Estimate annual equity needs.
- Set target payout based on the residual model.
- Generally, some dividend growth rate emerges. Maintain target growth rate if possible, varying capital structure somewhat if necessary.

Stock Repurchases

Repurchases: Buying own stock back from stockholders.

Reasons for repurchases:

- As an alternative to distributing cash as dividends.
- To dispose of one-time cash from an asset sale.
- To make a large capital structure change.

Advantages of Repurchases

- Stockholders can tender or not.
- Helps avoid setting a high dividend that cannot be maintained.
- Repurchased stock can be used in takeovers or resold to raise cash as needed.
- Income received is capital gains rather than higher-taxed dividends.
- Stockholders may take as a positive signal-- management thinks stock is undervalued.

Disadvantages of Repurchases

- May be viewed as a negative signal (firm has poor investment opportunities).
- IRS could impose penalties if repurchases were primarily to avoid taxes on dividends.
- Selling stockholders may not be well informed, hence be treated unfairly.
- Firm may have to bid up price to complete purchase, thus paying too much for its own stock.

Stock Dividends vs. Stock Splits

- Stock dividend: Firm issues new shares in lieu of paying a cash dividend. If 10%, get 10 shares for each 100 shares owned.

- Stock split: Firm increases the number of shares outstanding, say 2:1. Sends shareholders more shares.

Both stock dividends and stock splits increase the number of shares outstanding, so "the pie is divided into smaller pieces."

Unless the stock dividend or split conveys information, or is accompanied by another event like higher dividends, *the stock price falls so as to keep each investor's wealth unchanged*.

But splits/stock dividends may get us to an "optimal price range."

When should a firm consider splitting its stock?

- There's a widespread belief that the *optimal price range* for stocks is $20 to $80.

- Stock splits can be used to keep the price in the optimal range.

- Stock splits generally occur when management is confident, so are interpreted as *positive signals*.

EXAM-TYPE PROBLEMS

14-1. If you were to argue that the firm's cost of equity, k_s, increases as the dividend payout decreases, you would be making an argument _____ with MM's dividend irrelevance theory, and _____ with Gordon and Lintner's "bird-in-the-hand" theory.

a.   consistent; consistent

b.   inconsistent; consistent

c.   consistent; inconsistent

d.   inconsistent; inconsistent

e.   The argument above does not make sense, neither theory involves the cost of equity capital.

14-2. Which of the following statements is most correct?

a.   If the *dividend irrelevance theory* (which is associated with the names Modigliani and Miller) were exactly correct, and if this theory could be tested with "clean" data, then we would find, in a regression of stock price and dividend payout, a line with a slope of -1.0.

b.   The *tax preference* and *bird-in-the-hand* theories lead to identical conclusions as to the optimal dividend policy.

c.   If a company raises its dividend by an unexpectedly large amount, the announcement of this new and higher dividend is generally accompanied by an increase in the stock price. This is consistent with the bird-in-the-hand theory, and Modigliani and Miller used these findings to support their position on dividend theory.

d.   If it could be demonstrated that a *clientele effect* exists, this would suggest that firms could alter their dividend payment policies from year to year to take advantage of investment opportunities without having to worry about the effects of changing dividends on capital costs.

e.   Each of the above statements is false.

14-3. Driver Corporation faces an investment opportunity schedule (IOS) calling for a capital budget of $60 million. Its optimal capital structure is 60% equity and 40% debt. Its earnings before interest and taxes (EBIT) were $98 million for the year. The firm has $200 million in assets, pays an average of 10% on all its debt, and faces a marginal tax rate of 34 percent. If the firm maintains a residual dividend policy and will finance its capital budget so as to keep its optimal capital structure intact, what will be the amount of the dividends it pays out? ($23.4 million)

15-12 Sue Wilson, the new financial manager of New World Chemicals (NWC), a California producer of specialized chemicals for use in fruit orchards, must prepare a financial forecast for 1998. NWC's 1997 sales were $2 billion, and the marketing department is forecasting a 25 percent increase for 1998. Wilson thinks the company was operating at full capacity in 1997, but she is not sure about this. The 1997 financial statements, plus some other data, are given in Table IC15-1.

Table IC15-1. Financial Statements and Other Data on NWC
(Millions of dollars)

A. 1997 Balance Sheet

Cash & securities	$ 20	Accounts payable and accruals	$ 100
Accounts receivable	240	Notes payable	100
Inventory	240	Total current liabilities	$ 200
Total current assets	$ 500	Long-term debt	100
Net fixed assets	500	Common stock	500
		Retained earnings	200
Total assets	$1,000	Total liabilities and equity	$1,000

B. 1997 Income Statement

Sales	$2,000.00
Less: Variable costs	1,200.00
Fixed costs	700.00
Earnings before interest and taxes	$ 100.00
Interest	16.00
Earnings before taxes	$ 84.00
Taxes (40%)	33.60
Net income	$ 50.40
Dividends (30%)	$ 15.12
Addition to retained earnings	$ 35.28

C. Key ratios

	NWC	Industry	Comment
Basic earnings power	10.00%	20.00%	
Profit margin	2.52%	4.00%	
Return on equity	7.20%	15.60%	
Days sales outstanding (360 days)	43.20 days	32.00 days	
Inventory turnover	8.33×	11.00×	
Fixed assets turnover	4.00×	5.00×	
Total assets turnover	2.00×	2.50×	
Debt/assets	30.00%	36.00%	
Times interest earned	6.25×	9.40×	
Current ratio	2.50×	3.00×	
Payout ratio	30.00%	30.00%	

Assume that you were recently hired as Wilson's assistant, and your first major task is to help her develop the forecast. She asked you to begin by answering the following set of questions.

a. Assume (1) that NWC was operating at full capacity in 1997 with respect to all assets, (2) that all assets must grow proportionally with sales, (3) that accounts payable and accruals will also grow in proportion to sales, and (4) that the 1997 profit margin and dividend payout will be maintained. Under these conditions, what will the company's financial requirements be for the coming year? Use the AFN equation to answer this question.

b. Now estimate the 1998 financial requirements using the projected financial statement approach. Assume (1) that each type of asset, as well as payables, accruals, and fixed and variable costs, grow at the same rate as sales; (2) that the payout ratio is held constant at 30 percent; and (3) that external funds needed are financed 50 percent by notes payable and 50 percent by long-term debt (no new common stock will be issued).

c. Why do the two methods produce somewhat different AFN forecasts? Which method provides the more accurate forecast?

d. Calculate NWC's forecasted ratios, and compare them with the company's 1997 ratios and with the industry averages. How does NWC compare with the average firm in its industry, and is the company expected to improve during the coming year?

e. Suppose you now learn that NWC's 1997 receivables and inventory were in line with required levels, given the firm's credit and inventory policies, but that excess capacity existed with regard to fixed assets. Specifically, fixed assets were operated at only 75 percent of capacity.

(1) What level of sales could have existed in 1997 with the available fixed assets? What would the fixed assets/sales ratio have been if NWC had been operating at full capacity?

(2) How would the existence of excess capacity in fixed assets affect the additional funds needed during 1998?

f.   Without actually working out the numbers, how would you expect the ratios to change in the situation where excess capacity in fixed assets exists? Explain your reasoning.

g.   Based on comparisons between NWC's days sales outstanding (DSO) and inventory turnover ratios with the industry average figures, does it appear that NWC is operating efficiently with respect to its inventory and accounts receivable? If the company were able to bring these ratios into line with the industry averages, what effect would this have on its AFN and its financial ratios? (Note: Inventory and receivables will be discussed in detail in Chapter 16.)

h.   The relationship between sales and the various types of assets is important in financial forecasting. The financial statement method, under the assumption that each asset item grows at the same rate as sales, leads to an AFN forecast that is reasonably close to the forecast using the AFN equation. Explain how each of the following factors would affect the accuracy of financial forecasts based on the AFN equation: (1) excess capacity, (2) base stocks of assets, such as shoes in a shoe store, (3) economies of scale in the use of assets, and (4) lumpy assets.

I.   (1) How could regression analysis be used to detect the presence of the situations described above and then to improve the financial forecasts? Plot a graph of the following data, which is for a typical well-managed company in NWC's industry, to illustrate your answer.

	Sales	Inventories
1995	$1,280	$118
1996	1,600	138
1997	2,000	162
1998E	2,500	192

(2) On the same graph that plots the above data, draw a line which shows how the regression line would have to appear to justify the use of the AFN formula and the projected financial statement forecasting method. As a part of your answer, show the growth rate in inventory that results from a 10 percent increase in sales from a sales level of (a) $200 and (b) $2,000 based on both the actual regression line and a *hypothetical* regression line which is linear and which goes through the origin.

j.   How would changes in these items affect the AFN? (1) The dividend payout ratio, (2) the profit margin, (3) the capital intensity ratio, and (4) if NWC begins buying from its suppliers on terms which permit it to pay after 60 days rather than after 30 days. (Consider each item separately and hold all other things constant.)

CHAPTER 15
Financial Forecasting

- Forecast sales
- Project the assets needed to support sales
- Project internally generated funds
- Project outside funds needed
- Decide how to raise funds
- See effects of plan on ratios

1997 Balance Sheet
(Millions of $)

Cash & sec.	$ 20	Accts. pay. & accruals	$ 100
Accounts rec.	240	Notes payable	100
Inventories	240	Total CL	$ 200
Total CA	$ 500	L-T debt	100
		Common stk	500
Net fixed assets	500	Retained earnings	200
Total assets	$1,000	Total claims	$1,000

1997 Income Statement
(Millions of $)

Sales	$2,000.00
Less: Var. Costs (60%)	1,200.00
Fixed Costs	700.00
EBIT	$ 100.00
Interest	16.00
EBT	$ 84.00
Taxes (40%)	33.60
Net income	$ 50.40
Dividends (30%)	$15.12
Add'n to RE	$35.28

Key Ratios

	NWC	Industry	Condition
BEP	10.00%	20.00%	Poor
Profit Margin	2.52%	4.00%	"
ROE	7.20%	15.60%	"
DSO	43.20 days	32.00 days	"
Inv. turnover	8.33x	11.00x	"
F.A. turnover	4.00x	5.00x	"
T.A. turnover	2.00x	2.50x	"
Debt/ assets	30.00%	36.00%	Good
TIE	6.25x	9.40x	Poor
Current ratio	2.50x	3.00x	"
Payout ratio	30.00%	30.00%	O.K.

Key Assumptions

- Operating at full capacity in 1997.
- Each type of asset grows proportionally with sales.
- Payables and accruals grow proportionally with sales.
- 1997 profit margin (2.52%) and payout (30%) will be maintained.
- Sales are expected to increase by $500 million. (%ΔS = 25%)

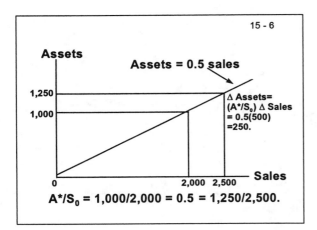

Assets

Assets = 0.5 sales

Δ Assets= (A^*/S_0) Δ Sales = 0.5(500) =250.

$A^*/S_0 = 1{,}000/2{,}000 = 0.5 = 1{,}250/2{,}500.$

Assets must increase by $250 million. What is the AFN, based on the AFN equation?

$$AFN = (A^*/S_0)\Delta S - (L^*/S_0)\Delta S - M(S_1)(1 - d)$$
$$= (\$1,000/\$2,000)(\$500)$$
$$- (\$100/\$2,000)(\$500)$$
$$- 0.0252(\$2,500)(1 - 0.3)$$
$$= \$180.9 \text{ million.}$$

Assumptions about How AFN Will Be Raised

- The payout ratio will remain at 30 percent (d = 30%).
- No new common stock will be issued.
- Any external funds needed will be raised as debt, 50% notes payable and 50% L-T debt.

1998 Forecasted Income Statement

	1997	Factor	1998 Forecast
Sales	$2,000	x1.25	$2,500
Less: VC	1,200	x1.25	1,500
FC	700	x1.25	875
EBIT	$100		$125
Interest	16	→	16
EBT	$84		$109
Taxes (40%)	34		44
Net. income	$50		$65
Div. (30%)	$15		$19
Add. to RE	$35		$46

1998 1st Pass Balance Sheet (Assets)

	1997	Factor	1st Pass
Cash	$20	x1.25	$25
Accts. rec.	240	x1.25	300
Inventories	240	x1.25	300
Total CA	$500		$625
Net FA	500	x1.25	625
Total assets	$1,000		$1,250

At full capacity, so all assets must increase in proportion to sales.

1998 1st Pass Balance Sheet (Claims)

	1997	Factor	1st Pass
AP/accruals	$100	x1.25	$125
Notes payable	100	→	100
Total CL	$200		$225
L-T debt	100	→	100
Common stk.	500	→	500
Ret. earnings	200	+46*	246
Total claims	$1,000		$1,071

*From income statement.

What is the additional financing needed (AFN)?

- Forecasted total assets = $1,250
- Forecasted total claims = $1,071
- Forecast AFN = $ 179

NWC must have the assets to make forecasted sales. The balance sheet must balance. So, we must raise $179 externally.

How will the AFN be financed?

Additional notes payable =
0.5($179) = $89.50

Additional L-T debt =
0.5($179) = $89.50

But this financing will add to interest expense, which will lower NI and retained earnings. We will generally ignore financing feedbacks.

1998 2nd Pass Balance Sheet (Assets)

	1st Pass	AFN	2nd Pass
Cash	$25	→	$25
Accts. rec.	300	→	300
Inventories	300	→	300
Total CA	$625	→	$625
Net FA	625	→	625
Total assets	$1,250	→	$1,250

No change in asset requirements.

1998 2nd Pass Balance Sheet (Claims)

	1st Pass	AFN	2nd Pass
AP/accruals	$125	→	$125
Notes payable	100	+89.5	190
Total CL	$225		$315
L-T debt	100	+89.5	189
Common stk.	500	→	500
Ret. earnings	246	→	246
Total claims	$1,071		$1,250

Equation AFN = $181 vs. $179. Why different?

■ Equation method assumes a constant profit margin.

■ Financial statement method is more flexible. More important, it allows different items to grow at different rates.

Ratios

	1997	1998(E)	Industry	
BEP	10.00%	10.00%	20.00%	Poor
Profit Margin	2.52%	2.60%	4.00%	"
ROE	7.20%	8.71%	15.60%	"
DSO (days)	43.20	43.20	32.00	"
Inv. turnover	8.33x	8.33x	11.00x	"
F.A. turnover	4.00x	4.00x	5.00x	"
T.A. turnover	2.00x	2.00x	2.50x	"
D/A ratio	30.00%	40.32%	36.00%	"
TIE	6.25x	7.81%	9.40x	"
Current ratio	2.50x	1.98x	3.00x	"
Payout ratio	30.00%	30.00%	30.00%	O.K.

Suppose in 1997 fixed assets had been operated at only 75% of capacity.

$$\text{Capacity Sales} = \frac{\text{Actual sales}}{\text{\% of capacity}}$$

$$= \frac{\$2,000}{0.75} = \$2,667.$$

With the existing fixed assets, sales could be $2,667. Since sales are forecasted at only $2,500, no new fixed assets are needed.

How would the excess capacity situation affect the 1998 AFN?

- The projected increase in fixed assets was $125, the AFN would decrease by $125.

- Since no new fixed assets will be needed, AFN will fall by $125, to

$179 - $125 = $54.

Q.   If sales went up to $3,000, not $2,500, what would the F.A. requirement be?

A.   Target ratio = FA/Capacity sales
              = 500/2,667 = 18.75%.

Have enough F.A. for sales up to $2,667, but need F.A. for another $333 of sales:

ΔFA = 0.1875(333) = $62.4.

How would excess capacity affect the forecasted ratios?

1. Sales wouldn't change but assets would be lower, so turnovers would be better.

2. Less new debt, hence lower interest, so higher profits, EPS, ROE (when financing feedbacks considered).

3. Debt ratio, TIE would improve.

1998 Forecasted Ratios: S_{98} = $2,500

| | % of 1997 Capacity | | |
	100%	75%	Industry
BEP	10.00%	11.11%	20.00%
Profit Margin	2.60%	2.60%	4.00%
ROE	8.71%	8.71%	15.60%
DSO (days)	43.20	43.20	32.00
Inv. turnover	8.33x	8.33x	11.00x
F.A. turnover	4.00x	5.00x	5.00x
T.A. turnover	2.00x	2.22x	2.50x
D/A ratio	40.32%	33.69%	36.00%
TIE	7.81%	7.81x	9.40x
Current ratio	1.98x	2.48x	3.00x

How is NWC performing with regard to its receivables and inventories?

- DSO is higher than the industry average, and inventory turnover is lower than the industry average.

- Improvements here would lower current assets, reduce capital requirements, and further improve profitability and other ratios.

Declining A/S Ratio

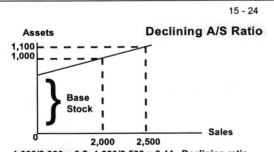

1,000/2,000 = 0.5; 1,000/2,500 = 0.44. Declining ratio shows economies of scale. Going from S = 0 to S = 2,000 requires 1,000 of assets. Next 500 of sales requires only 100 of assets.

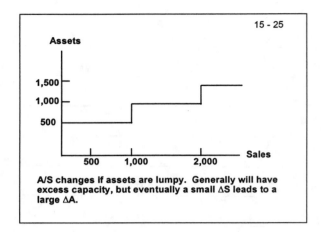

A/S changes if assets are lumpy. Generally will have excess capacity, but eventually a small ΔS leads to a large ΔA.

Summary: How different factors affect the AFN forecast.

- **Excess capacity:**
  - Existence lowers AFN.
- **Base stocks of assets:**
  - Leads to less-than-proportional asset increases.
- **Economies of scale:**
  - Also leads to less-than-proportional asset increases.
- **Lumpy assets:**
  - Leads to large periodic AFN requirements, recurring excess capacity.

Regression Analysis for Asset Forecasting

- Get historical data on a good company, then fit a regression line to see how much a given sales increase will require in way of asset increase.

Example of Regression

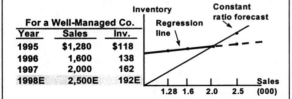

For a Well-Managed Co.		
Year	Sales	Inv.
1995	$1,280	$118
1996	1,600	138
1997	2,000	162
1998E	2,500E	192E

Constant ratio overestimates inventory required to go from $S_1 = 2,000$ to $S_2 = 2,500$.

Regression with 10B for Our Example

- Same as finding beta coefficients.
- Clear all
  - 1280 Input   118Σ+
  - 1600 Input   138Σ+
  - 2000 Input   162Σ+
- 0 ■ $\hat{y}$, m → 40.0 = Inventory at sales = 0.
- ■ SWAP → 0.0611 = Slope coefficient.

Inventory = 40.0 + 0.0611 Sales.

LEAVE CALCULATOR ALONE!

Equation is now in the calculator. Let's use it by inputting new sales of $2,500 and getting forecasted inventory:

2500 ■ $\hat{y}$, m → 192.66.

The constant ratio forecast was inventory = 300, so the regression forecast is lower by $107. This would free up $107 for use elsewhere, which would improve profitability and raise P_0.

How would increases in these items affect the AFN?

- **Higher dividend payout ratio?**
  Increase AFN : Less retained earnings.
- **Higher profit margin?**
  Decrease AFN: Higher profits, more retained earnings.
- **Higher capital intensity ratio, A^*/S_0?**
  Increase AFN: Need more assets for given sales increase.
- **Pay suppliers in 60 days rather than 30 days?**
  Decrease AFN: Trade creditors supply more capital, i.e., L^*/S_0 increases.

_____

_____

_____

_____

_____

_____

_____

EXAM-TYPE PROBLEMS

15-1. Snowball & Company has the following balance sheet:

Current assets	$ 7,000	A/P & Accruals	$ 1,500
Fixed assets	3,000	S-T (3 month) Loans	2,000
		Common Stock	1,500
		Ret. Earnings	5,000
Total Assets	$10,000	Total Claims	$10,000

Snowball's after-tax profit margin is 11%, and the company pays out 60 percent of its earnings as dividends. Its sales last year were $10,000; its assets were used to full capacity; no economies of scale exist in the use of assets; and the profit margin and payout ratio are expected to remain constant. The company uses the AFN equation to estimate funds requirements, and it plans to raise any required external capital as short-term bank loans. If sales grow by 50 percent, what will Snowball's current ratio be after it has raised the necessary expansion funds? (1.34)

15-2. Hogan Inc. generated EBIT of $240,000 this past year using assets of $1,100,000. The interest rate on its existing long-term debt of $640,000 is 12.5 percent and the firm's tax rate is 40 percent. The firm paid a dividend of $1.27 on each of its 37,800 shares outstanding from net income of $96,000. The total book value of equity is $446,364 of which the common stock account equals $335,000. The firm's shares sell for $28.00 per share in the market. The firm forecasts a 10% increase in sales, assets, and EBIT next year, and a dividend of $1.40 per share. If the firm needs additional capital funds, it will raise 60% with debt and 40% with equity. Spontaneous liabilities are estimated at $15,000 for next year, representing an increase of 10% over this year. Except for spontaneous liabilities, the firm uses no other sources of current liabilities and will continue this policy in the future. What will be the AFN Hogan will need to balance its projected balance sheet using the projected balance sheet method? ($51,156)

15-3. Which of the following statements is most correct?

a. If the capital intensity ratio is high, this permits sales to grow more rapidly without much outside capital.

b. The lower the profit margin, the lower the additional funds needed because less assets are needed to support existing sales.

c.   When positive economies of scale are present, linear balance sheet relationships no longer hold. As sales increase, a proportionately greater stock of assets is required to support the higher sales level.

d.   Technological considerations often require firms to add fixed assets in large, discrete units. Such assets are called lumpy assets and they affect the firm's financial requirements through the fixed assets/sales ratio at different sales levels.

e.   The projected balance sheet method accounts for changing balance sheet ratios and thus, cyclical changes in the actual sales/assets ratio do not have an impact on financing requirements.

16-11 Dan Barnes, financial manager of Ski Equipment Inc. (SKI), is excited, but apprehensive. The company's founder recently sold his 51 percent controlling block of stock to Kent Koren, who is a big fan of EVA (Economic Value Added). EVA is found by taking the after-tax operating profit and then subtracting the dollar cost of all the capital the firm uses:

$$EVA = EBIT(1 - T) - \text{Capital costs}$$
$$= EBIT(1 - T) - WACC \text{ (Capital employed)}.$$

If EVA is positive, then the firm is creating value. On the other hand, if EVA is negative, the firm is not covering its cost of capital, and stockholders' value is being eroded. Koren rewards managers handsomely if they create value, but those whose operations produce negative EVAs are soon looking for work. Koren frequently points out that if a company can generate its current level of sales with less assets, it would need less capital. That would, other things held constant, lower capital costs and increase its EVA.

Shortly after he took control of SKI, Kent Koren met with SKI's senior executives to tell them of his plans for the company. First, he presented some EVA data which convinced everyone that SKI has not been creating value in recent years. He then stated, in no uncertain terms, that this situation must change. He noted that SKI's designs of skis, boots, and clothing are acclaimed throughout the industry, but something is seriously amiss elsewhere in the company. Costs are too high, prices are too low, or the company employs too much capital, and he wants SKI's managers to correct the problem or else.

Barnes has long felt that SKI's working capital situation should be studied--the company may have the optimal amounts of cash, securities, receivables, and inventories, but it may also have too much or too little of these items. In the past, the production manager resisted Dan's efforts to question his holdings of raw materials inventories, the marketing manager resisted questions about finished goods, the sales staff resisted questions about credit policy (which affects accounts receivable), and the treasurer did not want to talk about her cash and securities balances. Koren's speech made it clear that such resistance would no longer be tolerated.

Dan also knows that decisions about working capital cannot be made in a vacuum. For example, if inventories could be lowered without adversely affecting operations, then less capital would be required, the dollar cost of capital would decline, and EVA would increase. However, lower raw materials inventories might lead to production slowdowns and higher costs, while lower finished goods inventories might lead to the loss of profitable sales. So, before inventories are changed, it will be necessary to study operating as well as financial effects. The situation is the same with regard to cash and receivables.

a.   Dan plans to use the ratios in Table IC16-1 as the starting point for discussions with SKI's operating executives. He wants everyone to think about the pros and cons of changing each type of current asset and how changes would interact to affect profits and EVA. Based on the Table IC16-1 data, does SKI seem to be following a relaxed, moderate, or restricted working capital policy?

Table IC16-1. Selected Ratios: SKI and Industry Average

	SKI	Industry
Current	1.75x	2.25x
Quick	0.83x	1.20x
Debt/assets	58.76%	50.00%
Turnover of cash and securities	16.67x	22.22x
Days sales outstanding	45.00	32.00
Inventory turnover	4.82x	7.00x
Fixed assets turnover	11.35x	12.00x
Total assets turnover	2.08x	3.00x
Profit margin on sales	2.07%	3.50%
Return on equity (ROE)	10.45%	21.00%

b.   How can one distinguish between a relaxed but rational working capital policy and a situation where a firm simply has a lot of current assets because it is inefficient? Does SKI's working capital policy seem appropriate?

c.   What might SKI do to reduce its cash and securities without harming operations?

d.   What is "float," and how is it affected by the firm's cash manager (treasurer)?

        In an attempt to better understand SKI's cash position, Dan developed a cash budget. Data for the first two months of the year are shown in Table IC16-2. (Note that Dan's preliminary cash budget does not account for interest income or interest expense.) He has the figures for the other months, but they are not shown in Table IC16-2.

Table IC16-2. SKI's Cash Budget for January and February

		NOV	DEC	JAN	FEB	MAR	APR
I. COLLECTIONS AND PURCHASES WORKSHEET							
(1)	Sales (gross)	$71,218	$68,212.00	$65,213.00	$52,475.00	$42,909	$30,524
Collections:							
(2)	During month of sale (0.2)(0.98)(month's sales)			12,781.75	10,285.10		
(3)	During first month after sale 0.7(previous month's sales)			47,748.40	45,649.10		
(4)	During second month after sale 0.1(sales 2 months ago)			7,121.80	6,821.20		
(5)	Total collections (Lines 2+3+4)			$67,651.95	$62,755.40		
Purchases:							
(6)	0.85(forecasted sales 2 months from now)		$44,603.75	$36,472.65	$25,945.40		
(7)	Payments (1-month lag)			44,603.75	36,472.65		
II. CASH GAIN OR LOSS FOR MONTH							
(8)	Collections (from Section I)			$67,651.95	$62,755.40		
(9)	Payments for purchases (from Section I)			44,603.75	36,472.65		
(10)	Wages and salaries			6,690.56	5,470.90		
(11)	Rent			2,500.00	2,500.00		
(12)	Taxes						
(13)	Total payments			$53,794.31	$44,443.55		
(14)	Net cash gain (loss) during month (Line 8 - Line 13)			$13,857.64	$18,311.85		
III. CASH SURPLUS OR LOAN REQUIREMENT							
(15)	Cash at beginning of month if no borrowing is done			$ 3,000.00	$16,857.64		
(16)	Cumulative cash (cash at start, + gain or - loss = Line 14 + Line 15)			16,857.64	35,169.49		
(17)	Target cash balance			1,500.00	1,500.00		
(18)	Cumulative surplus cash or loans outstanding to maintain $1,500 target cash balance (Line 16 - Line 17)			$15,357.64	$33,669.49		

e.   Should depreciation expense be explicitly included in the cash budget? Why or why not?

f.   In his preliminary cash budget, Dan has assumed that all sales are collected and, thus, that SKI has no bad debts. Is this realistic? If not, how would bad debts be dealt with in a cash budgeting sense? (Hint: Bad debts will affect collections but not purchases.)

g.   Dan's cash budget for the entire year, although not given here, is based heavily on his forecast for monthly sales. Sales are expected to be extremely low between

May and September but then increase dramatically in the fall and winter. November is typically the firm's best month, when SKI ships equipment to retailers for the holiday season. Interestingly, Dan's forecasted cash budget indicates that the company's cash holdings will exceed the targeted cash balance every month except for October and November, when shipments will be high but collections will not be coming in until later.

Based on the ratios in Table IC16-1, does it appear that SKI's target cash balance is appropriate? In addition to possibly lowering the target cash balance, what actions might SKI take to better improve its cash management policies, and how might that affect its EVA?

h. What reasons might SKI have for maintaining a relatively high amount of cash?

I. What are the three categories of inventory costs? If the company takes steps to reduce its inventory, what effect would this have on the various costs of holding inventory?

j. Is there any reason to think that SKI may be holding too much inventory? If so, how would that affect EVA and ROE?

k. If the company reduces its inventory without adversely affecting sales, what effect should this have on the company's cash position (1) in the short run and (2) in the long run? Explain in terms of the cash budget and the balance sheet.

l. Dan knows that SKI sells on the same credit terms as other firms in its industry. Use the ratios presented in Table IC16-1 to explain whether SKI's customers pay more or less promptly than those of its competitors. If there are differences, does that suggest that SKI should tighten or loosen its credit policy? What four variables make up a firm's credit policy, and in what direction should each be changed by SKI?

m. Does SKI face any risks if it tightens its credit policy?

n. If the company reduces its DSO without seriously affecting sales, what effect would this have on its cash position (1) in the short run and (2) in the long run? Answer in terms of the cash budget and the balance sheet. What effect would this have on EVA in the long run?

CHAPTER 16
Managing Current Assets

- Alternative working capital policies
- Cash management
- Inventory management
- Accounts receivable management

Definitions

- Gross W.C.: Total current assets.
- Net W.C.: Current assets - Current liabilities.
- W.C. Policy: Decisions as to (1) the level of each type of current asset, and (2) how current assets will be financed.
- W.C. Management: Controlling cash, inventories, and A/R, plus S-T liability management.

Selected Ratios--SKI Inc.

	SKI	Industry
Current	1.75x	2.25x
Quick	0.83x	1.20x
Debt/Assets	58.76%	50.00%
Turnover of cash & securities	16.67x	22.22x
DSO (days)	45.00	32.00
Inv. turnover	4.82x	7.00x
F.A. turnover	11.35x	12.00x
T.A. turnover	2.08x	3.00x
Profit margin	2.07%	3.50%
ROE	10.45%	21.00%

SKI appears to have large amounts of working capital given its level of sales.

How does SKI's working capital policy compare with the industry?

- Working capital policy is reflected in current ratio, quick ratio, turnover of cash and securities, inventory turnover, and DSO.

- These ratios indicate SKI has large amounts of working capital relative to its level of sales. SKI is either very conservative or inefficient.

Is SKI inefficient or just conservative?

- A conservative (relaxed) policy may be appropriate if it leads to greater profitability.

- However, SKI is not as profitable as the average firm in the industry. This suggests the company has excessive working capital.

Cash doesn't earn a profit, so why hold it?

1. **Transactions:** Must have some cash to operate.
2. **Precaution:** "Safety stock." But lessened by line of credit, marketable securities.
3. **Compensating balances:** For loans and/or services provided.
4. **Speculation:** To take advantage of bargains, to take discounts, etc. Reduced by credit lines, securities.

What's the goal of cash management?

- To meet above objectives, especially to have cash for transactions, yet not have any excess cash.

- To minimize transactions balances in particular, and also needs for cash to meet other objectives.

Ways to Minimize Cash Holdings

- Use a lockbox.
- Insist on wire transfers from customers.
- Synchronize inflows and outflows.
- Use a remote disbursement account.

(Cont...)

- Increase forecast accuracy to reduce need for "safety stock" of cash.
- Hold marketable securities (also reduces need for "safety stock").
- Negotiate a line of credit (also reduces need for "safety stock").

What is "Float" and how is it affected by the firm's cash manager?

- Float is the difference between cash as shown on the firm's books and on its bank's books.
- If SKI collects checks in 2 days but those to whom SKI writes checks don't process them for 6 days, then SKI will have 4 days of net float.
- If a firm with 4 days of net float writes and receives $1 million of checks per day, it would be able to operate with $4 million less capital than if it had zero net float.

Cash Budget: The Primary Cash Management Tool

- **Purpose:** Forecasts cash inflows, outflows, and ending cash balances. Used to plan loans needed or funds available to invest.
- **Timing:** Daily, weekly, or monthly, depending upon purpose of forecast. Monthly for annual planning, daily for actual cash management.

Data Required for Cash Budget

1. Sales forecast.
2. Information on collections delay.
3. Forecast of purchases and payment terms.
4. Forecast of cash expenses, taxes, etc.
5. Initial cash on hand.
6. Target cash balance.

SKI's Cash Budget for January and February

	Net Cash Inflows	
	January	**February**
Collections	**$67,651.95**	**$62,755.40**
Purchases	44,603.75	36,472.65
Wages	6,690.56	5,470.90
Rent	2,500.00	2,500.00
Total payments	**$53,794.31**	**$44,443.55**
Net CF	**$13,857.64**	**$18,311.85**

Cash Budget (Continued)

	January	February
Cash at start	$3,000.00	$16,857.64
Net CF (slide 13)	13,857.64	18,311.85
Cumulative cash	$16,857.64	$35,169.49
Less: target cash	1,500.00	1,500.00
Surplus	$15,357.64	$33,669.49

Should depreciation be explicitly included in the cash budget?

- No. Depreciation is a noncash charge. Only cash payments and receipts appear on cash budget.
- However, depreciation does affect taxes, which appear in the cash budget.

What are some other potential cash inflows besides collections?

- Proceeds from the sale of fixed assets.
- Proceeds from stock and bond sales.
- Interest earned.
- Court settlements.

How can interest earned or paid on surplus/loan be incorporated in the cash budget?

- Interest earned: Add line in the collections section.
- Interest paid: Add line in the payments section.
- Found as interest rate x surplus/loan part of cash budget for preceding month.
- Note: Interest on any other debt would need to be incorporated as well.

How could bad debts be worked into the cash budget?

- Collections would be reduced by the amount of the bad debt losses.
- For example, if the firm had 3% bad debt losses, collections would total only 97% of sales.
- Lower collections would lead to higher borrowing requirements.

SKI's forecasted cash budget indicates that the company's cash holdings will exceed the targeted cash balance every month, except for October and November.

- Cash budget indicates the company is holding too much cash.

- SKI could improve its EVA by either investing cash in more productive assets, or by returning cash to its shareholders.

What reasons might SKI have for maintaining a relatively high amount of cash?

- If sales turn out to be considerably less than expected, SKI could face a cash shortfall.
- A company may choose to hold large amounts of cash if it does not have much faith in its sales forecast, or if it is very conservative.
- The cash may be used, in part, to fund future investments.

Categories of Inventory Costs

- **Carrying Costs:** Storage and handling costs, insurance, property taxes, depreciation, and obsolescence.
- **Ordering Costs:** Cost of placing orders, shipping and handling costs.
- **Costs of Running Short:** Loss of sales, loss of customer goodwill, and the disruption of production schedules.

Reducing the average amount of inventory generally reduces carrying costs, increases ordering costs, and may increase the costs of running short.

Is SKI holding too much inventory?

- SKI's inventory turnover (4.82) is considerably lower than the industry average (7.00). The firm is carrying a lot of inventory per dollar of sales.

- By holding excessive inventory, the firm is increasing its costs which reduces its ROE. Moreover, this additional working capital must be financed, so EVA is also lowered.

If SKI reduces its inventory, without adversely affecting sales, what effect will this have on its cash position?

- Short run: Cash will increase as inventory purchases decline.

- Long run: Company is likely to take steps to reduce its cash holdings.

Do SKI's customers pay more or less promptly than those of its competitors?

- SKI's DSO (45 days) is well above the industry average (32 days).

- SKI's customers are paying less promptly.

- SKI should consider tightening its credit policy in order to reduce its DSO.

Elements of Credit Policy

1. **Cash Discounts:** Lowers price. Attracts new customers and reduces DSO.
2. **Credit Period:** How long to pay? Shorter period reduces DSO and average A/R, but it may discourage sales.
3. **Credit Standards:** Tighter standards tend to reduce sales, but reduce bad debt expense. Fewer bad debts reduces DSO.
4. **Collection Policy:** How tough? Tougher policy will reduce DSO but may damage customer relationships.

Does SKI face any risk if it tightens its credit policy?

YES! A tighter credit policy may discourage sales. Some customers may choose to go elsewhere if they are pressured to pay their bills sooner.

If SKI succeeds in reducing DSO without adversely affecting sales, what effect would this have on its cash position?

- **Short run:** If customers pay sooner, this increases cash holdings.
- **Long run:** Over time, the company would hopefully invest the cash in more productive assets, or pay it out to shareholders. Both of these actions would increase EVA.

EXAM-TYPE PROBLEMS

16-1. Ziltest Company's treasurer had $1 million of excess funds which were invested in marketable securities. At the time the investment was made, it was known that the funds would be needed in 6 months to fund an ongoing construction project. Six-month T-bills with a face value of $10,000 sold for $9,708.74 to yield a 6 percent nominal annual rate. As an alternative, the treasurer could purchase 7% coupon, semiannual payment, 10-year Treasury bonds at par. Seeking to earn a higher yield, he purchased the T-bonds. At the end of 6 months, when the funds were needed for construction, interest rates had risen to 9.5% on the T-bonds. The treasurer was forced to liquidate the T-bond holdings at a lower price. What was the absolute value of the dollar difference between the T-bond's purchase price and selling price? ($154,192.20)

16-2. Which of the following statement completions is most correct? If the yield curve is upward sloping, then a firm's marketable securities portfolio, assumed to be held for liquidity purposes, should be

a. Weighted toward long-term securities because they pay higher rates.

b. Weighted toward short-term securities because they pay higher rates.

c. Weighted toward U.S. Treasury securities to avoid interest rate risk.

d. Weighted toward short-term securities to avoid interest rate risk.

e. Balanced between long- and short-term securities to minimize the effects of either an upward or a downward shift in interest rates.

16-3. Which of the following statements is most correct?

a. If a firm's volume of credit sales declines then its DSO will also decline.

b. If a firm changes its credit terms from 1/20, net 40 days, to 2/10, net 60 days, the impact on sales can't be determined because the increase in the discount is offset by the longer net terms which tends to reduce sales.

c. The DSO of a firm with seasonal sales can vary because while the sales per day figure is usually based on the total annual sales, the accounts receivable balance will be high or low depending on the season.

d. An aging schedule is used to determine what portion of customers pay cash and what portion buy on credit.

e. Aging schedules can be constructed from the summary data provided in the firm's financial statements.

16-4. Jarrett Enterprises is considering whether to pursue a restricted or relaxed current asset investment policy. The firm's annual sales are $400,000; its fixed assets are $100,000; debt and equity are each 50% of total assets. EBIT is $36,000, the interest rate on the firm's debt is 10%, and the firm's tax rate is 40%. With a restricted policy, current assets will be 15% of sales. Under a relaxed policy, current assets will be 25% of sales. What is the difference in the projected ROEs between the restricted and relaxed policies? (5.4%)

16-5. Porta Stadium Inc. has annual sales of $40,000,000 and keeps average inventory of $10,000,000. On average the firm has accounts receivable of $8,000,000. The firm buys all raw materials on credit and its trade credit terms are net 30 days. It pays on time. The firm's managers are searching for ways to shorten the cash conversion cycle. If sales can be maintained at existing levels but inventory can be lowered by $2,000,000 and accounts receivable lowered by $1,000,000, what will be the net change in the cash conversion cycle? Use a 360-day year. (Hint: See Appendix 16A.) (27 days shorter)

17-18 Bats and Balls (B&B) Inc., a baseball equipment manufacturer, is a small company with seasonal sales. Each year before the baseball season, B&B purchases inventory which is financed through a combination of trade credit and short-term bank loans. At the end of the season, B&B uses sales revenues to repay its short-term obligations. The company is always looking for ways to become more profitable, and senior management has asked one of its employees, Ann Taylor, to review the company's current asset financing policies. Putting together her report, Ann is trying to answer each of the following questions:

a.   B&B tries to match the maturity of its assets and liabilities. Describe how B&B could adopt a more aggressive or more conservative financing policy.

b.   What are the advantages and disadvantages of using short-term credit as a source of financing?

c.   Is it likely that B&B could make significantly greater use of accruals?

d.   Assume that B&B buys on terms of 1/10, net 30, but that it can get away with paying on the 40th day if it chooses not to take discounts. Also, assume that it purchases $3 million of components per year, net of discounts. How much free trade credit can the company get, how much costly trade credit can it get, and what is the percentage cost of the costly credit? Should B&B take discounts?

e.   Would it be feasible for B&B to finance with commercial paper?

f.   Suppose B&B decided to raise an additional $100,000 as a 1-year loan from its bank, for which it was quoted a rate of 8 percent. What is the effective annual cost rate assuming (1) simple interest, (2) discount interest, (3) discount interest with a 10 percent compensating balance, and (4) add-on interest on a 12-month installment loan? For the first 3 of these assumptions, would it matter if the loan were for 90 days, but renewable, rather than for a year?

g.   How large would the loan actually be in each of the cases in Part f?

h.   What are the pros and cons of borrowing on a secured versus an unsecured basis? If inventories or receivables are to be used as collateral, how would the loan be handled?

CHAPTER 17
Financing Current Assets

- Working capital financing policies
- A/P (trade credit)
- Commercial paper
- S-T bank loans

Working Capital Financing Policies

- **Moderate:** Match the maturity of the assets with the maturity of the financing.
- **Aggressive:** Use short-term financing to finance permanent assets.
- **Conservative:** Use permanent capital for permanent assets and temporary assets.

Moderate Financing Policy

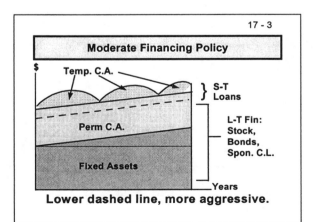

Lower dashed line, more aggressive.

Conservative Financing Policy

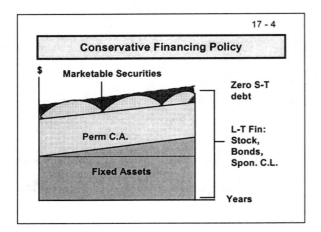

$ — Marketable Securities

Zero S-T debt

Perm C.A.

Fixed Assets

L-T Fin: Stock, Bonds, Spon. C.L.

Years

What is short-term credit, and what are the major sources?

- S-T credit: Any debt scheduled for repayment within one year.
- Major sources:
  - Accounts payable (trade credit)
  - Bank loans
  - Commercial paper
  - Accruals

- Is S-T credit riskier than L-T?

  To company, yes. Required repayment always looms. May have trouble rolling over loans.

- Advantages of short-term credit:

  Low cost-visualize yield curve. Can get funds relatively quickly. Can repay without penalty.

BLUEPRINTS: CHAPTER 17

The Dryden Press

Is there a cost to accruals? Do firms have much control over amount of accruals?

■ Accruals are free in that no explicit interest is charged.

■ Firms have little control over the level of accruals. Levels are influenced more by industry custom, economic factors, and tax laws.

What is trade credit?

■ Trade credit is credit furnished by a firm's suppliers.

■ Trade credit is often the largest source of short-term credit, especially for small firms.

■ Spontaneous, easy to get, but cost can be high.

B&B buys $3,030,303 gross, or $3,000,000 net, on terms of 1/10, net 30, and pays on Day 40. How much free and costly trade credit, and what's the cost of costly trade credit?

Net daily purchases = $3,000,000/360
= $8,333.

Gross/Net Breakdown

- Company buys goods worth $3,000,000. That's the cash price.
- They must pay $30,303 more if they don't take discounts.
- Think of the extra $30,303 as a financing cost similar to the interest on a loan.
- Want to compare that cost with the cost of a bank loan.

Payables level if take discount:
Payables = $8,333 (10) = $83,333.

Payables level if don't take discount:
Payables = $8,333 (40) = $333,333.

Credit Breakdown:
Total trade credit = $333,333
Free trade credit =   83,333
Costly trade credit = $250,000

Nominal Cost of Costly Trade Credit

Firm loses 0.01($3,030,303) = $30,303 of discounts to obtain $250,000 in extra trade credit, so

$$k_{Nom} = \frac{\$30,303}{\$250,000} = 0.1212 = 12.12\%.$$

But the $30,303 is paid all *during* the year, not at year-end, so EAR rate is higher.

Nominal Cost Formula, 1/10, net 40

$$k_{Nom} = \frac{\text{Discount \%}}{1 - \text{Discount \%}} \times \frac{360}{\text{Days taken - Discount period}}$$

$$= \frac{1}{99} \times \frac{360}{99} = 0.0101 \times 12$$

$$= 0.1212 = 12.12\%.$$

Pays 1.01% 12 times per year.

Effective Annual Rate, 1/10, net 40

Periodic rate = 0.01/0.99 = 1.01%.

Periods/year = 360/(40 - 10) = 12.

$$EAR = (1 + \text{Periodic rate})^n - 1.0$$
$$= (1.0101)^{12} - 1.0 = 12.82\%.$$

Commercial Paper (CP)

- Short term notes issued by large, strong companies. B&B couldn't issue CP--it's too small.
- CP trades in the market at rates just above T-bill rate.
- CP is bought with surplus cash by banks and other companies, then held as a marketable security for liquidity purposes.

A bank is willing to lend B&B $100,000 for 1 year at an 8 percent nominal rate. What is the EAR under the following five loans?

1. Simple annual interest, 1 year.
2. Simple interest, paid monthly.
3. Discount interest.
4. Discount interest with 10 percent compensating balance.
5. Installment loan, add-on, 12 months.

Why must we use EAR to evaluate the alternative loans?

- Nominal (quoted) rate = 8% in all cases.
- We want to compare loan cost rates and choose lowest cost loan.
- We must make comparison on EAR = Equivalent (or Effective) Annual Rate basis.

Simple Annual Interest, 1-Year Loan

"Simple interest" means not discount or add-on.

Interest = 0.08($100,000) = $8,000.

$$k_{Nom} = EAR = \frac{\$8,000}{\$100,000} = 0.08 = 8.0\%.$$

On a simple interest loan of one year, k_{Nom} = EAR.

Simple Interest, Paid Monthly

Monthly interest = (.08/12)(100,000)
= $666.67.

```
        0        1                    12
        |--------|------ ... ---------|
   100,000   -666.67              -667.67
                                 -100,000.00
```

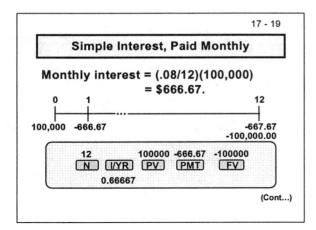

```
      12           100000  -666.67  -100000
   [ N ] [ I/YR ]  [ PV ]  [ PMT ]  [ FV ]
            0.66667
```

(Cont...)

---

k_{Nom} = **(Monthly rate)(12)**
= **0.66667(12)** = **8.00%.**

$$EAR = \left(1 + \frac{0.08}{12}\right)^{12} - 1 = 8.30\%.$$

or: 8■NOM%, 12■P/YR, ■EFF% = 8.30%.

Note: If interest were paid quarterly, then:

$$EAR = \left(1 + \frac{0.08}{4}\right)^{4} - 1 = 8.24\%.$$

Daily, EAR = 8.33%.

8% Discount Interest, 1 Year

Interest deductible = 0.08($100,000)
= $8,000.
Usable funds = $100,000 - $8,000
= $92,000.

```
    0          i = ?              1
    |--------------------------|
 92,000                    -100,000
```

```
      1            92     0    -100
   [ N ] [ I/YR ] [ PV ] [ PMT ] [ FV ]
         8.6957% = EAR
```

Discount Interest (Continued)

$$\text{Amt. borrowed} = \frac{\text{Amount needed}}{1 - \text{Nominal rate (decimal)}}$$

$$= \frac{\$100,000}{0.92} = \$108,696.$$

Need $100,000. Offered loan with terms of 8% discount interest, 10% compensating balance.

$$\text{Face amount of loan} = \frac{\text{Amount needed}}{1 - \text{Nominal rate} - \text{CB}}$$

$$= \frac{\$100,000}{1 - 0.08 - 0.1} = \$121,951.$$

(Cont...)

$$\text{Interest} = 0.08\,(\$121,951) = \$9,756.$$

$$\text{Cost} = \frac{\text{Interest paid}}{\text{Amount received}}\,.$$

$$\text{EAR} = \frac{\$9,756}{\$100,000} = 9.756\%.$$

EAR correct only if borrow for 1 year.

(Cont...)

8% Discount Interest with 10% Compensating Balance (Continued)

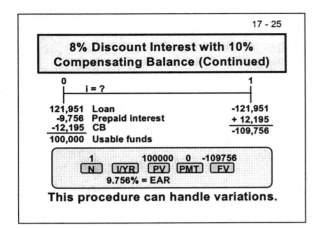

```
0        i = ?                        1
|----------------------------------|
121,951   Loan              -121,951
 -9,756   Prepaid interest  + 12,195
-12,195   CB                -109,756
100,000   Usable funds
```

```
   1            100000   0   -109756
[ N ]  [I/YR]  [PV]  [PMT]  [FV]
        9.756% = EAR
```

This procedure can handle variations.

1-Year Installment Loan, 8% "Add-On"

Interest = 0.08($100,000) = $8,000.

Face amount = $100,000 + $8,000 = $108,000.

Monthly payment = $108,000/12 = $9,000.

Average loan outstanding = $100,000/2 = $50,000.

Approximate cost = $8,000/$50,000 = 16.0%.

(Cont...)

Installment Loan

To find the EAR, recognize that the firm has received $100,000 and must make monthly payments of $9,000. This constitutes an ordinary annuity as shown below:

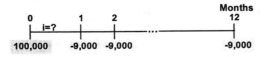

```
                                    Months
0        1       2             12
|   i=?  |       |    ...       |
100,000  -9,000  -9,000         -9,000
```

12		100000	-9000	0
N	I/YR	PV	PMT	FV

1.2043% = rate per month

k_{Nom} = APR = (1.2043)(12) = **14.45%**.
EAR = $(1.012043)^{12}$ - 1 = **15.45%**.

14.45 ■ NOM ⟶ enters nom rate
12 ■ P/YR ⟶ enters 12 pmts/yr
■ EFF% = 15.4489 = **15.45%**.

1 ■ P/YR to reset calculator.

What is a secured loan?

■ In a secured loan, the borrower pledges assets as collateral for the loan.

■ For short-term loans, the most commonly pledged assets are receivables and inventories.

Securities are great collateral, but generally not available.

What are the differences between pledging and factoring receivables?

■ If receivables are pledged, the lender has recourse against both the original buyer of the goods and the borrower.

■ When receivables are factored, they are generally sold, and the buyer (lender) has no recourse to the borrower.

17 - 31

What are three forms of inventory financing?

- Blanket lien.

- Trust receipt.

- Warehouse receipt.

- The form used depends on the type of inventory and situation at hand.

17 - 32

Legal stuff is vital.

- Security agreement: Standard form under Uniform Commercial Code. Describes when lender can claim collateral.

- UCC Form-1: Filed with Secretary of State to establish claim. Future lenders do search, won't lend if prior UCC-1 is on file.

EXAM-TYPE PROBLEMS

17-1. The Lasser Company needs to finance an increase in its working capital for the coming year. Lasser is reviewing the following three options: (1) The firm can borrow from its bank on a simple interest basis for one year at 13%. (2) It can borrow on a 3-month, but renewable, loan at a 12% nominal rate. The loan is a simple interest loan, completely paid off at the end of each quarter, then renewed for another quarter. (3) The firm can increase its accounts payable by not taking discounts. Lasser buys on credit terms of 1/30, net 60 days. What is the effective annual cost (not the approximate cost) of the least expensive type of credit, assuming 360 days per year? (12.55%)

17-2. Which of the following statements is most correct?

a. Under normal conditions the shape of the yield curve implies that the interest cost of short-term debt is greater than that of long-term debt, although short-term debt has other advantages that make it desirable as a financing source.

b. Flexibility is an advantage of short-term credit but this is somewhat offset by the higher flotation costs associated with the need to repeatedly renew short-term credit.

c. A short-term loan can usually be obtained more quickly than a long-term loan but the penalty for early repayment of a short-term loan is significantly higher than for a long-term loan.

d. Statements about the flexibility, cost, and riskiness of short-term versus long-term credit are dependent on the type of credit that is actually used.

e. Short-term debt is often less costly than long-term debt and the major reason for this is that short-term debt exposes the borrowing firm to much less risk than long-term debt.

17-3. A chain of lighting fixture stores, LCG Corporation, purchases inventory with a net price of $750,000 each day. The company purchases the inventory under the credit terms of 2/20, net 50. LCG always takes the discount, but takes the full 20 days to pay its bills. What is the average accounts payable for LCG? ($15,000,000)

18-18 Citrus Products Inc. is a medium-sized producer of citrus juice drinks with groves in Indian River County, Florida. Until now, the company has confined its operations and sales to the United States, but its CEO, George Gaynor, wants to expand into Europe. The first step would be to set up sales subsidiaries in Spain and Portugal, then to set up a production plant in Spain, and, finally, to distribute the product throughout the European common market. The firm's financial manager, Ruth Schmidt, is enthusiastic about the plan, but she is worried about the implications of the foreign expansion on the firm's financial management process. She has asked you, the firm's most recently hired financial analyst, to develop a 1-hour tutorial package that explains the basics of multinational financial management. The tutorial will be presented at the next board of director's meeting. To get you started, Schmidt has supplied you with the following list of questions.

a.   What is a multinational corporation? Why do firms expand into other countries?

b.   What are the six major factors which distinguish multinational financial management from financial management as practiced by a purely domestic firm?

c.   Consider the following illustrative exchange rates.

	U.S. Dollars Required to Buy One Unit of Foreign Currency
Spanish peseta	0.0075
Portuguese escudo	0.0063

(1) Are these currency prices direct quotations or indirect quotations?

(2) Calculate the indirect quotations for pesetas and escudos.

(3) What is a cross rate? Calculate the two cross rates between pesetas and escudos.

(4) Assume Citrus Products can produce a liter of orange juice and ship it to Spain for $1.75. If the firm wants a 50 percent markup on the product, what should the orange juice sell for in Spain?

(5) Now, assume Citrus Products begins producing the same liter of orange juice in Spain. The product costs 200 pesetas to produce and ship to Portugal, where it can be sold for 400 escudos. What is the dollar profit on the sale?

(6) What is exchange rate risk?

d. Briefly describe the current international monetary system. How does the current system differ from the system that was in place prior to August 1971?

e. What is a convertible currency? What problems arise when a multinational company operates in a country whose currency is not convertible?

f. What is the difference between spot rates and forward rates? When is the forward rate at a premium to the spot rate? At a discount?

g. What is interest rate parity? Currently, you can exchange 1 peseta for 0.0080 dollar in the 30-day forward market, and the risk-free rate on 30-day securities is 4 percent in both Spain and the United States. Does interest rate parity hold? If not, which securities offer the highest expected return?

h. What is purchasing power parity? If grapefruit juice costs $2.00 a liter in the United States and purchasing power parity holds, what should be the price of grapefruit juice in Portugal?

I. What impact does relative inflation have on interest rates and exchange rates?

j. Briefly discuss the international capital markets.

k. To what extent do average capital structures vary across different countries?

l. What is the impact of multinational operations on each of the following financial management topics?

(1) Cash management.

(2) Capital budgeting decisions.

(3) Credit management.

(4) Inventory management.

CHAPTER 18
Multinational Financial Management

- Multinational vs. domestic financial management
- Exchange rates and trading in foreign exchange
- International monetary system
- International money and capital markets

What is a multinational corporation?

A corporation that operates in two or more countries.

Why do firms expand into other countries?

1. To seek new markets.
2. To seek raw materials.
3. To seek new technology.
4. To seek production efficiency.
5. To avoid political and regulatory hurdles.
6. To diversify.

What are the six major factors that distinguish multinational from domestic financial management?

1. Different currency denominations.
2. Economic and legal ramifications.
3. Language differences.
4. Cultural differences.
5. Role of governments.
6. Political risk.

Consider the following exchange rates:

	U.S. $ to buy 1 Unit
Spanish peseta	0.0075
Portuguese escudo	0.0063

■ Are these currency prices direct or indirect quotations?

● Since they are prices of foreign currencies expressed in dollars, they are direct quotations.

What is an indirect quotation?

The number of units of foreign currency needed to purchase one U.S. dollar, or the reciprocal of a direct quotation.

Calculate the indirect quotations for pesetas and escudos.

	# of Units of Foreign Currency per U.S. $
Spanish peseta	133.3
Portuguese escudo	158.7

Peseta: 1/0.0075 = 133.3
Escudo: 1/0.0063 = 158.7

What is a cross rate?

The exchange rate between any two currencies. Cross rates are actually calculated on the basis of various currencies relative to the U.S. dollar.

Calculate the two cross rates between pesetas and escudos.

■ Cross rate $= \dfrac{\text{Pesetas}}{\text{Dollar}} \times \dfrac{\text{Dollars}}{\text{Escudo}}$

= 133.3 x 0.0063
= 0.84 pesetas/escudo.

■ Cross rate $= \dfrac{\text{Escudos}}{\text{Dollar}} \times \dfrac{\text{Dollars}}{\text{Peseta}}$

= 158.7 x 0.0075
= 1.19 escudos/peseta.

Note:

- The two cross rates are reciprocals of one another.
- They can be calculated by dividing either the direct or indirect quotations.

The firm can produce a liter of orange juice and ship it to Spain for $1.75. If the firm wants a 50% markup on the product, what should the juice sell for in Spain?

Price = (1.75)(1.50)(133.3)

= 349.91 pesetas.

Now the firm begins producing the orange juice in Spain. The product costs 200 pesetas to produce and ship to Portugal, where it can be sold for 400 escudos. What is the dollar profit on the sale?

200 pesetas = 200(1.19) = 238 escudos.

400 - 238 = 162 escudos profit.

158.7 escudos = 1 U.S. dollar.

Dollar profit = 162/158.7 = $1.02.

What is exchange rate risk?

The risk that the value of a cash flow in one currency translated to another currency will decline due to a change in exchange rates.

For example, in the last slide, a weakening escudo (strengthening dollar) would lower the dollar profit.

Describe the current and former international monetary systems.

- The current system is a floating rate system.
- Prior to 1971, a fixed exchange rate system was in effect.
  - The U.S. dollar was tied to gold.
  - Other currencies were tied to the dollar.

What is a convertible currency?

- A currency is convertible when the issuing country promises to redeem the currency at current market rates.
- Convertible currencies are traded in world currency markets.

What problems arise when a firm operates in a country whose currency is not convertible?

- It becomes very difficult for multi-national companies to conduct business because there is no easy way to take profits out of the country.
- Often, firms will barter for goods to export to their home countries.

What is the difference between spot rates and forward rates?

- Spot rates are the rates to buy currency for immediate delivery.
- Forward rates are the rates to buy currency at some agreed-upon date in the future.

When is the forward rate at a premium to the spot rate?

- If the U.S. dollar buys fewer units of a foreign currency in the forward than in the spot market, the foreign currency is selling at a premium.
- In the opposite situation, the foreign currency is selling at a discount.
- The primary determinant of the spot/forward rate relationship is relative interest rates.

What is interest rate parity?

Interest rate parity holds that investors should expect to earn the same return in all countries after adjusting for risk.

$$\frac{f_t}{e_0} = \frac{1 + k_h}{1 + k_f}.$$

f_t = t-period forward exchange rate
e_0 = today's spot rate
k_h = periodic interest rate in the home country
k_f = periodic interest rate in the foreign country

Assume 1 peseta = \$0.008 in 30-day forward market and k_{Nom} for 30-day risk-free securities in Spain and U.S. = 4%. Does interest rate parity hold?

No.

f_t = \$0.008
k_h = 4%/12 = 0.333%
k_f = 4%/12 = 0.333%

(Cont...)

$$\frac{f_t}{e_0} = \frac{1 + k_h}{1 + k_f}$$

$$\frac{\$0.008}{e_0} = \frac{1.0033\%}{1.0033\%}$$

$$\frac{\$0.008}{e_0} = 1.$$

Therefore, if interest rate parity holds then e_0 = \$0.008. However, we were given earlier that e_0 = \$0.0075.

What security offers highest return?

Spanish security.
1. Convert $1,000 to pesetas in spot market. $1,000 x 133.333 = 133,333 pesetas.
2. Invest 133,333 pesetas in 30-day Spanish security. In 30 days receive 133,333 pesetas x 1.00333 = 133,777 pesetas.
3. Agree today to exchange 133,777 pesetas 30 days from now at forward rate. 133,777/125 = $1,070.22.
4. 30-day return = $70.22/$1,000 = 7.02%, nominal annual return = 12 x 7.02% = 84.24%.

What is purchasing power parity (PPP)?

Purchasing power parity implies that the level of exchange rates adjusts so that identical goods cost the same amount in different countries.

$$P_h = P_f(e_0) \text{ or } e_0 = P_h/P_f.$$

If grapefruit juice costs $2.00/liter in U.S. and PPP holds, what is price of grapefruit juice in Portugal?

$$PPP = e_0 = P_h/P_f$$
$$\$0.0063 = \$2.00/P_f$$
$$P_f = \$2.00/\$0.0063 = 317.46 \text{ escudos.}$$

What impact does relative inflation have on interest rates and exchange rates?

- Lower inflation leads to lower interest rates, so borrowing in low-interest countries may appear attractive to multinational firms.
- However, currencies in low-inflation countries tend to appreciate against those in high-inflation rate countries, so the effective interest cost increases over the life of the loan.

Describe the international money and capital markets.

- Eurodollar markets
  - a source of dollars outside the U.S.
- International bonds
  - Foreign bonds: Sold by foreign borrower, but denominated in the currency of the country of issue.
  - Eurobonds: Sold in country other than the one in whose currency it is denominated.

To what extent do average capital structures vary across different countries?

- Previous studies suggested that average capital structures vary among the large industrial countries.
- However, a recent study, which controlled for differences in accounting practices, suggests that capital structures are more similar across different countries than previously thought.

18 - 28

What is the impact of multinational operations on each of the following topics?

Cash Management

- Distances are greater.
- Access to more markets for loans and for temporary investments.
- Cash is often denominated in different currencies.

---

18 - 29

Capital Budgeting Decisions

- Foreign operations are taxed locally, and then funds repatriated may be subject to U.S. taxes.
- Foreign projects are subject to political risk.
- Funds repatriated must be converted to U.S. dollars, so exchange rate risk must be taken into account.

---

18 - 30

Credit Management

- Credit is more important, because commerce to lesser-developed countries often relies on credit.
- Credit for future payment may be subject to exchange rate risk.

Inventory Management

- Inventory decisions can be more complex, especially when inventory can be stored in locations in different countries.

- Some factors to consider are shipping times, carrying costs, taxes, import duties, and exchange rates.

EXAM-TYPE PROBLEMS

18-1. In 1985, a particular Japanese imported automobile sold for 1,476,000 yen or $8,200. If the car still sells for the same amount of yen today but the current exchange rate is 144 yen per dollar, what is the car selling for today in U.S. dollars? ($10,250)

18-2. Sunware Corporation, a U.S.-based importer, makes a purchase of crystal glassware from a firm in Germany for 39,960 marks, or $24,000, at the spot rate of 1.665 marks per dollar. The terms of the purchase are net 90 days, and the U.S. firm wants to cover this trade payable with a forward market hedge to eliminate its exchange rate risk. Suppose the firm completes a forward hedge at the 90-day forward rate of 1.682 marks. If the spot rate in 90 days is actually 1.638 marks, how much will the U.S. firm have saved in U.S. dollars by hedging its exchange rate exposure? ($638.17)

18-3. Six months ago, a Swiss investor bought a 6-month U.S. Treasury bill at a price of $9,708.74, with a maturity value of $10,000. The exchange rate at that time was 1.420 Swiss francs per dollar. Today, at maturity, the exchange rate is 1.324 for Swiss francs. What is the nominal annual rate of return to the Swiss investor? (-7.93%)

18-4. A refrigerator costs $899 in the United States. The same set costs 1,425 DM. If purchasing power parity holds, what is the spot exchange rate between the mark and the dollar? ($0.631 per DM or 1.585 DM per U.S. dollar)

18-5 3-month T-bills have a nominal rate of 5 percent, while default-free Swiss bonds that mature in 3 months have a nominal rate of 3.5 percent. In the spot exchange market, one Swiss franc equals $0.6935. If interest rate parity holds, what is the 3-month forward exchange rate? ($0.6961)

```
┌─────────────────────────────────────────────────────────────┐
│                  BLUEPRINTS: CHAPTER 19                      │
│              DERIVATIVES AND RISK MANAGEMENT                 │
└─────────────────────────────────────────────────────────────┘
```

19-7   Assume that you have just been hired as a financial analyst by Tropical Sweets Inc., a mid-sized California company that specializes in creating exotic candies from tropical fruits such as mangoes, papayas, and dates. The firm's CEO, George Yamaguchi, recently returned from an industry corporate executive conference in San Francisco, and on e of the sessions he attended was on the pressing need for smaller companies to institute corporate risk management programs. Since no one at Tropical Sweets is familiar with the basics of derivatives and corporate risk management, Yamaguchi has asked you to prepare a brief report that the firm's executives could use to gain at least a cursory understanding of the topics.

To begin, you gathered some outside materials on derivatives and corporate risk management and used these materials to draft a list of pertinent questions that need to be answered. In fact, one possible approach to the paper is to use a question-and-answer format. Not that the questions have been drafted, you have to develop the answers.

a.   What is an option? What is the single most important characteristic of an option?

b.   Options have a unique set of terminology. Define the following terms: call option; put option; exercise price; striking, or strike, price; option price; expiration date; formula value; covered option; naked option; in-the-money call; out-of-the-money call; and LEAP.

c.   Consider Tropical Sweet's call option with a $25 strike price. The following table contains historical values for this option at different stock prices:

Stock Price	Call Option Price
$25	$ 3.00
30	7.50
35	12.50
40	16.50
45	21.00
50	25.50

(1) Create a table which shows (a) stock price, (b) striking price, (c) formula value, (d) option price, and (e) the parium of option price over formula value.

(2) What happens to the premium of option price over formula value as the stock price rises? Why?

d.　　In 1973, Fischer Black and Myron Scholes developed the Black-Scholes Option Pricing Model (OPM).

(1) What assumptions underlie the OPM?

(2) Write out the three equations that constitutes the model.

(3) What is the value of the following call option according to the OPM?

> Stock price = $27.00
> Exercise price = $25.00
> Time to expiration = 6 months
> Risk-free rate = 6.0%
> Stock return variance = 0.11.

e.　　What impact does each of the following call option parameters have on the value of a call option?

(1) Current stock price

(2) Exercise price

(3) Option's term to maturity

(4) Risk-free rate

(5) Variability of the stock price

f.　　What is corporate risk management? Why is it important to all firms?

g.　　Risks that firms face can be categorized in many ways. Define the following types of risk: speculative risks, pure risks; demand risks; input risks; financial risks; property risks; personnel risks; environmental risks; liability risks; and insurable risks.

h.　　What are the three steps of corporate risk management?

l.   What are some actions that companies can take to minimize or reduce risk exposures?

j.   What is financial risk exposure? Describe the following concepts and techniques that can be used to reduce financial risks: derivatives; futures markets; hedging; and swaps.

k.   Describe how commodity futures markets can be used to reduce input price risk.

CHAPTER 19
Derivatives and Risk Management

■ Derivative securities.

■ Fundamentals of risk management.

■ Using derivatives to reduce interest rate risk.

What is an option?

An option is a contract which gives its holder the right, but not the obligation, to buy (or sell) an asset at some predetermined price within a specified period of time.

What is the single most important characteristic of an option?

■ It does not obligate its owner to take any action. It merely gives the owner the right to buy or sell an asset.

Option Terminology

- **Call option:** An option to buy a specified number of shares of a security within some future period.
- **Put option:** An option to sell a specified number of shares of a security within some future period.
- **Exercise (or strike) price:** The price stated in the option contract at which the security can be bought or sold.

- **Option price:** The market price of the option contract.
- **Expiration date:** The date the option matures.
- **Formula value:** The value of a call option if it were exercised today = Current stock price - Strike price.

- **Covered option:** A call option written against stock held in an investor's portfolio.
- **Naked (uncovered) option:** An option sold without the stock to back it up.
- **In-the-money call:** A call whose exercise price is less than the current price of the underlying stock.

■ **Out-of-the-money call:** A call option whose exercise price exceeds the current stock price.

■ **LEAPs:** Long-term Equity AnticiPation securities that are similar to conventional options except that they are long-term options with maturities of up to 2 1/2 years.

Consider the following data:

Stock Price	Call Option Price
$25	$ 3.00
30	7.50
35	12.00
40	16.50
45	21.00
50	25.50

Exercise price = $25.

Create a table which shows (a) stock price, (b) strike price, (c) formula value, (d) option price, and (e) premium of option price over the formula value.

Price of Stock (a)	Strike Price (b)	Formula Value of Option (a) - (b)
$25.00	$25.00	$0.00
30.00	25.00	5.00
35.00	25.00	10.00
40.00	25.00	15.00
45.00	25.00	20.00
50.00	25.00	25.00

Table (Continued)

Formula Value of Option (c)	Mkt. Price of Option (d)	Premium (d) - (c)
$ 0.00	$ 3.00	$ 3.00
5.00	7.50	2.50
10.00	12.00	2.00
15.00	16.50	1.50
20.00	21.00	1.00
25.00	25.50	0.50

What happens to the premium of the option price over the formula value as the stock price rises?

- The premium of the option price over the formula value declines as the stock price increases.
- This is due to the declining degree of leverage provided by options as the underlying stock price increases, and the greater loss potential of options at higher option prices.

What are the assumptions of the Black-Scholes Option Pricing Model?

- The stock underlying the call option provides no dividends during the call option's life.
- There are no transactions costs for the sale/purchase of either the stock or the option.
- k_{RF} is known and constant during the option's life.

(Cont...)

- Security buyers may borrow any fraction of the purchase price at the short-term risk-free rate.
- No penalty for short selling and sellers receive immediately full cash proceeds at today's price.
- Call option can be exercised only on its expiration date.
- Security trading takes place in continuous time, and stock prices move randomly in continuous time.

What are the three equations that make up the OPM?

$$V = P[N(d_1)] - Xe^{-k_{RF}t}[N(d_2)].$$

$$d_1 = \frac{\ln(P/X) + [k_{RF} + (\sigma^2/2)]t}{\sigma\sqrt{t}}.$$

$$d_2 = d_1 - \sigma\sqrt{t}.$$

What is the value of the following call option according to the OPM? Assume: P = $27; X = $25; k_{RF} = 6%; t = 0.5 years: σ^2 = 0.11

$$V = \$27[N(d_1)] - \$25e^{-(0.06)(0.5)}[N(d_2)].$$

$$d_1 = \frac{\ln(\$27/\$25) + [(0.06 + 0.11/2)](0.5)}{(0.3317)(0.7071)}$$

$$= 0.5736.$$

$$d_2 = d_1 - (0.3317)(0.7071) = d_1 - 0.2345$$

$$= 0.5736 - 0.2345 = 0.3391.$$

$N(d_1) = N(0.5736) = 0.5000 + 0.2168$
$= 0.7168.$
$N(d_2) = N(0.3391) = 0.5000 + 0.1327$
$= 0.6327.$

Note: Values obtained from Table A-5 in text.

$V = \$27(0.7168) - \$25e^{-0.03}(0.6327)$
$= \$19.3536 - \$25(0.97045)(0.6327)$
$= \$4.0036.$

What impact do the following para-meters have on a call option's value?

■ **Current stock price:** Call option value increases as the current stock price increases.

■ **Exercise price:** As the exercise price increases, a call option's value decreases.

■ **Option period:** As the expiration date is lengthened, a call option's value increases (more chance of becoming in the money.)

■ **Risk-free rate:** Call option's value tends to increase as k_{RF} increases (reduces the PV of the exercise price).

■ **Stock return variance:** Option value increases with variance of the underlying stock (more chance of becoming in the money).

What is corporate risk management?

Corporate risk management relates
to the management of unpredictable
events that would have adverse
consequences for the firm.

Why is corporate risk management important to all firms?

All firms face risks, but the lower
those risks can be made, the more
valuable the firm, other things held
constant. Of course, risk reduction
has a cost.

Definitions of Different Types of Risk

- **Speculative risks:** Those that offer the chance of a gain as well as a loss.
- **Pure risks:** Those that offer only the prospect of a loss.
- **Demand risks:** Those associated with the demand for a firm's products or services.
- **Input risks:** Those associated with a firm's input costs.

(Cont...)

- **Financial risks:** Those that result from financial transactions.
- **Property risks:** Those associated with loss of a firm's productive assets.
- **Personnel risk:** Risks that result from human actions.
- **Environmental risk:** Risk associated with polluting the environment.
- **Liability risks:** Connected with product, service, or employee liability.
- **Insurable risks:** Those which typically can be covered by insurance.

What are the three steps of corporate risk management?

Step 1. Identify the risks faced by the firm.

Step 2. Measure the potential impact of the identified risks.

Step 3. Decide how each relevant risk should be dealt with.

What are some actions that companies can take to minimize or reduce risk exposures?

- Transfer risk to an insurance company by paying periodic premiums.
- Transfer functions which produce risk to third parties.
- Purchase derivatives contracts to reduce input and financial risks.

(Cont...)

- ■ Take actions to reduce the probability of occurrence of adverse events.
- ■ Take actions to reduce the magnitude of the loss associated with adverse events.
- ■ Avoid the activities that give rise to risk.

What is a financial risk exposure?

- ■ Financial risk exposure refers to the risk inherent in the financial markets due to price fluctuations.
- ■ Example: A firm holds a portfolio of bonds, interest rates rise, and the value of the bonds falls.

Financial Risk Management Concepts

- ■ Derivative: Security whose value stems or is derived from the value of other assets. Swaps, options, and futures are used to manage financial risk exposures.
- ■ Futures: Contracts which call for the purchase or sale of a financial (or real) asset at some future date, but at a price determined today. Futures (and other derivatives) can be used either as highly leveraged speculations or to hedge and thus reduce risk. (Cont...)

■ **Hedging:** Generally conducted where a price change could negatively affect a firm's profits.

- **Long hedge:** involves the purchase of a futures contract to guard against a price increase.

- **Short hedge:** involves the sale of a futures contract to protect against a price decline in commodities or financial securities.

(Cont...)

■ **Swaps:** Involve the exchange of cash payment obligations between two parties, usually because each party prefers the terms of the other's debt contract. Swaps can reduce each party's financial risk.

How can commodity futures markets be used to reduce input price risk?

The purchase of a commodity futures contract will allow a firm to make a future purchase of the input at today's price, even if the market price on the item has risen substantially in the interim.

EXAM-TYPE PROBLEMS

19-1. A call option on the stock of Gemrock Jewelers has a market price of $13. The stock sells for $40 a share, and the option has an exercise price of $32 a share.

a. What is the formula value of the call option? ($8)

b. What is the premium on the option? ($5)

19-2. Assume you have been given the following information on Kazmirski Corporation:

Current stock price = $24   Exercise price of option = $24
Time to maturity of option = 6 months Risk-free rate = 7%
Variance of stock price = 0.10 d_1 = 0.26833
d_2 = 0.04472 $N(d_1)$ = 0.60572
$N(d_2)$ = 0.51783

Using the Black-Scholes Option Pricing Model, what would be the value of the option? ($2.54)

19-3. What is the implied interest rate on a Treasury bond ($100,000) futures contract that settled at 99-14? If interest rates decreased by ½ percent, what would be the contract's new value? (8.06%; $104,500.68)

```
┌─────────────────────────────────────────────────────────────┐
│                BLUEPRINTS: CHAPTER 20                         │
│   HYBRID FINANCING: PREFERRED STOCK, LEASING, WARRANTS,       │
│                    AND CONVERTIBLES                           │
└─────────────────────────────────────────────────────────────┘
```

20-11 Martha Millon, financial manager for Fish & Chips Inc., has been asked to perform a lease-versus-buy analysis on a new computer system. The computer costs $1,200,000, and, if it is purchased, Fish & Chips could obtain a term loan for the full amount at a 10 percent cost. The loan would be amortized over the 4-year life of the computer, with payments mad at the end of each year. The computer is classified as special purpose, and hence it falls into the MACRS 3-year class. If the computer is purchased, a maintenance contract must be obtained at a cost of $25,000.payable at the beginning of each year.

After 4 years the computer will be sold, and Millon's best estimate of its residual value at that time is $125,000. Because technology is changing rapidly, however, the residual value is very uncertain.

As an alternative, National Leasing is willing to write a 4-year lease on the computer, including maintenance, for payments of $340,000 at the beginning of each year. Fish & Chips' marginal federal-plus-state tax rate is 40 percent. Help Millon conduct her analysis by answering the following questions.

a. (1) Why is leasing sometimes referred to as "off balance sheet" financing?

   (2) What is the difference between a capital lease and an operating lease?

   (3) What effect does leasing have on a firm's capital structure?

b. (1) What is Fish & Chips' present value cost of owning the computer? (Hint: Set up a table whose bottom line is a "time line" which shows the net cash flows over the period t = 0 to t = 4, and then find the PV of these net cash flows, or the PV cost of owning.)

   (2) Explain the rationale for the discount rate you used to find the PV.

c. (1) What is Fish & Chip's present value cost of leasing the computer? (Hint: Again, construct a time line.)

(2) What is the net advantage to leasing? Does our analysis indicate that the firm should buy or lease the computer? Explain.

d. Now assume that Millon believes the computer's residual value could be as low as $0 or as high as $250,000, but she stands by $125,000 as her expected value. She concludes that the residual value is riskier than the other cash flows in the analysis, and she wants to incorporate this differential risk into her analysis. Describe how this could be accomplished. What effect would it have on the lease decision?

e. Millon knows that her firm has been considering moving its headquarters to a new location for some time, and she is concerned that these plans may come to fruition prior to the expiration of the lease. If the move occurs, the company would obtain completely new computers, and hence Millon would like to include a cancellation clause in the lease contract. What effect would a cancellation clause have on the riskiness of the lease?

20-12 Martha Millon, financial manager of Fish & Chips Inc., is facing a dilemma. The firm was founded 5 years ago to develop a new fast-food concept, and although Fish & Chips has done well, the firm's founder and chairman believes that an industry shake-out is imminent. To survive, the firm must capture market share now, and this requires a large infusion of new capital.

Because the stock price may rise rapidly, Millon does not want to issue new common stock. On the other hand, interest rates are currently very high by historical standards, and, with the firm's B rating, the interest payments on a new debt issue would be too much to handle if sales took a downturn. Thus, Millon has narrowed her choice to bonds with warrants or convertible bonds. She has asked you to help in the decision process by answering the following questions.

a. How does preferred stock differ from common equity and debt?

b. What is floating rate preferred?

c. How can a knowledge of call options help one understand warrants and convertibles?

d. One of Millon's alternative is to issue a bond with warrants attached. Fish & Chips' current stock price is $10, and its cost of 20-year, annual coupon debt without warrants is estimated by its investment bankers to be 12 percent. The banker suggest attaching 50 warrants to each bond, with each warrant having an exercise price of $12.50. It is estimated that each warrant, when detached an traded separately, will have a value of $1.50.

(1) What coupon rate should be set on the bond with warrants if the total package is to sell for $1,000?

(2) Suppose the bonds are issued and the warrants immediately trade for $2.50 each. What does this imply about the terms of the issue? Did the company "win" or lose"?

(3) When would you expect the warrants to be exercised?

(4) Will the warrants bring in additional capital when exercised? If so, how much and what type of capital?

(5) Because warrants lower the cost of the accompanying debt, shouldn't all debt be issued with warrants? What is the expected cost of the bond with warrants if the warrants are expected to be exercised in 5 years, when Fish & Chips' stock price is expected to be $17.50? How would you expect the cost of the bond with warrants to compare with the cost of straight debt? With the cost of common stock?

e. As an alternative to the bond with warrants, Millon is considering convertible bonds. The firm's investment bankers estimate that Fish & Chips could sell a 20-year, 10 percent annual coupon, callable convertible bond for its $1,000 par value, whereas a straight debt issue would require a 12 percent coupon. Fish & Chips current stock price is $10, its last dividend was $0.74, and the dividend is expected to grow at a constant rate of 8 percent. The convertible could be converted into 80 shares of Fish & Chips stock at the owner's option.

(1) What conversion price, P_c, is implied in the convertible's terms?

(2) What is the straight debt value of the convertible? What is the implied value of the convertibility feature?

(3) What is the formula for the bond's conversion value in any year? Its value at Year 0? At Year 10?

(4) What is meant by the term "floor value" of a convertible? What is the convertible's expected floor value in Year 0? In Year 10?

(5) Assume that Fish & Chips intends to force conversion by calling the bond when its conversion value is 20 percent above its par value, or at 1.2($1,000) = $1,200. When is the issue expected to be called? Answer to the closest year.

(6) What is the expected cost of the convertible to Fish & Chips? Does this cost appear consistent with the riskiness of the issue? Assume conversion in Year 5 at a conversion value of $1,200.

f.   Millon believes that the costs of both the bond with warrants and the convertible bond are essentially equal, so her decision must be based on other factors. What are some of the factors that she should consider in making her decision?

CHAPTER 20
Hybrid Financing: Preferred Stock, Leasing, Warrants, and Convertibles

- Preferred stock
- Leasing
- Warrants
- Convertibles
- Recent innovations

Leasing

- Leasing is sometimes referred to as "off balance sheet" financing because if a lease is not "capitalized" it is not shown on the balance sheet.
- Leasing is a substitute for debt financing and, thus, uses up a firm's debt capacity.

(Cont...)

- Capital leases are differentiated from operating leases:
  - Capital leases do not provide for maintenance service.
  - Capital leases are not cancelable.
  - Capital leases are fully amortized.

Analysis: Lease vs. Borrow-and-Buy

Data:
- New machine costs $1,200,000.
- 3-year MACRS class life; 4-year economic life.
- Tax rate of 40%.
- k_d = 10%.
- Maintenance of $25,000/year, payable at beginning of each year.
- Residual value in Year 4 of $125,000.
- 4-year lease includes maintenance.
- Lease payment is $340,000/year, payable at beginning of each year.

Depreciation Schedule

Depreciable basis = $1,200,000

Year	MACRS Rate	Depreciation Expense	End-of-Year Book Value
1	0.33	$ 396,000	$804,000
2	0.45	540,000	264,000
3	0.15	180,000	84,000
4	0.07	84,000	0
	1.00	$1,200,000	

Cost of Owning Analysis
(In Thousands)

	0	1	2	3	4
Cost of asset	(1,200.0)				
Dep. tax savings[1]		158.4	216.0	72.0	33.6
Maint. (AT)[2]	(15.0)	(15.0)	(15.0)	(15.0)	
Res. value (AT)[3]					75.0
Net cash flow	(1,215.0)	143.4	201.0	57.0	108.6

PV cost of owning (@ 6%) = -$766,948.

(Cont...)

Notes:

[1] **Depreciation is a tax deductible expense, so it produces a tax savings of T(Depreciation). Year 1 = 0.4($396) = $158.4.**

[2] **Each maintenance payment of $25 is deductible so the after-tax cost of the lease is (1 - T)($25) = $15.**

[3] **The ending book value is $0 so the full $125 salvage (residual) value is taxed.**

Cost of Leasing Analysis (In Thousands)

	0	1	2	3	4
Lease pmt (AT)[1]	-204	-204	-204	-204	

PV cost of leasing (@ 6%) = -$749,294.

Note:

[1]Each lease payment of $340 is deductible, so the after-tax cost of the lease is (1 - T)($340) = -$204.

Net Advantage of Leasing

$$NAL = \frac{PV\ cost}{of\ owning} - \frac{PV\ cost}{of\ leasing}$$

$$= \$766,948 - \$749,294$$

$$= \$17,654.$$

Suppose computer's residual value could be as low as $0 or as high as $250,000, but expected value is $125,000. How could the riskiness of the SV be incorporated in the analysis? What effect would this have on lease decision?

To account for risk, the rate used to discount the SV would be increased; therefore, the cost of owning would be even higher. Leasing becomes even more attractive.

What effect would a cancellation clause have on the riskiness of the lease?

A cancellation clause lowers the risk of the lease to the lessee, but increases the risk to the lessor.

How does preferred stock differ from common equity and debt?

- Preferred dividends are fixed, but they may be omitted without placing the firm in default.
- Most preferred stocks prohibit the firm from paying common dividends when the preferred is in arrears.
- Usually cumulative up to a limit.

What is floating rate preferred?

- Dividends are indexed to the rate on treasury securities instead of being fixed.
- Excellent S-T corporate investment:
  - Only 30% of dividends are taxable to corporations.
  - The floating rate generally keeps issue trading near par.

- However, if the issuer is risky, the floating rate preferred stock may have too much price instability for the liquid asset portfolios of many corporate investors.

How can a knowledge of call options help one understand warrants and convertibles?

- A warrant is a long-term call option.
- A convertible consists of a fixed rate bond plus a call option.

Given the following facts, what coupon rate must be set on a bond with warrants if the total package is to sell for $1,000?

- P_0 = $10.
- k_d of 20-year annual payment bond without warrants = 12%.
- 50 warrants with an exercise price of $12.50 each are attached to bond.
- Each warrant's value will be $1.50.

Step 1: Calculate V_{Bond}

$V_{Package} = V_{Bond} + V_{Warrants}$ = $1,000.

$V_{Warrants}$ = 50($1.50) = $75.

V_{Bond} + $75 = $1,000

$\quad\quad V_{Bond}$ = $925.

Step 2: Find Coupon Payment and Rate

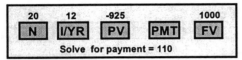

20	12	-925		1000
N	I/YR	PV	PMT	FV

Solve for payment = 110

Therefore, the required coupon rate is $110/$1,000 = 11%.

If after issue the warrants immediately sell for $2.50 each, what would this imply about the value of the package?

■ The package would actually have been worth

$V_{package}$ = $925 + 50($2.50) = $1,050,

which is $50 more than the actual selling price.

■ The firm could have set lower interest payments whose PV would be smaller by $50 per bond, or it could have offered fewer warrants with a higher exercise price.

■ Current stockholders are giving up value to the warrant holders.

Assume that the warrants expire 10 years after issue. When would you expect them to be exercised?

■ Generally, a warrant will sell in the open market at a premium above its theoretical value (it can't sell for less).

■ Therefore, warrants tend not to be exercised until just before they expire.

- In a stepped-up exercise price, the exercise price increases in steps over the warrant's life. Because the value of the warrant falls when the exercise price is increased, step-up provisions encourage in-the-money warrant holders to exercise just prior to the step-up.
- Since no dividends are earned on the warrant, holders will tend to exercise voluntarily if a stock's dividend rises enough.

Will the warrants bring in additional capital when exercised?

- When exercised, each warrant will bring in the exercise price, $12.50.
- This is equity capital and holders will receive one share of common stock per warrant.
- The exercise price is typically set at 10% to 30% above the current stock price on the issue date.

Because warrants lower the cost of the accompanying debt issue, should all debt be issued with warrants?

No. As we shall see, the warrants have a cost which must be added to the coupon interest cost.

What is the expected return to the holders of the bond with warrants (or the expected cost to the company) if the warrants are expected to be exercised in 5 years when P = $17.50?

■ The company will exchange stock worth $17.50 for one warrant plus $12.50. The opportunity cost to the company is $17.50 - $12.50 = $5.00.

■ Bond has 50 warrants, so on a par bond basis, opportunity cost = 50($5.00) = $250.

■ Here is the cash flow time line:

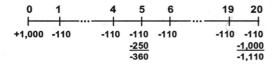

```
    0    1        4    5    6        19    20
    |----|---...--|----|----|---...--|-----|
 +1,000 -110    -110 -110 -110    -110  -110
                      -250              -1,000
                      -360              -1,110
```

Input the cash flows in the calculator to find IRR = 12.93%. This is the pre-tax cost of the bond and warrant package.

■ The cost of the bond with warrants package is higher than the 12% cost of straight debt because part of the expected return is from capital gains, which are riskier than interest income.

■ The cost is lower than the cost of equity because part of the return is fixed by contract.

Assume the following convertible bond data:

- 20-year, 10% annual coupon, callable convertible bond will sell at its $1,000 par value; straight debt issue would require a 12% coupon.
- Call the bonds when conversion value > $1,200.
- $P_0 = \$10$; $D_0 = \$0.74$; $g = 8\%$.
- Conversion ratio = CR = 80 shares.

What conversion price (P_c) is built into the bond?

$$P_c = \frac{\text{Par value}}{\text{\# Shares received}}$$

$$= \frac{\$1,000}{80} = \$12.50.$$

The conversion price is typically set 10% to 30% above the stock price on the issue date.

What is (1) the convertible's straight debt value and (2) the implied value of the convertibility feature?

Straight debt value:

20	12		100	1000
N	I/YR	PV	PMT	FV

Solution: -850.61

Implied Convertibility Value

■ Because the convertibles will sell for $1,000, the implied value of the convertibility feature is

$1,000 - $850.61 = $149.39.

$$\frac{\$149.39}{80\ shares} = \$1.87\ per\ share.$$

■ The convertibility value corresponds to the warrant value in the previous example.

What is the formula for the bond's expected conversion value in any year?

Conversion value = $C_t = CR(P_0)(1 + g)^t$.

t = 0

$C_0 = 80(\$10)(1.08)^0 = \$800$.

t = 10

$C_{10} = 80(\$10)(1.08)^{10}$
$= \$1,727.14$.

What is meant by the floor value of a convertible?

■ The floor value is the higher of the straight debt value and the conversion value.

■ Straight debt value$_0$ = $850.61.

■ C_0 = $800.

Floor value at Year 0 = $850.61.

- Straight debt value$_{10}$ = $887.00.
- C_{10} = $1,727.14.

> Floor value$_{10}$ = $1,727.14.

- Convertible will generally sell above its floor value prior to maturity because convertibility option has an additional value.

The firm intends to force conversion when C = 1.2($1,000) = $1,200. When is the issue expected to be called?

8	-800	0	1200
N	I/YR	PV	PMT	FV

Solution: n = 5.27

What is the convertible's expected cost of capital to the firm? Assume conversion in Year 5 at $1,200.

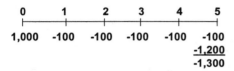

0	1	2	3	4	5
1,000	-100	-100	-100	-100	-100
					-1,200
					-1,300

Input the cash flows in the calculator and solve for IRR = 13.08%.

Does the cost of the convertible appear to be consistent with the riskiness of the issue?

■ For consistency, need $k_d < k_c < k_e$.

■ Why?

■ The convertible bond's risk is a blend of the risk of debt and equity, so k_c should be in between the cost of debt and equity.

■ Check the values:

$k_d = 12\%$ and $k_c = 13.08\%$.

$$k_s = \frac{D_0(1+g)}{P_0} + g = \frac{\$0.74(1.08)}{\$10} + 0.08$$

$$= 16.0\%.$$

Since k_c is between k_d and k_s, the consistency requirement is met.

Besides cost, what other factors should be considered?

■ The firm's future needs for capital:
  ● Exercise of warrants brings in new equity capital without the need to retire low-coupon debt.
  ● Conversion brings in no new funds, and low-coupon debt is gone when bonds are converted. However, debt ratio is lowered, so new debt can be issued.

- **Does the firm want to commit to 20 years of debt?**

  - **Conversion removes debt, while the exercise of warrants does not.**

  - **If stock price does not rise over time, then neither warrants nor convertibles would be exercised. Debt would remain outstanding.**

EXAM-TYPE PROBLEMS

20-1. Redstone Corporation is considering a leasing arrangement to finance some special manufacturing tools that it needs for production during the next three years. A planned change in the firm's production technology will make the tools obsolete after three years. The firm will depreciate the cost of the tools on a straight-line basis. The firm can borrow $4,800,000, the purchase price, at 10 percent to buy the tools or make three equal end-of-year lease payments of $2,100,000. The firm's tax rate is 40 percent and the firm's before-tax cost of debt is 10 percent. Annual maintenance costs associated with ownership are estimated at $240,000. What is the net advantage to leasing (NAL)? (+106.19--in thousands)

20-2. Insight Incorporated just issued 20-year convertible bonds at a price of $1,000 each. The bonds pay 9 percent annual coupon interest, have a par value of $1,000, and are convertible into 40 shares of the firm's common stock. Investors would require a return of 12 percent on the firm's bonds if they were not convertible. The current market price of the firm's stock is $18.75 and the firm just paid a dividend of $0.80. Earnings and dividends are expected to grow at a rate of 7 percent into the foreseeable future. What is the expected pure-bond value, B_t, and conversion value, C_t, at the end of Year 5? ($795.67; $1,051.91)

20-3. Johnson Beverage's common stock sells for $27.83, pays a dividend of $2.10, and has an expected long-term growth rate of 6 percent. The firm's pure-debt bonds pay 10.8 percent. Johnson is planning a convertible bond issue. The bonds will have a 20-year maturity, pay $100 interest annually, have a par value of $1,000, and a conversion ratio of 25 shares per bond. The bonds will sell for $1,000 and will be callable after 10 years. Assuming that the bonds will be converted at Year 10, when they become callable, what will be the expected return on the convertible when it is issued? (11.44%)

21-7   Smitty's Home Repair Company, a regional hardware chain which specializes in "do-it-yourself" material and equipment rentals, is cash rich because of several consecutive good years. One of the alternative used for the excess funds is an acquisition. Linda Wade, Smitty's treasurer and your boss, has been asked to place a value on a potential target, Hill's Hardware, a small chain which operates in an adjacent state, and she has enlisted your help.

The following table below indicates Wade's estimates of Hill's earnings potential if it cam under Smitty's management (in millions of dollars):

	1998	1999	2000	2001
Net sales	$60.0	$90.0	$112.5	$127.5
Cost of goods sold (60%)	36.0	54.0	67.5	76.5
Selling/administrative expense	4.5	6.0	7.5	9.0
Interest expense	3.0	4.5	4.5	6.0
Necessary retained earnings	0.0	7.5	6.0	4.5

The interest expense listed here includes the interest (1) on Hill's existing debt, (2) on new debt that Smitty's would issue to help finance the acquisition, and (3) on new debt expected to be issued over time to help finance expansion within the new "H Division," the code name given to the target firm. The retentions represent earnings that will be reinvested within the H Division to help finance its growth.

Hill's Hardware currently uses 40 percent debt financing, and it pays federal-plus-state taxes at a 30 percent rate. Security analysts estimate Hill's beta to be 1.2. If the acquisition were to take place, Smitty's would increase Hill's debt ratio to 50 percent, which would increase its beta to 1.3. Further, because Smitty's is highly profitable, taxes on the consolidated firm would be 40 percent. Wade realizes that Hill's Hardware also generates depreciation cash flows, but she believes that these funds would have to be reinvested within the division to replace worn-out equipment.

Wade estimates the risk-free rate to be 9 percent and the market risk premium to be 4 percent. She also estimates that net cash flows after 2001 will grow at a constant rate of 6 percent. Smitty's management is new to the merger game, so Wade has been asked to answer some basic questions about mergers as well as to perform the merger analysis. To structure the task, Wade has developed the following questions, which you must answer and then defend to Smitty's board.

a.	Several reasons have been proposed to justify mergers. Among the more prominent are (1) tax considerations, (2) risk reduction, (3) control, (4) purchase of assets at below-replacement cost, (5) synergy, and (6) globalization. In general, which of the reasons are economically justifiable? Which are not? Which fit the situation at hand? Explain.

b.	Briefly describe the differences between a hostile merger and a friendly merger.

c.	Use the data developed in the table to construct the H Division's cash flow statements for 1998 through 2001. Why is interest expense deducted in merger cash flow statements, whereas it is not normally deducted in a capital budgeting cash flow analysis? Why are earnings retentions deducted in the cash flow statement?

d.	Conceptually, what is the appropriate discount rate to apply to the cash flows developed in part c? What is your actual estimate of this discount rate?

e.	What is the estimated terminal value of the acquisition; that is, what is the estimated value of the h division's cash flows beyond 2001? What is hill's value to Smitty's? Suppose another firm were evaluating hill's as an acquisition candidate. Would they obtain the same value? Explain.

f.	Assume that Hill's has 10 million shares outstanding. These shares are traded relatively infrequently, but the last trade, made several weeks ago, was at a price of $9 per share. Should Smitty's make an offer for Hill's? If so, how much should it offer per share?

g.	What merger-related activities are undertaken by investment bankers?

CHAPTER 21
Mergers, LBOs, Divestitures, and Holding Companies

- Types of mergers
- Merger analysis
- Role of investment bankers
- Corporate alliances, LBOs, divestitures, and holding companies

Why do mergers occur?

- Synergy: Value of the whole exceeds sum of the parts. Could arise from:
  - Operating economies
  - Financial economies
  - Differential management efficiency
  - Increased market power
  - Taxes (use accumulated losses)

- Break-up value: Assets would be more valuable if sold to some other company.

What are some questionable reasons for mergers?

- Diversification
- Purchase of assets at below replacement cost
- Get bigger using debt-financed mergers to help fight off takeovers

Differentiate between hostile and friendly mergers

- Friendly merger:
  - The merger is supported by the managements of both firms.

- Hostile merger:
  - Target firm's management resists the merger.
  - Acquirer must go directly to the target firm's stockholders, try to get 51% to tender their shares.
  - Often, mergers that start out hostile end up as friendly, when offer price is raised.

Merger Analysis (In Millions)

Cash Flow Statements after Merger Occurs

	1998	1999	2000	2001
Net sales	$60.0	$90.0	$112.5	$127.5
Cost of goods sold (60%)	36.0	54.0	67.5	76.5
Selling/admin. expenses	4.5	6.0	7.5	9.0
Interest expense	3.0	4.5	4.5	6.0
EBT	$16.5	$25.5	$ 33.0	$ 36.0
Taxes (40%)	6.6	10.2	13.2	14.4
Net income	$ 9.9	$15.3	$ 19.8	$ 21.6
Retentions	0.0	7.5	6.0	4.5
Cash flow	$ 9.9	$ 7.8	$ 13.8	$ 17.1

Conceptually, what is the appropriate discount rate to apply to target's cash flows?

- Estimated cash flows are residuals which belong to acquirer's shareholders.
- They are riskier than the typical capital budgeting cash flows. Because fixed interest charges are deducted, this increases the volatility of the residual cash flows.

(Cont...)

- Because the cash flows are risky equity flows, they should be discounted using the cost of equity rather than the WACC.

- The cash flows reflect the target's business risk, not the acquiring company's.

- However, the merger will affect the target's leverage and tax rate, hence its financial risk.

Terminal Value Calculation

1. **First, find the new discount rate:**

$$k_{s(Target)} = k_{RF} + (k_M - k_{RF})b_{Target}$$
$$= 9\% + (4\%)1.3 = 14.2\%.$$

2. **Terminal value** $= \dfrac{(2001\ \text{Cash flow})(1 + g)}{k_s - g}$

$$= \dfrac{\$17.1(1.06)}{0.142 - 0.06}$$

$$= \$221.0 \text{ million.}$$

Net Cash Flow Stream Used in Valuation Calculation (In Millions)

	1998	1999	2000	2001
Annual cash flow	$9.9	$7.8	$13.8	$ 17.1
Terminal value				221.0
Net cash flow	$9.9	$7.8	$13.8	$238.1

$$\text{Value} = \dfrac{\$9.9}{(1.142)^1} + \dfrac{\$7.8}{(1.142)^2} + \dfrac{\$13.8}{(1.142)^3} + \dfrac{\$238.1}{(1.142)^4}$$

$$= \$163.9 \text{ million.}$$

Would another acquiring company obtain the same value?

- No. The input estimates would be different, and different synergies would lead to different cash flow forecasts.

- Also, a different financing mix or tax rate would change the discount rate.

Target firm has 10 million shares outstanding at a price P_0 of $9.00 per share. What should the offering price be?

Maximum price $= \dfrac{\text{Value of Acquisition}}{\text{Shares Outstanding}}$

$= \dfrac{\$163.9 \text{ million}}{10 \text{ million}}$

$= \$16.39/\text{share}.$

Range = $9 to $16.39/share.

- The offer could range from $9 to $16.39 per share.
- At $9 all the merger benefits would go to the acquirer's shareholders.
- At $16.39, all value added would go to the target's shareholders.
- See graph on Slide #21-15.

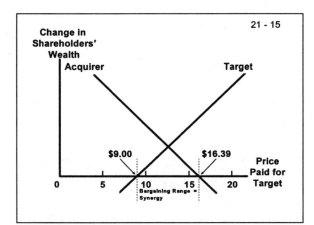

Points About Graph

■ Nothing magic about crossover price.

■ Actual price would be determined by bargaining. Higher if target is in better bargaining position, lower if acquirer is.

■ If target is good fit for many acquirers, other firms will come in, price will be bid up. If not, could be close to $9. (Cont...)

■ Acquirer might want to make high "preemptive" bid to ward off other bidders, or low bid and then plan to go up. Strategy.

■ Do target's managers have 51% of stock and want to remain in control?

■ What kind of personal deal will target's managers get?

Do mergers really create value?

■ The evidence strongly suggests:

● Acquisitions do create value as a result of economies of scale, other synergies, and/or better management.

● Shareholders of target firms reap most of the benefits, i.e., move to right in merger graph (Slide 21-15), because of competitive bids.

Functions of Investment Bankers in Mergers

- Arranging mergers
- Assisting in defensive tactics
- Establishing a fair value
- Financing mergers
- Risk arbitrage

EXAM-TYPE PROBLEMS

(The following information applies to the next four questions.)

Magiclean Corporation is considering an acquisition of Dustvac Company. Dustvac has a capital structure of 50 percent debt, 50 percent equity, with a current book value of $10 million in assets. Dustvac's pre-merger beta is 1.36 and is not likely to be altered as a result of the proposed merger. Magiclean's pre-merger beta is 1.02 and both it and Dustvac face a 40 percent tax rate. Magiclean's capital structure is 40 percent debt and 60 percent equity, and it has $24 million in total assets. The net cash flows from Dustvac available to Magiclean's stockholders are estimated at $4.0 million for each of the next three years and a terminal value of $19.0 million in Year 4. Additionally, new debt issued by the combined firm would yield 10 percent before tax, and the combined firm's cost of equity is estimated at 12.59 percent. Currently, the risk-free rate is 6.0 percent and the market risk premium is 5.88 percent.

21-1. What is the merged firm's WACC? (9.76%)

21-2. What is the merged firm's new beta? (1.12)

21-3. What is the appropriate discount rate Magiclean should use to value the equity cash flows from Dustvac? (14%)

21-4. If the acquisition price of Dustvac is 155 percent of Dustvac's current book value of assets, should Magiclean proceed with the acquisition? (NPV = +$5,036,053)

SOLUTIONS TO EXAM-TYPE PROBLEMS

CHAPTER 1

1-1. d.

1-2. e.

CHAPTER 2

2-1. b.

2-2. *Florida muni bond*

A-T yield on FLA bond = 8%. (The munis are tax exempt.)

AT&T bond

A-T yield on AT&T bond = 11% - Taxes = 11% - 11%(0.4) = 6.6%.

Alternately,

AT&T bond

Invest $20,000 @ 11% = $2,200 interest.

Pay 40% tax, so A-T income = $2,200(1 - T) = $2,200(0.6) = $1,320.
A-T rate of return = $1,320/$20,000 = 6.6%.

AT&T preferred stock

A-T yield = 9% - Taxes = 9% - 0.3(9%)(0.4) = 9% - 1.08% = 7.92%.

Therefore, invest in the Florida muni bonds which yield 8% after taxes.

Note: This problem can be made harder by asking for the tax rate that would cause the company to prefer the AT&T bonds or the preferred stock.

2-3. a.

EBIT	$1,250,000
Interest	0
EBT	$1,250,000
Taxes (40%)	500,000
Net income	$ 750,000

b. Net cash flow = Net income + Depreciation
$$= \$750,000 + \$300,000$$
$$= \$1,050,000.$$

c. Operating cash flow = EBIT(1 - T) + Depreciation
$$= \$1,250,000(0.6) + \$300,000$$
$$= \$1,050,000.$$

CHAPTER 3

3-1. ROE = Profit margin × Total assets turnover × Equity multiplier
= NI/Sales × Sales/TA × TA/Equity.

Now we need to determine the inputs for the equation from the data that were given. On the left we set up an income statement, and we put numbers in it on the right:

Sales (given)	$20,000
- Cost	NA
EBIT (given)	$ 2,000
- Interest (given)	500
EBT	$ 1,500
- Taxes (30%)	450
Net income	$ 1,050

Now we can use some ratios to get some more data:

Total assets turnover = S/TA = 2.5 (given).

D/A = 70%, so E/A = 30%, and therefore A/E = 1/(E/A) = 1/0.3 = 3.33.

Now we can complete the Du Pont equation to determine ROE:
ROE = $1,050/$20,000 × 2.5 × 3.33 = 43.75%.

3-2. a. Current NI = 0.05 × $5,000,000 = $250,000.

Current ROE = NI/Equity = $250,000/$4,000,000 = 6.25%.

Current DSO = Receivables/(Sales/360)
= $2,250,000/($5,000,000/360) = 162 days.

Reduce DSO to 60 days.

Freed up cash = 102 × $5,000,000/360 = $1,416,667.

Alternatively,

Accounts receivable /($5,000,000/360) = 60
Accounts receivable = $833,333.

Δ in A/R = $2,250,000 - $833,333 = $1,416,667.

Reduce Common Equity: $4,000,000 - $1,416,667 = $2,583,333.

New ROE = $250,000/$2,583,333 = 9.68%.

Change in ROE = 9.68% - 6.25% = 3.43%.

b. (1) Doubling the dollar amounts would not affect the answer; it would still be 3.43%.

(2) Target DSO = 70 days.
   Freed up cash = 92 × $5,000,000/360 = $1,277,778.

   Reduce Common Equity: $4,000,000 - $1,277,778 = $2,722,222.

   New ROE = $250,000/$2,722,222 = 9.18%.

   Change in ROE = 9.18% - 6.25% = 2.93%.

(3) This would provide the same answer as in Part a.

   Sales/Receivables = 6
   $5,000,000/Receivables = 6
   Receivables = $5,000,000/6 = $833,333.

   Thus, receivables would be reduced by $1,416,667.

(4) Original EPS = NI/Shares = $250,000/250,000 = $1.00.

   New EPS calculation: Assume book value = Market value. (M/B = 1).

   Price = $4,000,000/250,000 shares = $16. Stock is selling for $16 per share.

   Thus, must buy back $\dfrac{\$1,416,667}{\$16}$ = 88,542 shares.

   Number of shares outstanding = 250,000 - 88,542
                                = 161,458 shares.

$$\text{New EPS} = \frac{\$250,000}{161,458} = \$1.55.$$

Δ in EPS = \$1.55 - \$1.00 = \$0.55 per share.

(5) From Part 4, Book value = \$16 per share.
Market value = 2 × \$16 = \$32.

Thus, firm must buy back \$1,416,667/\$32 = 44,271 shares.

Number of shares outstanding = 250,000 - 44,271 = 205,729 shares.

New EPS = \$250,000/205,729 = \$1.22.

Δ in EPS = \$1.22 - \$1.00 = \$0.22 per share.

c. We could have started with lower receivables and higher fixed assets or inventory, then had you calculate the fixed assets or inventory turnover ratios. Then, we could have the company move to lower fixed assets or inventory turnover reducing equity by like amounts, and then had you determine the effects on ROE and EPS under different conditions. In any of these cases, we could have used the funds generated to retire debt, which would have lowered interest charges, and consequently, increased net income and EPS. (Note that information would have had to be given on interest and EBIT too.)

If we had to increase assets, then we would have had to finance this increase by adding either debt or equity, which would have lowered ROE and EPS, other things held constant.

3-3. a.

3-4. TIE = EBIT/I, so find EBIT and I.
Interest = \$800,000 × 0.1 = \$80,000.
Net income = \$3,200,000 × 0.06 = \$192,000.
Pre-tax income = \$192,000/(1 - T) = \$192,000/0.6 = \$320,000.
EBIT = \$320,000 + \$80,000 = \$400,000.
TIE = \$400,000/\$80,000 = 5.0×.

3-5. Before:
Equity multiplier = 1/(1 - D/A) = 1/(1 - 0.5) = 2.0.
ROE = (PM)(Assets turnover)(EM) = (10%)(0.25)(2.0) = 5%.

After:
    ROE $= 2(5\%) = 10\%$
    $10\% = (12\%)(0.25)(EM)$
    EM $= 3.33$.

$$\frac{A}{E} = \frac{3.33}{1.00}$$
    $A = D + E$
    $3.33 = D + 1.00$
    $D = 2.33$.

$D/A = 2.33/3.33 = 0.70 = 70\%$.

3-6. a. ROA $= \dfrac{NI}{S} \times \dfrac{S}{A}$

$12.5\% = 3\% \times \dfrac{S}{A}$

$\dfrac{S}{A} = 4.167$.

b. ROE $= \dfrac{NI}{S} \times \dfrac{S}{A} \times \dfrac{A}{E}$

$16\% = 3\% \times 4.167 \times EM$
    EM $= 1.28$.

c. From Part b, we know that A/E = 1.28; therefore, the firm's ratio of equity to assets is 1/1.28 = 0.78125 ≈ 78%. Consequently, the firm's debt ratio = D/A = 1 - E/A = 1 - 0.78 = 0.22 = 22%.

CHAPTER 4

4-1. c.

4-2. First, note that we will use the equation $k_t = 4\% + IP_t + MRP_t$. We have the data needed to find the IPs:

$IP_5 = (9\% + 6\% + 4\% + 4\% + 4\%)/5 = 27\%/5 = 5.4\%$.

$IP_2 = (9\% + 6\%)/2 = 7.5\%$.

Now we can substitute into the equation:

$k_5 = 4\% + 5.4\% + MRP = 12\%.$

$k_2 = 4\% + 7.5\% + MRP = 12\%.$

Now we can solve for the MRPs, and find the difference between them:

$MRP_5 = 12\% - 9.4\% = 2.6\%.$

$MRP_2 = 12\% - 11.5\% = 0.5\%.$

Difference = 2.6% - 0.5% = 2.1%.

4-3. $k_{T-8} = 6.6\%$; $k_{C-8} = 9.3\%$; $LP_{C-8} = 0.6\%.$

$k = k^* + IP + DRP + LP + MRP.$

$k_{T-8} = 6.6\% = k^* + IP + MRP$; $DRP = LP = 0.$

$k_{C-8} = 9.3\% = k^* + IP + DRP + 0.6\% + MRP.$

Because both bonds are 8-year bonds the inflation premium and maturity risk premium on both bonds are equal. The only difference between them is the liquidity and default risk premiums.

$k_{C-8} = 9.3\% = k^* + IP + MRP + 0.6\% + DRP.$

But we know from above that $k^* + IP + MRP = 6.6\%$; therefore,

$k_{C-8} = 9.3\% = 6.6\% + 0.6\% + DRP$
$DRP = 2.1\%.$

CHAPTER 5

5-1.   a.

5-2.   c.

5-3.   Before: $1.15 = 0.95(b_R) + 0.05(1.0)$
                $0.95(b_R) = 1.10$
                        $b_R = 1.158.$

After: $b_p = 0.95(b_R) + 0.05(2.0) = 1.10 + 0.10 = 1.20.$

5-4.   Electro b = 1.7; Stanton b = 0.6; k_M = 14%; k_{RF} = 7.8%.

Electro k = k_{RF} + (k_M - k_{RF})b
         = 7.8% + (14% - 7.8%)1.7
         = 18.34%.

Stanton k = k_{RF} + (k_M - k_{RF})b
         = 7.8% + (14% - 7.8%)0.6
         = 11.52%.

Δk = 18.34% - 11.52%
    = 6.82%.

CHAPTER 6

6-1.   d.

6-2.   **Time line:**

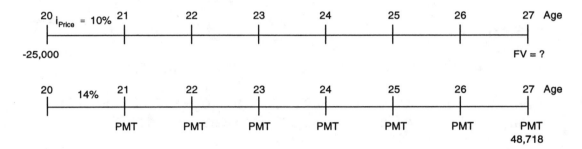

Tabular solution:

Price of car on 27th birthday.

FV = $25,000(FVIF$_{10\%, 7}$) = $25,000(1.9487) = $48,718.

Annual investment required.

FV of annuity = FVA$_n$ = PMT(FVIFA$_{i,n}$)
         $48,718 = PMT(FVIFA$_{14\%,7}$)
             PMT = $48,718/10.7305 = $4,540.14.

Financial calculator solution:

Price of car on 27th birthday.

Inputs: N = 7; I = 10; PV = -25000; PMT = 0.
Output: FV = $48,717.93 ≈ $48,718.

Annual investment required.

Inputs: N = 7; I = 14; PV = 0; FV = 48718.
Output: PMT = -$4,540.15.

6-3. **Time line:**

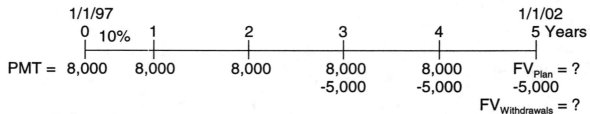

Tabular solution:

Easy way. $5,000(FVIFA$_{10\%,3}$) = $5,000(3.3100) = $16,550.

Hard way.   Target FV = $8,000(FVIFA$_{10\%,5}$)(1.10) = $53,725. Find FV of cash flow stream of $8,000 for Years 0-2; $3,000, for Years 3-4; and -$5,000 for Year 5; and subtract from $53,725. The answer is $16,550.

Financial calculator solution:

Calculate the FV of the withdrawals which is how much her actual account fell short of her plan.

END mode   Inputs: N = 3; I = 10; PV = 0; PMT = -5000.
                      Output: FV = $16,550.

Alternative solution:

Calculate FV of original plan.

BEGIN mode   Inputs: N = 5; I = 10; PV = 0; PMT = -8000.
                        Output: FV = $53,724.88.

Calculate FV of actual deposit less withdrawals, take the difference.

Inputs: $CF_0 = 8000$; $CF_1 = 8000$; $N_j = 2$; $CF_2 = 3000$; $N_j = 2$; $CF_3 = -5000$; $I = 10$.

Outputs: NFV = $37,174.88.

Difference: $53,724.88 - $37,174.88 = $16,550.

6-4. **Time line:**

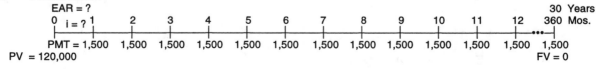

Financial calculator solution:

Calculate periodic rate.

Inputs: N = 360; PV = -120000; PMT = 1500; FV = 0.
Output: I = 1.235% per period.

Use interest rate conversion feature.

Inputs: NOM% = $1.235 \times 12 = 14.82$; P/YR = 12.
Output: EFF% = 15.868 ≈ 15.87%.

6-5. Steps:

1. He will save for 10 years, then receive payments for 25 years.

2. He wants a payment of $40,000 per year in today's dollars for first payment only. Real income will decline. Inflation will be 5%. Enter N = 10, I = 5, PV = -40000, PMT = 0, and press FV to get FV = $65,155.79.

3. He now has $100,000 in an account which pays 8%, annual compounding. We need to find the FV of the $100,000 after 10 years. Enter N = 10, I = 8, PV = -100000, PMT = 0, and press FV to get FV = $215,892.50.

4. He wants to withdraw, or have payments of, $65,155.79 per year for 25 years, with the first payment made at the beginning of the first retirement year. So, we have a 25-year annuity due with PMT = $65,155.79, at an interest rate of 8%. (The interest rate is 8% annually, so no adjustment is required.) Set the calculator to BEGIN MODE, then enter N = 25, I = 8, PMT = 65155.79, FV = 0, and press PV to get PV = $751,165.35. This amount must be on hand to make the 25 payments.

5. Since the original $100,000, which grows to $215,892.50, will be available, we must save enough to accumulate $751,165.35. Need $751,165.35 - $215,892.50 = $535,272.85.

6. The $535,272.85 is the FV of a 10-year ordinary annuity. The payments will be deposited in the bank and earn 8% interest. Therefore, set the calculator to END MODE and enter N = 10, I = 8, PV = 0, FV = 535272.85, and press PMT to find PMT = $36,949.61 ≈ $36,950.

6-6. a. $i_{PER} = \dfrac{i_{Nom}}{m}$

$$= \frac{0.10}{4} = 0.025 = 2.5\%.$$

b. i_{Nom} = stated interest = 10%.

c. $EAR = \left(1 + \dfrac{i_{Nom}}{m}\right)^m - 1$

$$= \left(1 + \frac{0.10}{4}\right)^4 - 1$$

$$= 0.1038 = 10.38\%.$$

CHAPTER 7

7-1. **Time line:**

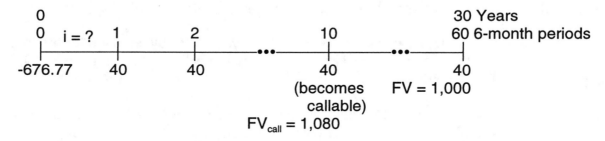

Investors would expect to earn either the YTM or the YTC, and the expected return on the old bonds is the cost GSU would have to pay in order to sell new bonds.

Financial calculator solution:

Calculate the YTM on the old bonds.

Inputs: N = 2(30) = 60; PV = -676.77; PMT = 80/2 = 40; FV = 1000.
Output: I = 6% = $k_d/2$. 6% is the semiannual or periodic rate.

YTM = 2(6%) = 12%.

Calculate the YTC for comparison.

Inputs: N = 2(5) = 10; PV = -676.77; PMT = 80/2 = 40; FV = 1080.
Output: I = 9.70% = $k_d/2$.

YTC = 2(9.70%) = 19.40%.

Would investors expect the company to call the bonds? No. The company currently pays interest of only 8% on its debt. New debt would cost GSU at least 12%. It would be foolish for the company to call the bonds, because investors would logically expect to earn the current YTM of 12% on new bonds. So k_d = 12% is the best estimate of the nominal annual interest rate GSU would have to pay on the new bonds.

7-2.   **Time line:**

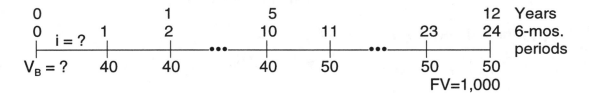

Financial calculator solution:

We are comparing securities with different payment patterns, semiannual and quarterly. To properly value the student loan securities, we must match the opportunity cost rate on the bonds with the payment period on the student loan securities, which is semiannual. Thus, convert the quarterly (periodic) rate on the bonds to a semiannual effective rate.
    Since the bonds are selling at par value, the 9% coupon rate is also the market rate. The semiannual periodic rate is then 9%/2 = 4.5%. There are 2 compounding periods (quarters) in a half year.

Calculate the opportunity cost semiannual EAR of the quarterly payment bonds (using the interest rate conversion feature).

Inputs: P/YR = 2; NOM% = 9/2 = 4.5.
Output: EFF% = 4.55% = semiannual effective rate.

Calculate the present value of the student loan package, V_B, using the semiannual effective rate (using cash flow register).

Inputs: $CF_0 = 0$; $CF_1 = 40$; $N_j = 10$; $CF_2 = 50$; $N_j = 13$; $CF_3 = 1050$; $I = 4.55$.
Output: NPV = V_B = $985.97.

7-3. **Time line:**

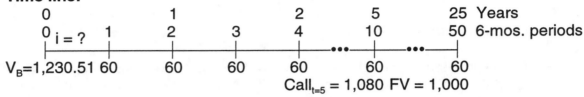

Calculate the nominal yield to call.

The bonds are selling at a premium because the coupon interest rate is above the market rate. Under the expectation of a flat yield curve, the bonds will most likely be called so that the firm can issue new, cheaper bonds. The FV is the call price and the period is 5 years or 10 semiannual periods.

Financial calculator solution:

Calculate the semiannual interest rate and convert to a nominal annual rate.

Inputs: N = 10; PV = -1230.51; PMT = 60; FV = 1080.
Output: I = 3.85% periodic rate (semiannual).

The nominal annual rate equals 2 × 3.85% = 7.70%. Thus, the before-tax cost of debt is 7.70%.

7-4. **Time line:**

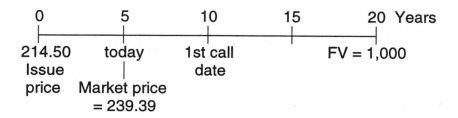

Financial calculator solution:

Calculate the original YTM when the bonds were issued.

Inputs: N = 20; PV = -214.50; PMT = 0; FV = 1000.
Output: I = 8.0%.

Calculate the current market rate using the current market price of $239.39.

Inputs: N = 15; PV = -239.39; PMT = 0; FV = 1000.
Output: I = 10.0%.

At a current market price of $239.39, market rates are 10%. Since market rates have risen, the bond will not likely be called. So today, at Year 5, the YTM of 10% is the most likely annual rate of return an investor who buys the bonds today will earn.

7-5. e.

7-6. d.

7-7.

```
  0                1               9          10 Years
  0 i = 6%  1      2               18    19   20 6-mos. periods
  ├─────────┼──────┼──── • • • ────┼─────┼────┤
PV = ?      50     50              50    50   50
                                        FV = 1,000
```

Financial calculator solution:

Calculate the PV of the bond so the current yield can then be calculated.

Inputs: N = 2 x 10 = 20; I = 12/2 = 6; PMT = 100/2 = 50; FV = 1000.
Output: PV = $885.30.

Calculate the current yield.

$$\text{Current yield} = \frac{\text{Interest}}{\text{Bond value}} = \frac{\$100}{\$885.30} = 11.30\%.$$

CHAPTER 8

8-1. Step 1: *Calculate required rate of return.*

$$k_s = \frac{\$2}{\$20} + 6\% = 10\% + 6\% = 16\%.$$

Step 2: *Calculate risk-free rate.*

$$16\% = k_{RF} + (15\% - k_{RF})1.2$$
$$k_{RF} = 10\%.$$

Step 3: *Calculate capital gain.*

New $k_s = 10\% + (15\% - 10\%)0.6 = 13\%.$

$$\hat{P}_{New} = \frac{\$2}{0.13 - 0.06} = \$28.57.$$

Therefore, the percentage capital gain is 43%, as calculated below.

$$\text{Capital gain} = \frac{\$28.57 - \$20.00}{\$20.00} = \frac{\$8.57}{\$20.00} = 43\%.$$

8-2. **Time line**:

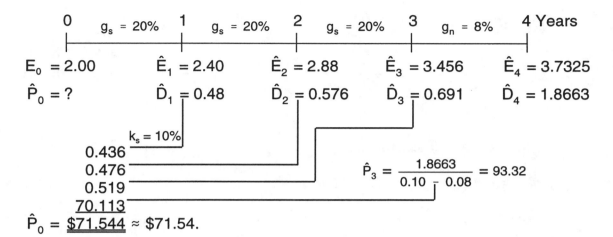

$\hat{P}_0 = \underline{\$71.544} \approx \$71.54.$

Tabular solution:

$\hat{P}_0 = \$0.48(PVIF_{10\%,1}) + \$0.576(PVIF_{10\%,2}) + \$0.691(PVIF_{10\%,3}) + \$93.32(PVIF_{10\%,3})$

$= \$0.48(0.9091) + \$0.576(0.8264) + \$0.691(0.7513) + \$93.32(0.7513)$

$= \$0.436 + \$0.476 + \$0.519 + \$70.113 = \$71.54.$

Financial calculator solution:

Inputs: $CF_0 = 0$; $CF_1 = 0.48$; $CF_2 = 0.576$; $CF_3 = 94.011$; $I = 10$.
Output: NPV = $\hat{P}_0 = \$71.54.$

8-3. e.

8-4. $k_{ps} = \dfrac{D_{ps}}{V_{ps}}$

$0.125 = \dfrac{\$8.75}{V_{ps}}$

$V_{ps} = \$70.$

CHAPTER 9

9-1. **Time line:**

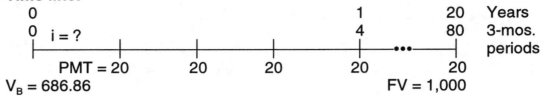

Financial calculator solution:

Calculate the <u>nominal</u> YTM of the bond.

Inputs: $N = 4 \times 20 = 80$; $PV = -686.86$; $PMT = 80/4 = 20$; $FV = 1000$.
Output: $I = 3.05\%$ periodic rate = quarterly rate.

Nominal annual rate = $3.05\% \times 4 = 12.20\%$.

Calculate k_d after-tax. $k_{d,AT} = 12.20\%(1 - T) = 12.20\%(1 - 0.4) = 7.32\%$.

9-2. Information given:

Net income = \$600; Debt = 0.4; Equity = 0.6; Dividend payout = 0.6.

Calculate the retained earnings break point.

Breakpoint$_{RE}$ = Retained earnings/Equity fraction
$\qquad\qquad\quad = [\$600(1 - 0.6)]/0.6 = \$240/0.6 = \$400$.

Since the \$600 capital budget exceeds the retained earnings breakpoint, $BP_{RE} = \$400$, Allison will need new equity capital. The firm will have \$240 of retained earnings which will be exhausted when the capital budget reaches \$400.

Use the dividend growth model to calculate k_e.
$$k_e = \frac{D_0(1 + g)}{P_0(1 - F)} + g = \frac{\$2.20(1.06)}{\$28(1 - 0.15)} + 0.06 = \frac{\$2.33}{\$23.80} + 0.06$$
$$= 0.0980 + 0.06 = 0.1580 = 15.8\%.$$

9-3. Step 1: *Calculate the break point for retained earnings, BP_{RE}.*

$$BP_{RE} = \frac{\text{Retained earnings}}{\text{Equity fraction}} = \frac{NI(1 - \text{Payout})}{0.45} = \frac{\$50(0.6)}{0.45} = \$66.67 \text{ million.}$$

Note that we are interested in the WACC at a capital budget of $100 million. The MCC or $WACC_2$ at this point will require use of new equity, k_e.

Step 2: *Calculate cost of new equity, k_e.*

$$k_e = \frac{D_1}{P_0(1 - F)} + g = \frac{\$3.00(1.10)}{\$50(1 - 0.15)} + 0.10$$

$$= \frac{\$3.30}{\$42.50} + 0.10 = 0.0776 + 0.10 = 0.1776 = 17.76\%.$$

Step 3: *Use the target capital structure weights to calculate $WACC_2$.*

$$WACC_2 = 0.55(0.10)(1 - 0.35) + 0.45(17.76\%) = 11.57\%.$$

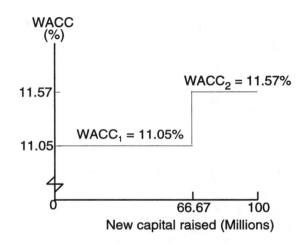

Note that the initial $WACC_1$ is 11.05% and is calculated as follows:

Debt: $k_{d,AT} = 10.0\%(1 - 0.35) = 6.50\%.$

Retained earnings: $k_s = D_1/P_0 + g = \dfrac{\$3.00(1.10)}{\$50.00} + 0.10$

$$= 0.066 + 0.10 = 0.1660 = 16.60\%.$$

$$WACC_1 = 0.55(6.50\%) + 0.45(16.60\%) = 3.575\% + 7.47\% = 11.045\% \approx 11.05\%.$$

9-4. Debt = 42%; Equity = 58%; YTM = 11%, T = 40%; WACC = 10.53%.
k_s = ?

$k_d (1 - T) = 11\%(1 - 0.4) = 6.6\%$.

$WACC = w_d k_d(1 - T) + w_{ce} k_s$
$10.53\% = 0.42(6.6\%) + (0.58)k_s$
$7.758\% = (0.58)k_s$
$\quad k_s = 13.38\%$.

CHAPTER 10

10-1. **Time line:**

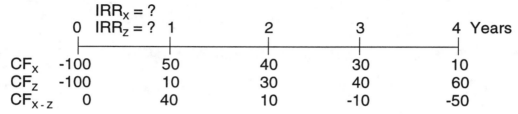

Cash flows S   -1,100   900   350   50   10
NPV_S = ? IRR_S = ?

Cash flows L   -1,100   0   300   500   850
NPV_L = ? IRR_L = ?

Financial calculator solution:

Calculate the NPV and IRR of each project then select the IRR of the higher NPV project.

Project S;   Inputs: CF_0 = -1100; CF_1 = 900; CF_2 = 350; CF_3 = 50; CF_4 = 10; I = 12.
Output: NPV_S = $24.53; IRR_S = 13.88%.

Project L;   Inputs: CF_0 = -1100; CF_1 = 0; CF_2 = 300; CF_3 = 500; CF_4 = 850; I = 12.
Output: NPV_L = $35.24; IRR_L = 13.09%.

Project L has the higher NPV and its IRR = 13.09%.

10-2. **Time line:**

IRR_X = ?
0   IRR_Z = ?   1   2   3   4 Years

CF_X -100   50   40   30   10
CF_Z -100   10   30   40   60
CF_{X-Z} 0   40   10   -10   -50

Financial calculator solution:

Calculate the IRR of each project.

Project X:

Inputs: $CF_0 = -100$; $CF_1 = 50$; $CF_2 = 40$; $CF_3 = 30$; $CF_4 = 10$.
Output: IRR = 14.489% ≈ 14.49%.

Project Z:

Inputs: $CF_0 = -100$; $CF_1 = 10$; $CF_2 = 30$; $CF_3 = 40$; $CF_4 = 60$.
Output: IRR = 11.79%.

Calculate the NPVs of the projects at k = 0 discount rate.

$NPV_{X,k=0\%} = -100 + 50 + 40 + 30 + 10 = 30$.

$NPV_{Z,k=0\%} = -100 + 10 + 30 + 40 + 60 = 40$.

Calculate the IRR of the residual project cash flows, i.e., Project$_{X-Z}$.

IRR_{X-Z}; Inputs: $CF_0 = 0$; $CF_1 = 40$; $CF_2 = 10$; $CF_3 = -10$; $CF_4 = -50$.
           Output: IRR = 7.167% ≈ 7.17%.

Using the calculator we can determine that there is a crossover point in the relevant part of an NPV profile graph. Project X has the higher IRR. Project Z has the higher NPV at k = 0. The crossover rate is 7.17%.

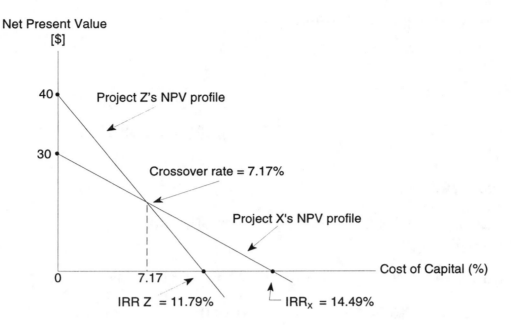

Net Present Value [$]

Project Z's NPV profile

Crossover rate = 7.17%

Project X's NPV profile

Cost of Capital (%)

IRR Z = 11.79%

IRR$_X$ = 14.49%

10-3. Time line:

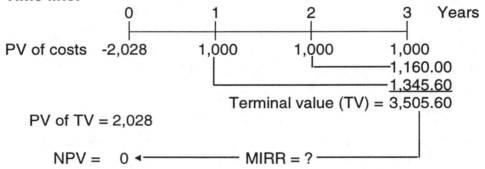

	0	1	2	3	Years
PV of costs	-2,028	1,000	1,000	1,000	

1,160.00

1,345.60

Terminal value (TV) = 3,505.60

PV of TV = 2,028

NPV = 0 ◄————— MIRR = ? —————

Step 1: *Calculate the historical beta.*

Regression method; Financial calculator: Different calculators have different list entry procedures and key stroke sequences.

Enter Nulook returns as the y-list:

Inputs: Item(1) = 9 INPUT; Item(2) = 15 INPUT; Item(3) = 36 INPUT.

Enter market returns as the x-list:

Inputs: Item(1) = 6 INPUT; Item(2) = 10 INPUT; Item(3) = 24 INPUT; use linear model.

Output: **m** or slope = 1.50 = historical beta.

Graphical/numerical method: Note that this method works precisely in this problem because the data points lie in a straight line. If the plotted data points don't lie in a straight line, regression is a better method.

Slope = Rise/Run = (36 - 9)/(24 - 6) = 27/18 = 1.5. Beta = 1.5.

Step 2: *Calculate cost of equity using CAPM and beta given inputs.*

$k_s = k_{RF} + (MRP)b = 7.0\% + (6.0\%)1.5 = 16.0\%$.

Financial calculator solution:

Step 3: *Calculate MIRR.*

Terminal value using TVM:

Inputs: N = 3; I = 16; PV = 0; PMT = -1000.
Output: FV = $3,505.60.

Terminal value using cash flows:

Inputs: CF_0 = 0; CF_1 = 1000; N_j = 3; I = 16.
Output: NFV = $3,505.60.

Note: Some calculators do not have the Net Future Value (NFV) function. You can still calculate the NFV or terminal value using cash flows to calculate NPV, then TVM to calculate NFV or TV from the NPV.

Calculate NPV of cash inflows.

Inputs: CF_0 = 0; CF_1 = 1000; N_j = 3; I = 16.
Output: NPV = -$2,245.89.

Now take the NPV of $2,245.89 and bring it forward at 16% for three periods to get the FV or terminal value.

Inputs: N = 3; I = 16; PV = -2245.89; PMT = 0.
Output: FV = $3,505.60.

MIRR using TVM:

Inputs: N = 3; PV = -2028; PMT = 0; FV = 3505.60.
Output: I = 20.01% = MIRR ≈ 20%.

CHAPTER 11

11-1. **Time line:**

Determine the residual cash flows by subtracting the cash flows of Project S from Project M:

	0	1	2	3	4 Years
Project M:	-700	265	265	265	265
Project S:	-200	85	140	130	
Project M - S:	-500	180	125	135	265

Financial calculator solution:

Calculate the IRR of the residual cash flows, Project$_{M-S}$.

Inputs: CF_0 = -500; CF_1 = 180; CF_2 = 125; CF_3 = 135; CF_4 = 265.
Output: IRR = 14.19%.

When each of the projects is evaluated at a cost of capital of 14.19%, the NPVs are approximately equal. This is the rate at which McQueen should be indifferent between the two projects.

Check answer by evaluating each project at a rate of 14.19%.

Project M:

Inputs: CF_0 = -700; CF_1 = 265; N_j = 4; I = 14.19.
Output: NPV = $69.14.

Project S:

Inputs: CF_0 = -200; CF_1 = 85; CF_2 = 140; CF_3 = 130; I = 14.19.
Output: NPV = $69.11.

11-2. **Time line:**

(In thousands)

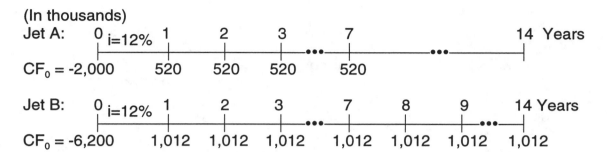

Jet A: 0 i=12% 1   2   3   7   14 Years

CF_0 = -2,000   520   520   520   520

Jet B: 0 i=12% 1   2   3   7   8   9   14 Years

CF_0 = -6,200 1,012 1,012 1,012 1,012 1,012 1,012 1,012

Financial calculator solution:

Calculate NPV of single, 7-year project for Jet A.

Inputs: CF_0 = -2000000; CF_1 = 520000; N_j = 7; I = 12.
Output: NPV = $373,153.40.

Calculate NPV of single, 14-year project for Jet B.

Inputs: CF_0 = -6200000; CF_1 = 1012000; N_j = 14; I = 12.
Output: NPV = $507,706.25.

Calculate the NPV of the 7-year project (Jet A), using replacement chain analysis.

Time line:

(In thousands)

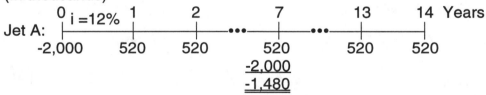

Jet A: 0 i =12% 1   2   7   13 14 Years

-2,000   520   520   520   520   520

<u>-2,000</u>
<u>-1,480</u>

Inputs: CF_0 = -2000000; CF_1 = 520000; N_j = 6; CF_2 = -1480000; CF_3 = 520000;
        N_j = 7; I = 12.
Output: NPV = $541,949.05.

By the replacement chain method, the Jet A project replicated is the higher NPV project, and will increase the firm's value by $541,949.05.

11-3. Old bonds:

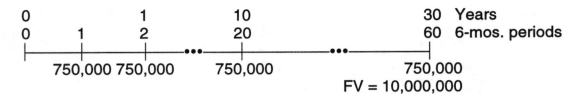

New bonds:

Step 1: *Calculate the number of bonds and the total initial costs of refunding (premium and flotation costs).*

Number of bonds = $10,000,000/$1,000 = 10,000 bonds.

Premium on old issue (10,000 × $100)	$1,000,000
Flotation costs new issue	400,000
Total initial costs	$1,400,000

Step 2: *Calculate the expected semiannual interest savings.*

Old interest expense (annual)	$1,500,000
New interest expense (annual)	1,350,000
Annual interest savings	$ 150,000
Semiannual interest savings	$ 75,000

Step 3: *Calculate the semiannual after-tax discount rate required to evaluate the refunding cash flows.*

Nominal annual rate after-tax = 13.5%(1 - 0) = 13.5%.

Semiannual after-tax rate = 13.5%/2 = 6.75%.

Step 4: *Calculate the NPV of the refunding, using the total initial costs, semiannual savings, and semiannual discount rate.*

Inputs: CF_0 = -1400000; CF_1 = 75000; N_j = 20 × 2 = 40; I = 6.75.
Output: NPV = -$370,367.22 ≈ -$370,367.

This project has a negative NPV, -$370,367. Market rates would have to drop further to make the refunding a positive NPV project.

CHAPTER 12

12-1. k_A = 12%; +3% risky projects; -3% low risk projects.

Time line:

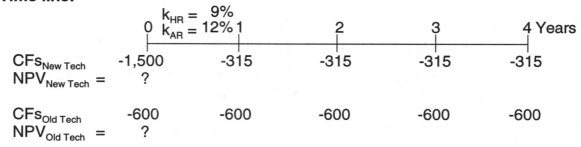

Recognize that (1) risky <u>outflows</u> must be discounted at <u>lower rates</u>, and (2) since Project New Tech has high risk, it should be discounted at a rate of 12% - 3% = 9%. Project Old Tech is of average risk and should be discounted at 12%.

Financial calculator solution:

Project New Tech

Inputs: CF_0 = -1500; CF_1 = -315; N_j = 4; I = 9.
Output: NPV = -$2,520.51.

Project Old Tech

Inputs: CF_0 = -600; CF_1 = -600; N_j = 4; I = 12.
Output: NPV = -$2,422.41.

Thus, the proper choice is to select the project with the lowest PV of costs which is Project Old Tech with a PV of costs = -$2,422.41.

12-2. *Calculate the breakpoints for retained earnings and debt.*

$$BP_{RE} = \frac{NI(1 - Payout)}{Equity\ fraction} = \frac{\$10,000,000(0.5)}{0.8} = \$6,250,000.$$

$$BP_{Debt} = \frac{Amount\ of\ Cheap\ Debt}{Debt\ fraction} = \frac{\$5,000,000}{0.2} = \$25,000,000.$$

Calculate the component costs of capital.

k_{d1} = 0.08(1 - 0.34) = 0.0528 = 5.28%. (After-tax cost of cheap debt.)

k_{d2} = 0.10(1 - 0.34) = 0.066 = 6.66%. (After-tax cost of costlier debt.)

$k_s = \dfrac{\$5.00}{\$50.00} + 0.10 = 0.20 = 20.0\%.$

$k_e = \dfrac{\$5.00}{\$50.00(1 - 0.15)} + 0.10 = 0.2176 = 21.76\%.$

Determine the weighted average cost of capital schedule using the optimal capital structure weights and component capital costs.

WACC$_1$ = 0.2(0.0528) + 0.8(0.20) = 0.1706 = 17.06%.

WACC$_2$ = 0.2(0.0528) + 0.8(0.2176) = 0.1846 = 18.46%.

WACC$_3$ = 0.2(0.066) + 0.8(0.2176) = 0.1873 = 18.73%.

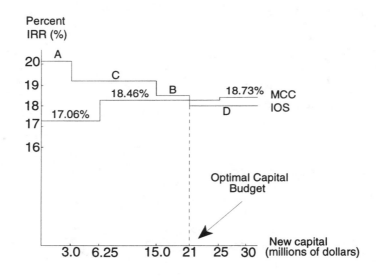

Investments A, B, and C have IRRs greater than the relevant WACC of 18.46%; therefore, they should be accepted. However, investment D has an IRR less than the relevant WACC and should be rejected. The optimal capital budget equals $21 million.

12-3. a.

12-4. d.

12-5. a.

12-6. *Calculate expected value of NPV.*

	Probability of Outcome, P_i	Unit Sales Volume	Sales Price	NPV (In 1000s)	$P_i(x)$	
Worst case	0.30	6,000	$3,600	-$6,000	0.3(-6,000) =	-1,800
Base case	0.50	10,000	4,200	13,000	0.5(13,000) =	6,500
Best case	0.20	13,000	4,400	28,000	0.2(28,000) =	5,600
					E(NPV) =	$10,300

Calculate standard deviation of NPV.

(Table in millions.)

	P_i		$(x - \bar{x})^2$		$P_i(x - \bar{x})^2$
Worst case	0.3	×	$(-6 - 10.3)^2$ = 265.69 =		79.707
Base case	0.5	×	$(13 - 10.3)^2$ = 7.29 =		3.645
Best case	0.2	×	$(28 - 10.3)^2$ = 313.29 =		62.658
				σ^2_{NPV} =	146.010

$\sigma_{NPV} = (146,010,000)^{1/2} = 12,083.$

Calculate coefficient of variation (CV) of NPV.

$CV_{NPV} = \sigma_{NPV}/E(NPV) = \$12,083/\$10,300 = 1.17.$

CHAPTER 13

13-1. d.

13-2. b.

13-3. $EPS_1 = \left[(\text{Sales} - \text{Variable costs} - \text{Fixed Costs} - \text{Interest})(1 - T)\right]/\text{Shares outstanding.}$

Step 1: *Calculate the amount of debt and interest expense.*

Debt = 0.60 × $400,000 = $240,000.

Interest = 0.12 × $240,000 = $28,800.

Step 2: *Solve for sales using the forecasted EPS.*

$$
\begin{aligned}
EPS_1 = \ \$4.00 &= [(S - 0.40S - \$80,000 - \$28,800)(1 - 0.40)]/10,000 \\
&= [(0.60S - \$108,800)(0.6)]/10,000 \\
\$4.00 &= (0.36S - \$65,280)/10,000 \\
\$105,280 &= 0.36S \\
\text{Sales} &= \$292,444.44 \approx \$292,445.
\end{aligned}
$$

Alternative method:

Note that Sales - VC - FC = EBIT. Calculate net income from EPS and shares outstanding and work back up the income statement.

$EPS_1 = [(\text{EBIT} - \text{Interest})(1 - T)]/\text{Shares outstanding.}$

Solve for net income, then EBT, interest (step 1 above), and EBIT.

Net Income = EPS × Shares outstanding = $4.00 × 10,000 = $40,000.

EBT = NI/(1 - T) = $40,000/0.6 = $66,667.

Interest (from above) = $28,800.

EBIT = EBT + Interest = $66,667 + $28,800 = $95,467.

Solve for sales using VC percentage, EBIT, and FC.

$$
\begin{aligned}
S &= 0.40S + \$95,467 + \$80,000 \\
0.6S &= \$175,467 \\
S &= \$175,467/0.6 = \$292,445.
\end{aligned}
$$

13-4. FC = $900,000; VC = $3.25/unit; P = $4.75; Q_{BE} = ?

$$Q_{BE} = \frac{F}{P - V}$$
$$= \frac{\$900,000}{\$4.75 - \$3.25}$$
$$= 600,000 \text{ units.}$$

CHAPTER 14

14-1. b.

14-2. e. The dividend irrelevance theory is MM's theory. The tax preference theory says that capital gains are preferred to dividends, while the bird-in-the-hand (G-L) theory says that dividends are preferred to capital gains. The clientele effect assumes that investors are attracted to a firm's particular dividend payout policy.

14-3. *Calculate the amount of debt and interest expense (in millions).*

Total assets = $200; 40% debt × $200 = $80 debt.

Interest expense = $80 × 0.10 = $8.

Calculate net income (in millions).

EBIT	$98.0
Less: Interest	8.0
EBT	$90.0
Less: Taxes (@34%)	30.6
Net income	$59.4

Calculate portion of projects financed with retained earnings.

IOS contains $60 million in positive NPV projects.

Retained earnings portion: $60M × 0.60 = $36 million
Debt portion: $60M × 0.40 = $24 million.

Calculate residual available for dividends.

$59.4 - $36.0 = $23.4 million in dividends.

CHAPTER 15

15-1. **Formula solution:**

Step 1: *Use the AFN formula to calculate AFN.*

$$
\begin{aligned}
\text{AFN} &= A^*/S_0(\Delta S) - L^*/S_0(\Delta S) - M(S_1)(1 - d) \\
&= \frac{\$10,000}{\$10,000}(\$5,000) - \frac{\$1,500}{\$10,000}(\$5,000) - 0.11(\$15,000)(1 - 0.6) \\
&= 1(\$5,000) - 0.15(\$5,000) - 0.11(\$15,000)(0.4) \\
&= \$5,000 - \$750 - \$660 = \$3,590.
\end{aligned}
$$

Step 2: *Calculate the new account levels for current assets and current liabilities.*

Current assets will increase by 50% to $7,000(1.5) = $10,500.

The AFN will be funded using short-term debt.

Current liabilities will increase to:

$$
\begin{aligned}
\text{A/P + Accruals} &= \$1,500(1.5) = \$2,250 \\
\text{S-T Debt} &= \$2,000 + \$3,590 = \underline{\quad 5,590} \\
\text{Total C.L.} &= \underline{\$7,840}
\end{aligned}
$$

Step 3: *Calculate the new current ratio.*

New current ratio = $10,500/$7,840 = 1.34.

15-2. Construct a partial projected income statement and balance sheet:

	Last Year	Basis	First Pass	AFN	Second Pass
EBIT	$ 240,000	× 1.10	$ 264,000		
Interest	80,000		80,000		
EBT	$ 160,000		$ 184,000		
Taxes (40%)	64,000		73,600		
NI	$ 96,000		$ 110,400		$ 110,400
NI avail. to common	$ 96,000		$ 110,400		
Divs. to common					
(37,800 × $1.27)	48,006	37,800 × $1.40	52,920		
Addition to RE	$ 47,994		$ 57,480		$ 57,480
Total assets	$1,100,000	× 1.10	$1,210,000		$1,210,000
Accruals	$ 13,636	× 1.10	$ 15,000		$ 15,000
Long-term debt	640,000		640,000	+ 30,694	670,694
Equity	335,000		335,000	+ 20,462	355,462
RE	111,364	+ 57,480	168,844		168,844
Total liab & equity	$1,100,000		$1,158,844		$1,210,000
AFN			51,156		

AFN financing:

The shortfall will be financed in accordance with the capital structure.

Long-term debt	0.60 × $51,156	= $30,694
Common stock	0.40 × $51,156	= 20,462
		$51,156

15-3. d.

CHAPTER 16

16-1. **Time line:**

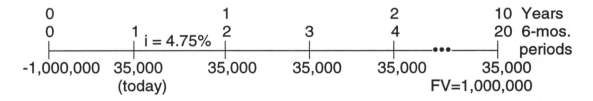

Financial calculator solution:

Calculate the market value of the bonds, V_B, today, at t = 1, on the time line above using the new market rate.

Inputs: N = 19; I = 9.5/2 = 4.75; PMT = 35000; FV = 1000000.
Output: PV = -$845,807.80.

Calculate the capital loss on the bonds.

The bonds were purchased at par for $1,000,000, but are resold 6 months later for considerably less.

Capital loss on bonds = $1,000,000 - $845,807.80 = $154,192.20.

16-2. d.

16-3. c.

16-4. Construct a simplified comparative balance sheet and income statement for the restricted and relaxed policies: (In thousands)

	15% of Sales Restricted	25% of Sales Relaxed
Balance sheet accounts:		
Current assets	$ 60	$ 100
Fixed assets	100	100
Total assets	$ 160	$ 200
Debt	$ 80	$ 100
Equity and retained earnings	80	100
Total liabilities and equity	$ 160	$ 200
Income statement accounts:		
EBIT	$ 36.0	$ 36.0
Less: Interest (10%)	8.0	10.0
EBT	$ 28.0	$ 26.0
Less: Taxes (40%)	11.2	10.4
Net income	$ 16.8	$ 15.6

Calculate ROEs under each policy.

ROE = NI/Equity.
ROE (restricted policy) = $16.8/$80 = 21.0%.
ROE (relaxed policy) = $15.6/$100 = 15.6%.

Difference in ROEs = 0.21 - 0.156 = 0.054 = 5.4%.

16-5. (Account balances stated in millions)

	Old	With Change

Inventory conversion period:

$$\text{ICP} = \frac{360}{\frac{40}{10}} = \frac{360}{4} = 90.$$

$$\text{ICP} = \frac{360}{\frac{40}{8}} = \frac{360}{5} = 72.$$

Receivables conversion period (or days sales outstanding):

$$\text{DSO} = \frac{8}{\frac{40}{360}} = \frac{8}{\frac{1}{9}} = 72.$$

$$\text{DSO} = \frac{7}{\frac{40}{360}} = \frac{7}{\frac{1}{9}} = 63.$$

Payables deferral period:

PDP = 30 days = -30   PDP = -30

CCC = 90 + 72 - 30 = 132 days.   CCC = 72 + 63 - 30 = 105 days.

Change in CCC = 132 - 105 = 27 days.

Net change is -27 days (CCC is 27 days shorter).

CHAPTER 17

17-1. **Financial calculator solution:**

(1)   Simple interest: 13.0%.   EAR = 13.0%.

(2)   Renewable loan: The rate on this loan is essentially a 12% nominal annual rate with quarterly compounding. Calculate the EAR.

Inputs: NOM% = 12; P/YR = 4.
Output: EFF% = 12.55%.

(3)   Trade credit: Terms 1/30, net 60.

Note that the approximate rate is really the rate per period multiplied by the number of periods, or a nominal annual rate.

1/99 × 360/(60 - 30) = 0.0101 × 12 = 12.12% approximate rate.

Calculate the EAR using the interest rate conversion feature.

Inputs: NOM% = 12.12; P/YR = 12.
Output: EFF% = 12.82%.

The least expensive type of credit is the quarterly renewable loan at a 12.55% effective annual rate.

17-2. d.

17-3. 20 × $750,000 = $15,000,000.

CHAPTER 18

18-1.   Exchange rate in 1985   = 1,476,000/$8,200 = 180 yen per dollar.
         Today's exchange rate   = 144 yen per dollar; 144/180 = 0.80.
       Today's price = $8,200/0.8 = $10,250.

Alternative method:

1,476,000/144 = $10,250.

18-2. **Time line:**

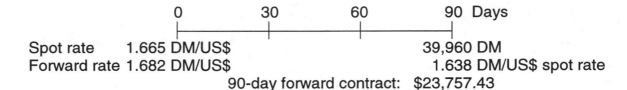

Calculate the cost of the forward contract at the forward rate.

39,960 DM/(1.682 DM/US$) = $23,757.43.

Calculate the cost of purchasing exchange currency at the spot rate in 90 days to satisfy the payable.

39,960 DM/1.638 DM/US$ = $24,395.60.

Calculate the savings from the forward market hedge.

$24,395.60 - $23,757.43 = $638.17 ≈ $638.

18-3. **Time line:**

$$0 \qquad\qquad\qquad\qquad\qquad\qquad 6 \text{ months}$$

US$:   -9,708.74   FV = 10,000
Spot rate: 1.42 SWF/US$ Spot rate = 1.324 SWF/US$
SWF: -13,786.41   FV = 13,240 SWF

PV of T-Bill in SWF is calculated as 9,708.74 × 1.42 = 13,786.41 SWF.

FV of T-Bill in SWF is calculated as 10,000 × 1.324 = 13,240 SWF.

Financial calculator solution:

Calculate the 6-month return to the Swiss investor after she has exchanged US$ for Swiss francs.

Inputs: N = 1; PV = -13786.41; PMT = 0; FV = 13240.
Output: I = -3.963%.

Annualized nominal rate of return = -3.963%(2) = -7.93%.

18-4. $e_0 = \dfrac{P_h}{P_f}$

$$= \frac{\$899}{1,425} = \$0.631 \text{ per DM or } \frac{1}{0.631} = 1.585 \text{ DM per U.S. dollar.}$$

18-5. *Convert the annual yields to quarterly yields.*

k_h = U.S. T-Bill (90-day): 5%/4 = 1.25%.
k_f = Swiss: 3.5%/4 = 0.875%.

Calculate the 3-month forward exchange rate.

$$\frac{f_t}{e_0} = \frac{(1 + k_h)}{(1 + k_f)}$$

$$\frac{f_t}{\$0.6935} = \frac{1.0125}{1.00875}$$

$$f_t = \$0.6961.$$

CHAPTER 19

19-1. a. Formula value = $\dfrac{\text{Current price}}{\text{of the stock}}$ - Strike price

                    = \$40 - \$32

                    = \$8.

    b. Premium = Market price of option - Formula value

                    = \$13 - \$8

                    = \$5.

19-2. $V = P[N(d_1)] - Xe^{-k_{RF}t}[N(d_2)]$

      $= \$24(0.60572) - \$24e^{(-0.07)(0.5)}(0.51783)$

      $= \$14.54 - \$24(0.9656)(0.51783)$

      $= \$14.54 - \$12.00$

      $= \$2.54.$

19-3. Furtures contract settled at 99 $14/32$% of \$100,000 contract value, so PV = $0.994375 \times \$1,000 = \$994.375 \times 100$ bonds = \$99,437.50. Using a financial calculator, we can solve for k_d as follows:

N = 40; PV = -994.375; PMT = 40; FV = 1000; and solve for I = $k_d/2$ = 4.02854%. k_d = 4.02854% $\times$ 2 = 8.0571% $\approx$ 8.06%.

If interest rates decrease by ½ percent to 7.56%, then we would solve for PV as follows:

N = 40; I = 7.56/2 = 3.78; PMT = 40; FV = 1000; and solve for PV = \$1,045.01 $\times$ 100 = \$104,500.68. Thus, the contract's value has increased from \$99,437.50 to \$104,500.68.

20-1. Annual depreciation = $4,800,000/3 = $1,600,000.

(In thousands)		Year		
	0	1	2	3
I. Cost of owning				
1. Net purchase price	($4,800)			
2. Maintenance cost		($240)	($240)	($240)
3. Maintenance tax savings (Line 2 × 0.4)		96	96	96
4. Depreciation		1,600	1,600	1,600
5. Depreciation tax savings (Line 4 × 0.4)		640	640	640
6. Net cash flow (1 + 2 + 3 + 5)	($4,800)	$496	$496	$496
7. PV cost of owning (@6%)	($3,474.19)			
II. Cost of leasing				
8. Lease payment		($2,100)	($2,100)	($2,100)
9. Lease payment tax savings		840	840	840
10. Net cash flow (8 + 9)	$ 0	($1,260)	($1,260)	($1,260)
11. PV cost of leasing (@6%)	($3,368.00)			

III. Cost comparison

12. Net advantage to leasing (In thousands):

$$\text{NAL} = \text{PV cost of owning - PV cost of leasing}$$
$$= \$3,474.19 - \$3,368.00 = \$106.19.$$

Time lines: *(In thousands)*

Buying:

```
      0   i = 6%   1          2          3 Years
      ├──────────┼──────────┼──────────┤
   -4,800        496        496        496
      PV=?
```

Leasing:

```
      0   i = 6%   1          2          3 Years
      ├──────────┼──────────┼──────────┤
              -1,260     -1,260     -1,260
      PV=?
```

Financial calculator solution: *(In thousands)*

The correct discount rate is the after-tax cost of debt $k_{d,AT} = 10\%(1 - 0.40) = 6.0\%$.

Calculate the NPV of both buying and leasing and determine the net advantage to leasing (NAL).

Buying:

Inputs: CF_0 = -4800; CF_1 = 496; N_j = 3; I = 6.
Output: NPV = -$3,474.19.

Leasing:

Inputs: CF_0 = 0; CF_1 = -1260; N_j = 3; I = 6.
Output: NPV = -$3,368.00.

NAL = $3,474.19 - $3,368.00 = $106.19. (Calculation is in thousands.)

20-2. **Time line:**

Financial calculator solution:

Calculate the pure-bond value, B_t, at Year 5. Since no assumption is made concerning future interest rates, the 12% required return on nonconvertible bonds is the appropriate rate.

Inputs: N = 15; I = 12; PMT = 90; FV = 1000.
Output: PV = $795.67.

Calculate the conversion value, C_t, at Year 5.

Conversion value = $C_5 = P_0(1 + g)^t(CR) = \$18.75(1.07)^5(40)$.

Inputs: N = 5; I = 7; PV = 18.75(40) = -750; PMT = 0.
Output: FV = $1,051.91.

The expected pure bond value at Year 5, $B_5 = \$795.67$.

The expected conversion value at Year 5, $C_5 = \$1,051.91$.

20-3. Time line:

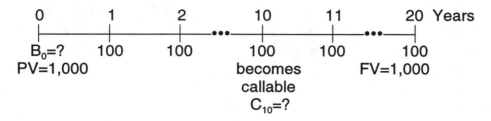

Financial calculator solution:

Calculate the expected stock price at Year 10, $\hat{P}_{10}$.

Inputs: N = 10; I = 6; PV = -27.83; PMT = 0.
Output: FV = $49.84.

Calculate the conversion value, C_t, at Year 10.

Information given: $P_0 = 27.83$; g = 6; t = 10; CR = 25.

$$
\begin{aligned}
\text{Conversion value, } C_{10} &= \$27.83(1.06)^{10}(\text{CR}) \\
&= \$49.84(25) = \$1,245.98 \approx \$1,246.
\end{aligned}
$$

Calculate the expected return using the expected conversion value at Year 10, C_{10}.

Inputs: N = 10; PV = -1000; PMT = 100; FV = 1246.
Output: I = 11.44%.

21-1. *Determine the capital structure of the merged firm (In millions).*

	Magiclean	Dustvac	Combined Firm	Capital Structure Weights
Debt	0.4(24) = 9.6	0.5(10) = 5.0	14.6	0.43
Equity	0.6(24) = 14.4	0.5(10) = 5.0	19.4	0.57
Total	24.0	10.0	34.0	1.00

Calculate the WACC.

$$\text{WACC} = 0.43(10\%)(1 - 0.4) + 0.57(0.1259) = 0.0258 + 0.0718$$
$$= 0.0976 = 9.76\%.$$

21-2. *Calculate the weighted average beta using the relative capital weights of the two firms (In millions).*

	Magiclean	Dustvac	Combined Firm
Total assets	24.0	10.0	34.0
Weight	24/34 = 0.706	10/34 = 0.294	1.0
Beta	1.02	1.36	1.12

$$\text{Beta}_{\text{New Firm}} = 0.706(1.02) + 0.294(1.36) = 0.720 + 0.40 = 1.12.$$

21-3. The net cash flows from Dustvac are equity cash flows. Magiclean should discount them with Dustvac's cost of equity, assuming that the merger will not significantly alter Dustvac's risk, which is stated in the problem. We can estimate its cost of equity using the Security Market Line (CAPM) and Dustvac's pre-merger beta.

$$k_{s(\text{Dustvac})} = k_{RF} + (k_M - k_{RF})\text{Beta}_{\text{premerger}} = 0.06 + (5.88\%)1.36 = 14.0\%.$$

21-4. **Time line:**

(In millions)

```
      0 i = 14% 1        2        3        4  Years
      |---------|--------|--------|--------|
   -15.5      4.0      4.0      4.0     19.0
   NPV=?
```

Acquisition price for Dustvac = 1.55($10,000,000) = $15,500,000.

Tabular solution:

$$\text{NPV} = \$4{,}000{,}000(\text{PVIFA}_{14\%,3}) + \$19{,}000{,}000(\text{PVIF}_{14\%,4}) - \$15{,}500{,}000$$
$$= \$4{,}000{,}000(2.3216) + \$19{,}000{,}000(0.5921) - \$15{,}500{,}000$$
$$= \$9{,}286{,}400 + \$11{,}249{,}900 - \$15{,}500{,}000$$
$$= \$5{,}036{,}300 \approx \$5{,}036{,}000.$$

Financial calculator solution:

Inputs: $CF_0 = -15500000$; $CF_1 = 4000000$; $N_j = 3$; $CF_2 = 19000000$; $I = 14$.
Output: NPV = $5,036,053.

(Difference in tabular and financial calculator results is due to rounding error.)

Since the NPV is positive, Magiclean should proceed with the acquisition.